RESEARCHING CRIMINOLOGY

RESEARCHING CRIMINOLOGY

Iain Crow and
Natasha Semmens

McGraw Hill Open University Press

Open University Press
McGraw-Hill Education
McGraw-Hill House
Shoppenhangers Road
Maidenhead
Berkshire
England
SL6 2QL

email: enquiries@openup.co.uk
world wide web: www.openup.co.uk

and Two Penn Plaza, New York, NY 10121—2289, USA

First published 2008

A catalogue record of this book is available from the British Library

ISBN-13: 978-0-33-521546-1 (pb) 978-0-33-521547-8 (hb)
ISBN-10: 0-33-522117-3 (pb) 0-33-522118-1 (hb)

Library of Congress Cataloging-in-Publication Data
CIP data applied for

Typeset by Kerrypress, Luton, Bedfordshire
Printed in Poland by OZGraf S.A.
www.polskabook.pl

The McGraw·Hill Companies

Contents

About the authors

Acknowledgements

Introduction

Part I: The principles of criminological research

1 **The research process**
What is research?
Researching criminology
Types of inquiry and types of data
Research as a process
Further reading

2 **The principles of researching criminology**
The research question: identifying the research question and exploring possible theoretical explanations
Choosing a research strategy
Method selection and data collection
Data analysis and inference
Conclusion
Further reading

3 **Designing criminological research**
What is research design and why is it important?
The main types of empirical inquiry
Some common kinds of research design
Choosing a research design: an example
Sampling
Researching criminology ethically
Conclusion
Further reading

4 **Criminological evaluation**
Defining terms
The evaluation paradigm
Evaluation and theory
Doing criminological evaluation
Further reading

Part II: Collecting and analysing material

5 **Researching by reading**
Introduction
Reading and reviewing the literature critically
Analysing other people's data
Analysing documents
Conclusion
Further reading
Appendix

6 **Researching by looking**
Introduction: watch and learn
The science of observation? Epistemology and research design
Methodological decisions
Data collection
Data analysis
The disadvantages of observation
Conclusion
Further Reading

7 **Researching by asking and listening**
Introduction
Interviewing
Group interviews and focus groups
Questionnaires
Further reading

8 **Analysing criminological research**
About analysis
Analysing quantitative material: an introduction
Analysing qualitative material: an introduction
Further reading
Appendix 1
Appendix 2

Part III: Real-world research

9 **Researching offenders and employment**
Background to the project
Theoretical context

The research
Results
Conclusion

10 Researching the Youth Court
Background to the project
Theoretical context
The research
Analysis
Results
Conclusion
Appendix

11 Researching a Community Safety Programme
Background to the project
Theoretical context
The research
Results
Conclusion

12 Researching the fear of crime
Background to the project
Theoretical context
The research
Results
Conclusion

13 Concluding comments
Taking it further

Glossary
Notes
References
Index

About the authors

Iain Crow is a reader in Research Methods at the University of Sheffield. He has previously worked at the Addiction Research Unit at the Institute of Psychiatry and was Head of Research at NACRO, the national organization for offender rehabilitation and crime prevention, until 1989. His teaching covers research methods and statistics, research ethics, and the treatment and rehabilitation of offenders. He has done research on drug use, race and criminal justice, offenders and unemployment, the Youth Court, community safety. He has also been involved with community-based programmes for offenders, and done research on such programmes. His other books include *The Treatment and Rehabilitation of Offenders, Criminal Justice 2000: Strategies for a New Century,* and *Unemployment, Crime and Offenders.*

Natasha Semmens has been a Lecturer in Criminology at the University of Sheffield since 2001. Her teaching covers research methods, white-collar crime and foundations in law and legal systems. Her research interests include the fear of crime, crime survey methodology, white-collar crime and cybercrime. She has also been involved in projects with the Home Office, NACRO and the UK Information Commissioner.

Acknowledgements

Inevitably such a book reflects our own approach to criminological research, but it also brings together material that reflects the teaching and research done by fellow criminologists in the School of Law at the University of Sheffield. It is therefore right and proper to acknowledge the fact that what is written here owes much to the work we have done with others. We should also say that teaching and learning go together, and that we have learned a lot about teaching research methods in criminology from the generations of students who have taken the modules we have taught, so we also wish to thank them.

We have used actual criminological examples to illustrate the points we are trying to convey as much as possible, and this means that we have drawn on the work of criminologists from many quarters. However, Part III of this book describes projects that we ourselves have done over the years. Most criminological research is a collaborative effort involving a team of people. We therefore owe a great debt of gratitude to those we have worked with on these projects, both for their contributions to the research we did together, but also for what we have learned by working with them.

Chapter 9, on the relationship between employment status and sentencing, is based on a study funded by the Economic and Social Research Council which was done in collaboration with Frances Simon. Frances was a statistician who had previously worked with the Home Office and her contribution to this particular study and to criminology generally has been immense, and deserving of the widest possible recognition.

Chapter 10 describes a project on the Youth Court funded by the Home Office, undertaken in collaboration with Charlotte Allen and Michael Cavadino. Charlotte subsequently went on to work in the Home Office Research, Development and Statistics Directorate, and Mick has since gone to the University of Central Lancashire.

Chapter 11 explains how a Joseph Rowntree Foundation-funded evaluation of three community safety projects was done. In the early days of this project, Paul Wiles played a key role before he went on to head the Home Office Research, Development and Statistics Directorate. Alan France was an important formative influence, and after Paul left became co-director of the project. He has since become Director of the Centre for Research and Social Policy. Sue Hacking and Mary Hart were other major contributors to the research, Sue on the quantitative side, and Mary working mainly on the qualitative material.

Chapter 12 describes a project which involved a collaboration with the British Crime Survey team at the Home Office. Pat Mayhew and Catriona Mirlees-Black were instrumental in setting up the collaboration back in 1999. Tracy Budd and Joanna Taylor (then Mattinson) provided valuable support and advice during the analysis stages. In the later stages of the project, Chris Kershaw was a source of continuing support. All have now moved on to work in other sections of the Home Office. This research was conducted for a PhD thesis and many academic colleagues offered priceless guidance and inspiration, including Jason Ditton, Steve Farrall and Ken Pease.

Finally, we would like to thank Chris Cudmore of McGraw-Hill for his help and encouragement, and for saving us from embarassment by looking over an early draft of the text.

Although, as we have explained, this book draws on the work of others, and brings together what we have learned from working with others, we lay no blame at their doors for what is written here. We take full responsibility for what is in the book, and they have every right to criticize us for anything we have got wrong.

Iain Crow and Natasha Semmens
University of Sheffield

Introduction

Almost the first question we asked ourselves before embarking on writing this book was why we wanted to do it. Surely there are plenty of research methods texts around already? Well, one answer is that although there are indeed a number of texts covering social research methods in general, there are not that many specifically oriented towards criminology and the needs of criminology students. Those that are around tend to be American, quite old, or collections of chapters by different authors rather than integrated texts.

The book has come about to a large extent as a result of our own teaching, and reflects our research experiences. In teaching undergraduate criminology students, and postgraduate students who had not encountered social research techniques previously or done any criminology, we felt there was a need for a textbook that would introduce them to the principles involved, the various methods used, and illustrate how these work in real criminological studies. In our work we have also encountered many practitioners, policy-makers, journalists and other commentators who have an interest in crime and criminal justice. We hope that the book will also be of value to them.

The book is in three parts, covering the main principles of criminological research, the collection and analysis of material, and examples of real criminological research projects that we have undertaken.

The principles that underpin criminological research are similar in many respects to those that form the basis for other forms of social inquiry. However, criminological investigation is often shaped by the fact that it deals with matters that are by their nature illegal and also often immoral, so criminological inquiry is often situated in a context that requires this to be taken into account. In Part I we start by introducing the research process. It would be misleading to think of research as simply an agglomeration of particular techniques and methods, and we emphasize the importance of seeing research as an integrated process. The book focuses mainly on the later stages of the process, and many of the topics mentioned in the opening chapter are considered in more detail subsequently. In Chapter 2, we consider the relationship between epistemology, theory and methods of inquiry. In Chapter 3, we look at how research is designed, and at the important matter of researching criminology in a way that is ethical. Chapter 4 focuses on a particular form of research design that has considerable importance in criminology: that which is directed towards evaluating the impact of various interventions which involve individuals, communities, or indeed national changes, such as new legislation.

Part II of the book, Chapters 5–8, covers the collection of research material. Most research comes down to looking at what happens (observing), reading, asking questions, and listening to what is said, and the chapters that comprise Part II reflect this. We also consider the analysis of research material here. All books have their limitations, and in this one we do not go into detail about how to analyse research data. An adequate consideration of how to analyse quantitative and qualitative data would require at least another one, if not two, books, and reference can be made to other sources for this purpose. However, having said already that research has to be seen as an integrated process, and that consideration must be given to how research material is to be analysed, we would be remiss if we did not give some attention to the kind of things that analysis involves, so that you can prepare adequately.

Reading books on research methods is all very well; they explain what should happen in theory, in ideal circumstances. But, as we ourselves have found, when you set out to do a criminological project, you often have to work it out for yourself. While it is necessary to understand what criminological research is about, how to make use of interviews and secondary sources, and what to do with the results, it is important to have a sense of how these things need to come together. Furthermore, it is one thing to know about such matters in the abstract; it is quite another to know how they work in reality. Throughout the earlier parts of the book we have tried to use examples wherever possible to illustrate various points, but this is not the same as understanding how a whole criminology project works. So Part III of the book, Chapters 9–12, describes some of the research that we have done. In doing this, we explain what the projects demonstrate, why we did things in a particular way, and what alternatives might have been used. The purpose of these chapters is to show how the principles described earlier are put into practice. They are four very different projects undertaken at different times. We explain the basis for each study, its design, the methods used, how the analysis was conducted, and how the results were interpreted and used.

The first study was conducted at a time of high unemployment, and examines the relationship between offenders' employment status and the sentence they received. Although carried out some years ago, the methodology is still relevant and could be applied to other similar inquiries. The second project is a study of the way that changes in the Youth Court were implemented. Although it illustrates how certain methods were used, it is also of interest because of the sensitive local and national political issues involved. The third study is one of those projects very common in criminology: an evaluation. However, it is an evaluation that was both problematic, and was at the centre of some far-reaching issues. The fourth project, covering fear of crime, describes how the understanding of that topic was extended by working alongside a major national survey to look at credit card fraud. In none of these examples are we saying that this is the only way of doing the research described. Criminological research is often a choice between options, and we explain why the studies happened the way they did.

Criminological research is usually a team effort, and that was very much the case with the projects described here. We did these projects in conjunction with fellow researchers, so we cannot take full credit for them, and duly acknowledge the part played by others. The full results of the studies can be found elsewhere and it is not the purpose of the final part of the book to reproduce the substance of the studies in all particulars. The aim is to illustrate the various methodological points that they raise, and in order to do this we make reference to some of the substantive material where necessary in order to make the methodology intelligible.

A Glossary of key terms is found at the back of the book.

Our hope is that this book will serve the dual purpose of helping readers to critically appraise criminological research that they encounter, and also perhaps to go on to experience the satisfaction that can be derived from researching criminology.

Part 1

The principles of criminological research

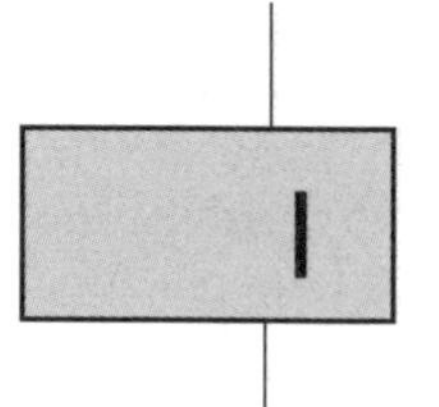

1 The research process

In this opening chapter we will be looking at what researching criminology involves as an integrated process. It is an overview of what is to come in the rest of the book and we will be raising a series of issues that will be covered in greater detail in subsequent chapters. The point of this first chapter is to explain how different elements of the research process hang together. Doing criminological research is not *just* a matter of using certain methods of inquiry; it is about the way such methods are used as part of a more wide-ranging enterprise that constitutes the scientific method.

What is research?

The term 'research' is used to refer to a wide range of activities. Sometimes it means nothing more than looking up information in established sources. So is there anything special about the kind of activity that takes place in academic institutions and certain research centres? How does academic research differ from, say, good journalism? Is it different in kind, or only in degree? Should we distinguish between academic researchers and researchers who work for non-academic organizations, such as market researchers?

There are no recognized standards or regulations that determine that one person is a bona fide researcher while another is not. We are not therefore going to attempt a prescriptive or proscriptive definition of research. But we are going to suggest that the kind of research engaged in by those who aspire to a genuine pursuit of knowledge has certain features. First, research is likely to be in some degree *original*; it is not merely looking up some information that is already known and reproducing that information. This does not necessarily mean that research requires the collection of new data at first hand. It may be a new analysis of existing data, or the re-interpretation of extant material; it may be a new synthesis.

Second, the kind of research that we are referring to will usually be *theoretically informed*: it attempts to advance a corpus of ideas and existing knowledge. It is not coming from nowhere and going to nowhere. From this it follows that research will also be *systematic* in nature. This does not mean that it has to follow a set of rules rigidly, but it will approximate to something called the scientific method. This requires a brief explanation because there is a tendency among some social researchers to equate the scientific method solely with a positivist notion of research based on natural science.[1] The scientific method is broader than this and applies in many disciplines, not just the natural sciences. It is more a way of approaching the process of inquiry. In particular, it is characterized by an interaction between theory and method. Another central concern of research is the extent to which any conclusions are *generalizable*. Here again we encounter the importance of a link between the methods used and the theoretical context. The kind of research that we are concerned with should also follow certain *ethical principles*. This involves having regard to such matters as informed consent, and ensuring that the rights of parties to the research are not violated. These are all matters to which we will return during the course of this book.

Research is about addressing questions, usually phrased in terms of hypotheses. We refer to theory for why we asked the questions, and to interpret the results. Research may take different forms. A distinction is commonly made, for example, between pure and applied research, and there are different types of applied research, such as evaluation research and action research. This book focuses on aspects of empirical investigation, based on the observation of social phenomena, rather than on *purely* abstract or theoretical inquiry, but this does not mean that such research is atheoretical.

Researching criminology

This book is about researching criminology, so the question arises as to whether there is anything particularly distinctive about criminological research. Criminological research has much in common with social research in general and the principles that apply in other areas of social science are also relevant to researching criminology. Consequently, much of this book could be read as being about social research methodology. However, researching criminology does have certain distinctive features. For a start, doing criminological research usually involves the study of things that are illegal. The criminological researcher is likely to learn about illegal acts and meet people who have committed such acts. Doing research on drug misuse, for example, may well mean being in the company of people in possession of illegal drugs. This can place researchers in difficult situations. Apart from the illegality of much of the subject matter, a criminological researcher is also quite possibly going to be dealing with sensitive issues, and with people who have had traumatic experiences. In some situations the research can have an emotional impact on the researcher, for example, undertaking research on sexual abuse is likely to be a harrowing experience. So the subject matter of criminology is distinctive and different from many other disciplines. This makes the observance of ethical principles especially important in criminology. It also means that the criminological researcher needs to develop a range of interpersonal skills. This is something often neglected in research methods textbooks. The emphasis is usually, and understandably, on theoretical and methodological matters; that is on what is colloquially regarded as 'academic' skills. But successful criminological research also means that the researcher has to be able to relate to people and organizations, to establish 'rapport', and sometimes empathy, while also retaining integrity as a researcher, and that is an important theme in this book.

The use of the term 'discipline' above is also important. Many would say that criminology is not a discipline in its own right. It is certainly the case that criminology draws on a number of different academic disciplines, including sociology, psychology, economics, geography, and law, to name just some. This disciplinary diversity means that the methods used in criminological research are likely to reflect the kinds of techniques used in the parent disciplines. Several of these parent disciplines use social science research methods, and will therefore have similar features, but it can lead to a rich diversity of approaches. Imagine, for example that you were undertaking a study of sentencing in the courts. A psychologist might use experimental techniques to present magistrates and judges with a series of cases in which the features of the cases are varied in such a way as to explore what is likely to influence sentencers most. A sociologist might spend time observing what happens in court, or looking at the backgrounds of sentencers and offenders. An economist might come up with models of sentencing that take account of various 'costs', a term which goes wider than just financial costs. Other kinds of study might look at how crime is distributed geographically. A feature of criminological research is that not only does it cover an important topic, but also has this richly diverse character.

Types of inquiry and types of data

Although much is written about research and ways of doing it, most empirical social inquiry involves three main kinds of data:

1 *Observation* – looking at things, people and events.
2 *Words* – verbal or textual communication in its various forms.
3 *Numbers* – counting things, people and events.

This forms the basis of Part II of the book, and we will therefore be considering all three of these activities in more detail there. First, however, it is worth referring to some important distinctions that are often found in criminology and in social research generally.

A distinction is often made between *quantitative* data, involving the use of numbers, and *qualitative* data, which usually means the use of words or images. The former is sometimes referred to as 'hard' data, and the latter as 'soft' data. Much social research is quantitative in nature, involving statistical analysis. Examples of such research include study of the criminal statistics and opinion polls, and major social surveys, such as the British Household Panel Survey, and the British Crime Survey. Quantitative research is sometimes, wrongly, seen as synonymous with a positivist approach to inquiry. Positivism, as we explain in a later chapter, is a more broadly based philosophy of science which involves using methods derived from the natural sciences, which does include numerical measurement, but this is far from being the whole story. On the other hand, methods which involve qualitative inquiry, such as ethnography, participant observation and discourse analysis, are often associated with a different perspective, most commonly referred to as interpretive inquiry, but encompassing such things as hermeneutics, ethnomethodology, phenomenology and structuralism. Such approaches tend to concentrate on understanding the *meaning* of social interaction.

The relationship between these different research perspectives might be viewed diagrammatically (Figure 1.1). The main point we want to make is that this simplistic distinction between positivist and interpretive inquiry is a crude, and even misleading one. Even those who are experts in statistical analysis are aware of its limitations, and would probably reject the label positivist, and those concerned with subcultural theory and ethnography also recognize the need to sample and count.

Returning to our identification of the three main components of research as observations, words and numbers, what we want to emphasize is that there is considerable interchange between them. Different research perspectives often have more in common with each other than may at first be apparent, each needing to have regard to such matters as the unit of observation, sampling and

Positivist | | Interpretive
Quantitative | | Qualitative
'Hard' | | 'Soft'
e.g. experiments | surveys | e.g. participant observation
[---]

Figure 1.1 Relationship between quantitative and qualitative data

problems of reliability and validity. For example, what people say or write may be converted into numbers by counting the number of times they say or do something. Conversely, numbers need to be examined for the meanings they contain. Although it is possible to associate quantitative and qualitative data with different epistemological positions, few modern researchers dogmatically assert that one type of data is inherently superior to the other; each is a way of trying to enhance our understanding, with advantages and disadvantages depending on the context in which they are used.

Most modern researchers in criminology and related social sciences are fairly eclectic about their research methods, and recognize the limitations of their data, however obtained. Indeed, many researchers would advocate the use of combined methods to improve the validity of their research. This has been the case for some time. Almost 20 years ago, Denzin (1988) described the use of 'triangulation' in research. He identified four basic kinds of triangulation. First was the triangulation of different types of data, which could involve time, space and people. The second was investigator triangulation, involving multiple observers of the same object. Next came theoretical triangulation, involving different perspectives in relation to the same set of objects. Finally, methodological triangulation was defined as a distinction between triangulation within a specific method, and triangulation combining dissimilar methods to examine the same thing. An example of within-methods triangulation might be to use more than one attitude scale within a study to look at alienation. A between-methods triangulation, on the other hand, might combine an attitude scale to study alienation with an observational study of behaviour.[2] To give a criminological example, imagine you want to know how magistrates sentence different types of offender. You could ask them how they would deal with various cases, while at the same time asking them questions about each case (within-methods interviewing). You could also interview magistrates, observe how cases are dealt with in court, and analyse a sample of cases using the court records (between-methods).

In recent years there has been a resurgence of interest in what is now called 'mixed methods' research, with recent journal articles and texts embracing a multi-method approach.[3] The studies described in the final part of this book all employ what Green and Preston (2005) refer to as 'methodological hybridity'. The use of numbers and measurement, as well as words, has always been an important component of both natural and social scientific research, and they are often used in combination. More problematic is what happens when sophisticated research techniques get into the hands of those who prefer research to provide simplistic, and preferably cheap, solutions.

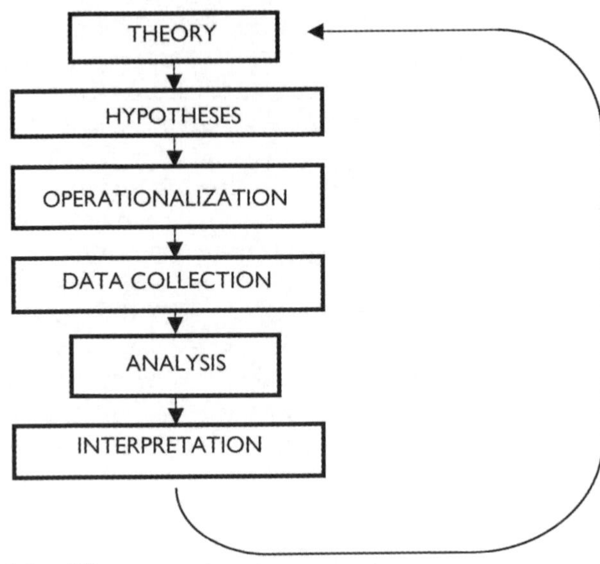

Figure 1.2 The research process

Research as a process

It follows from what has been said already that research is not simply the application of a particular *method*, such as a questionnaire. It is an integrated process involving theories, hypotheses, designs, methods and analyses. Only by having regard to the whole process is it possible to determine when it is appropriate to use particular methods, and to draw appropriate inferences from them. This process may be represented diagrammatically as shown in Figure 1.2.

The first thing to say about this model is that it is a simplified one, and it is something of an ideal. Research does not always move definably from one stage in the process to the next. It is not uncommon for the process to work in the other direction as well, moving from observation, through the elaboration of hypotheses to theoretical propositions. This is the approach taken by those who develop *grounded theory* (Glaser and Strauss 1967; Strauss and Corbin 1998). Nonetheless, the model is one that is broadly recognized, even by researchers who go about inquiry in very different ways.[4] For example, at least one researcher adopts the model in writing about how to undertake literature reviews (Cooper 1989). Let us now look at the various elements of this process.

Theory

A theory is a set of logically inter-related propositions. The *Concise Oxford Dictionary of Sociology* defines theory as 'an account of the world which goes beyond what we can see and measure' (Marshall 1994). The nature of social theory, and the role of theory in research, will be considered further in the next chapter. However, what needs to be noted here is that empirical criminological inquiry is seldom if ever theory-free, and it is one of the basic principles of this book that the theory underlying a criminological research project, and the methods used in undertaking the research are closely related.

Like all social research, criminological research usually starts with the posing of a question or the addressing of a problem. Research may come about in a number of ways. It may be a response to a specific problem, such as an apparent rise in a particular type of crime, or as a result of new criminal justice legislation. It may be that after reading an article, or reviewing the literature on a topic, a researcher believes there is a gap in the knowledge, or that previous research is wrong, or out of date. Not infrequently research is prompted by a perceived wrong or injustice, such as the belief that a particular group is being discriminated against. In all these instances it can seem that the theoretical basis for a particular investigation is self-evident, and it is all too easy for the theory that underlies a research project to be unexamined. Whatever prompted the research, the theoretical basis of inquiry should be critically analysed. A competent researcher considers the theoretical context of an inquiry, even if s/he is not undertaking research directly associated with the investigation of a particular theory.

Having said this, not all research is about the examination of 'grand' theory. Much research is usefully conducted at lower levels of theoretical analysis. Research may be exploratory in nature, concerned with the development and formulation of concepts and propositions, rather than putting a theory to the test. But even exploratory research should have a clearly defined focus (Glaser and Strauss 1967). The point is that some theoretical element is invariably present in empirical investigation, and the more clearly this is set out, the more valid and valuable the research will be.

Hypotheses

Theoretical propositions are often of a rather general, abstract, nature. For example, the proposition may be that certain groups in society are more alienated than others and therefore more predisposed towards committing crimes. This may be related to certain forms of social theory concerned with class and conflict, and clearly there is much here that needs examination, definition and clarification before the proposition and the theory on which it is based can be tested empirically. Hypotheses are empirically testable statements, usually involving relationships between concepts which form part of a theory. Examining a hypothesis involves applying clearly defined criteria which enable the hypothesis to be refuted or not. Traditionally hypotheses are not *accepted*, since there is usually the possibility that some other basis for rejecting the hypothesis could be found. Hence hypotheses, and by extension our empirical understanding, are frequently of a provisional nature. There are few laws in the social sciences in the same way as in the natural sciences.

To give an example, it has been theorized that because of the nature of our society and the role of the criminal justice system within it, the unemployed are more likely to be punished by imprisonment than those with jobs (Box 1987). This theoretical proposition has been tested (Crow and Simon 1987). A fuller description of how this was done is given in Chapter 9, but for the time being what needs to be noted is that in the course of this inquiry the investigators framed a number of hypotheses about what the empirical study would find. As often happens in an empirical inquiry, the investigators found that the relationships were more complex than theories sometimes suggest. Hence what you tend to get is a modification and enhancement of the hypotheses, laying the basis for further inquiry. This is why research so often ends with the conclusion that 'more research is needed'. It is not necessarily because researchers are touting for their next research grant; it should be because research is a continuous process of refinement and discovery, reflecting a constant exchange between theory and data.

For this reason hypotheses are pivotal in research, making it possible to relate data and observations to theoretical propositions. This is true of both quantitative and qualitative research. Kelle describes the process in qualitative research:

> Qualitative hypotheses, when they first come into a researcher's mind, are usually not highly specified and definite propositions about certain facts, but tentative and imprecise, sometimes very vague conjectures about possible relationships. (1997: 13)

Kelle goes on to spell out the methodological requirements for hypothesis testing, which apply as much to quantitative as to qualitative data:

1 Hypotheses must be empirically testable; that means they must be precise enough and have empirical content.
2 The codes which are used for hypothesis testing must denote clearly defined phenomena in a reliable and stable way.
3 The prerequisite of independent testing requires that a hypothesis is not tested with the same empirical material from which it is developed.

In statistics, the term hypothesis has a very specific meaning and the criteria for rejecting or not rejecting a hypothesis are mathematically determined. Usually what happens is that, in looking at relationships between **variables**, one starts with a 'null hypothesis' that there is no relationship, or no difference, and a calculation is then performed to see whether this null hypothesis can be rejected on the basis that it is unlikely to occur by chance at a stated level of probability. In order to test a hypothesis, either quantitatively or qualitatively, it is necessary to state precisely what is meant by what initially may be some rather abstract concepts (e.g. alienation), and rough ideas about the relationships between them; this is a process rather inelegantly known as operationalization.

Operationalization

This is a crucial part of the research process. It includes the following:

1. The definition of any concepts, and the basis for examining them have to be spelled out. In other words, it is necessary to say just what is meant by a term such as 'alienation', and how you are able to tell whether someone is more or less alienated.[5] If the hypothesis is that 'People without family commitments are inclined to be more radical than those with such commitments', then what is meant by 'family commitments' has to be specified, and we have to say what we mean by 'more radical'. Only when this is done will it be possible to construct a questionnaire that can be used on a sample to see whether (at a certain level of statistical probability) those without family commitments satisfy the criterion of 'radicalness' more than those who have family commitments.
2. Operationalizing a project involves developing a *research design*. In the example above, this may involve obtaining two groups of people who are comparable in certain respects, except that one group has family commitments and the other does not. More will be said about this in Chapter 3.
3. The advantages and disadvantages of alternative *methods* of inquiry have to be considered – whether to use a questionnaire, in-depth interviews, observation, or some other method. The methods judged to be most appropriate for testing a hypothesis are chosen and justified. In doing this, an important consideration will be the resources available to carry out the research; research is often a compromise between what would be ideal and what is practical.
4. Any scales, scores or other measures need to be developed and validated. For example, one may need to develop a scale of 'alienation' or 'radicalness'.

5 The basis for selecting a sample or samples needs to be considered.
6 Consideration also needs to be given to ethical concerns.

Data collection

Data collection involves a range of skills, and consideration of a number of issues, including:

1 The need to negotiate access to the data, either with organizations or the individuals concerned.
2 The constraints and opportunities inherent in the fieldwork environment. The choice of which methods to use is affected by the environment in which you will be working. For example, a study of homeless alcoholics is unlikely to be best pursued by administering a 30-page questionnaire in a day centre. If the homeless alcoholics are receiving in-patient treatment in hospital, such a method might be conceivable, but even then there may be better alternatives.
3 Exactly how the data are going to be obtained and recorded. This depends on such things as whether collection is to be done by extraction from records or documents, by interview, by questionnaire, or by observation. You may need to develop abstraction proformas, interview schedules, consider whether or not to use a tape recorder or other form of recording, and how such recordings are to be processed and analysed.
4 This in turn involves consideration of how the data is structured. If using a questionnaire, recording may be highly structured, but qualitative methods allow for structure to emerge during the course of study. For example, Schatzman and Strauss (1973: 99–100) refer to observational notes, theoretical notes, and methodological notes.[6]

Planning fieldwork and data collection in advance is a critical part of any study, because you seldom get a second chance to go back and do it again!

Data analysis

Because the theoretical issues and data collection are interesting and demanding, it is easy to put off consideration of how information is to be analysed until later. It is tempting to wait and see what you get, and then decide what to do with it. This is a dangerous line of thought that can result in you ending up with a pile of material that is not going to be half as useful as it could have been. If the data is to be analysed statistically, consideration needs to be given to how it will be coded, whether you have the right computer program, and, not least, whether you have sufficient statistical knowledge for the task that faces you. It is no good, for example, finding out that the technique you need to use is multi-level modelling if you have neither the software nor the knowledge to use it. If you need help from a statistician, it is better to contact someone in advance than put them on the spot at the last minute. Conversely, there is no point in spending time planning to use sophisticated multi-variate techniques if your data will not meet the statistical assumptions required for, say, a multiple regression, when simpler techniques will suffice. Qualitative analysis involves a constant checking of emerging concepts and their interpretation against the fieldwork material (see Rose 1982: 123–5), and you need to decide in advance such things as whether you are going to use a computer-based package to analyse qualitative material, and whether the data needs to be transcribed verbatim.

Inference and presentation

This is where you draw appropriate conclusions and relate findings back to the hypotheses and theoretical context considered earlier. The skill is to make the best use of the data without 'over-reading' it or trying to get your material to tell you things that it was never intended for. It may also include drawing out implications for policy and practice. The presentation and dissemination of findings are also important at this stage. This may involve providing feedback to agencies and individuals who have co-operated with you during the investigation. This can be done in the form of a presentation, or in a short and accessible summary of the research.[7] Producing feedback to participants fulfils several functions. First, it is a way of discharging your ethical obligations, handing back some of the information to where it came from. Second, it may provide the opportunity to have your conclusions implemented by practitioners and policy-makers. Finally, such presentations can be a useful rehearsal for presenting results to the wider world. This wider presentation will usually involve publication in some form. Presenting a paper at a conference is also a useful way of running through your research in preparation for publication.

Further reading

There are several books on methods of social research in general. These include Alan Bryman's *Social Research Methods* (*2004*), which covers both quantitative and qualitative methods. *Research Training for Social Scientists* (*2000*), edited by Dawn Burton, is reasonably comprehensive, starting with the philosophy of the social sciences, moving on through ethical issues, qualitative and quantitative methods, to writing and presenting research.

One of our main reasons for writing this book is the fact that there are not many texts concerned specifically with research methods in criminology. However, there are edited books containing chapters by various writers. *Doing Criminological Research* (*2000*), edited by Victor Jupp, Pamela Davies and Peter Francis, has chapters on a variety of issues, including formulating research problems, and understanding the politics of criminological research, as well as drawing on what can be learned from research undertaken by the various contributors. *Doing Research on Crime and Justice*, by Roy King and Emma Wincup, also has chapters drawing on the expertise and experience of well-known criminologists such as Anthony Bottoms, Sandra Walklate, Mike Maguire and George Mair.

2 The principles of researching criminology

In Chapter 1, we emphasized that criminological research usually starts with the posing of a research question. This question may be developed in response to an emergent crime problem or policy issue, or it may be the case that a researcher sees the need to fill a gap in the literature, or update it. It is important to recognize that from this earliest stage of research, theory underpins the research process. As the researcher goes on to develop hypotheses, operationalize concepts, collect and analyse data and then draw conclusions, theory continues to drive the research process and fundamentally influences the final outcomes. It is extremely important, therefore, for a competent researcher to consider the theoretical context of an inquiry, even if s/he is not undertaking research directly associated with the investigation of a particular theory.

In this chapter, we will explore in some depth the relationship between research and theory. We will discover that there are two different ways of understanding the term 'theory' in the context of research. Most commonly, we understand theories to consist of explanations which are developed to account for phenomena which we have observed or experienced. So, for example, subcultural theory emerged from investigations into gang behaviour and delinquency (Cohen 1973; Thrasher 1947). It is important to realize that such theories are developed over time, by different people, using different methodologies and are in constant need of testing. However, we also need to consider theory in terms of the theoretical approach we take to the research process itself. In so doing we must consider one of the most debated questions in social research: is it possible to investigate the social world in a scientific way?

This chapter does not contain a discussion of all the possible theoretical explanations available to the criminological researcher. Indeed, there are many useful books and resources which already do this and we refer to some of them in the Further Reading section at the end of the chapter. The aim of the chapter is to explain how the relationship between theory and research is essential in criminological research as a foundation for 'quality control'. As we saw in the previous chapter, research is judged on its validity and reliability and in the discussion that follows, we hope to illustrate that theory plays an essential role in the establishment of validity and reliability in

Table 2.1 Validity and reliability in research

Criteria	*Key concern*
Internal validity	Can we be sure that a causal relationship exists?
External validity	Can the results be generalized?
Ecological validity	Are my conclusions applicable to everyday, natural situations or have they been drawn from unnatural conditions (for example, laboratory-style environments)?
Construct validity	Does a measure accurately reflect the concept it is designed to measure?
Reliability	Are concepts and measures consistent and repeatable?

research. Table 2.1 provides a summary of the key concerns in validity and reliability which we hope will serve as a useful point of reference as you progress through the chapter. It is helpful to reflect on these 'standards' when thinking about the theoretical underpinnings of research.

The research question: identifying the research question and exploring possible theoretical explanations

A characteristic of criminological research is that the research question is theoretically informed, even if the research itself is not directly associated with the investigation of a particular theory. This sets criminological research apart from other types of research, for example market research, which is often more concerned with fact-finding and polling than it is to explain and understand a social phenomenon. The process of designing a theoretically informed research question, or set of questions, does not always happen in exactly the same way but there are a number of important principles which, if followed, should facilitate the development of clear, specific, useful questions.

Take some time to think, for a moment, about your own research interests. If you had to design a research study, what would you choose as a topic? What are you interested in finding out about and why? The chances are your initial idea will be expressed in very broad terms. You might be interested, for example, in the relationship between poverty and crime or the experiences of witnesses in the courtroom. Whatever your decision, you will have made it in accordance with your own knowledge, experience and values. However, before you can start thinking about designing your research strategy, it is necessary to refine your broad interests into specific questions for investigation. In order to do this, you are going to have to become well acquainted with the literature in the topic area you have selected. Contained within the literature may be empirical and theoretical perspectives on any given area and it is the job of the researcher to decide which items are relevant to the project being developed. By reading about a subject, you will be able to assess the current level of knowledge in an area and identify potential gaps in understanding (i.e. gaps in the existing theory).

All research, then, should have a theoretical element which may be derived from a well-established theory, such as opportunity theory or subcultural theory, or it may even be an explanatory perspective which does not have a technical label. The process of researching and reviewing literature bases may take place in both library and electronic environments. Invariably, you will begin by searching the appropriate bibliographic databases and citation indices using key words or terms (we discuss this in more depth in Chapter 5). Once you have drawn up a list of potentially useful sources, the process of locating, reading and following up additional sources begins. Often, this is a time-consuming process and it requires good organizational skills on the part of the researcher. Robson (2002) also recommends that techniques of 'networking' are employed to ensure that the researcher knows his/her area extensively. He notes that, in many cases, other researchers who have completed research in the area are able to provide useful resources or citations. So he encourages dissemination of 'work in progress' through presenting seminars, writing reviews for publication and participation in interdisciplinary collaborations/investigations, with a view to getting feedback and ideas.

Once the literature review has been completed, you should be in a position to refine your original broad research idea into a defensible research question. The ultimate research question should primarily be focused and clear, but it also needs to be both useful and answerable. In order to ensure this, the research question should be accompanied by a clear set of aims and objectives.

The aims of research will usually fall into one of three categories: to *describe* something, to *explore/understand* a phenomenon, or to *explain/measure* it (Robson 2002). Importantly, though, research studies can incorporate combinations of elements of description, explanation and exploration and therefore it is important for the researcher to be clear about his/her aims from the outset. A descriptive research study does not seek to go beyond the simple reporting of an observation. It is most likely to report a situation or trend (so, for example, the publication of a police force's clear-up rates in the past five years) or it may be the kind of study which observes a newly emerging phenomenon (or a new perspective on an existing one). Research which has the aim of explanation and measurement will seek to test specific hypotheses with a view to drawing conclusions which may be generalized (a good example is the study described in Chapter 9). Research which sets out to explore or understand something will be more open in nature and will not always be restricted to the testing of hypotheses (see, for example, the study described in Chapter 12). The objectives of research may range from the development of theory or knowledge in a particular area, to the development of methodology or technical tools, through to a contribution to policy or practice. Or, indeed, there may be several inter-linked objectives.

Theory (be it criminological, sociological or whatever) not only feeds into or underpins research, but also can emerge from research, if, indeed, that is the aim of the enterprise. It is the job of the researcher to establish at the outset what role theory will take in the study. In a descriptive study, for example, the role of theory may be minimal but it may have a more important part to play in exploratory or explanatory studies. Wherever theory does play a role, the researcher must finally decide at which *level of explanation* to operate. This simply refers to the possibility that one explanation may be the result of a number of distinct causes, which can be expressed as different explanations which work at different 'levels' (individual, group, community, society, etc.). One can look at the motivations of *individuals*, one can look at the different pressures or opportunities which are specific to certain *groups* or one can consider *population* characteristics. These different accounts are not mutually exclusive and researchers can validly draw hypotheses about crime at each different level. However, what a researcher cannot assume is that a causal factor operating at one level also operates at another. So, for example, populations with a high proportion of unemployed people may be more prone to crime than populations where the vast majority of people have paid employment, but this does not necessarily mean that unemployment necessarily motivates an individual person to steal. To deduce conclusions about individuals on the basis of population-level data is often referred to as the 'ecological fallacy' (Robinson 1950) and it is something which the researcher needs to avoid.

To recap, then, the initial stages of research design involve some important decisions which are inevitably underpinned by theoretical considerations. Up until now, our discussion has centred on the role of theories in relation to the topic of the research itself. The next stage of research design is to select a research strategy and that involves some quite different theoretical questions.

Choosing a research strategy

Crucially, the choice of research strategy, and later the methodology, should follow the process of research question development. Any research study which emerges from a backward process (deciding for example that you want to do a survey and then looking for a topic) is likely to be badly conceived and full of practical and theoretical problems. But what do we mean by a *research strategy*? Put simply, it is a term which we are using to describe the overall design of the research process in any given project; thus it is a kind of 'strategic plan' which serves as a framework for all of the methodological decisions which need to be made and the conclusions which are eventually drawn. There are several different strategies available to the criminological researcher and we will be considering them in depth in Chapter 3, but first it is important to understand the role of theory in the strategic planning process. We must come to understand how strategies are firmly rooted in *epistemology* and how the epistemological basis of all research projects inform the methodological decisions which are later made.

What is epistemology?

Epistemology is a branch of philosophy which examines the concept of 'knowledge' – what it is, where it comes from and whether absolute, 'true' knowledge can be achieved. It is important in the context of research because a researcher's epistemological position will influence the methodological choices s/he makes. The focus of epistemology, in very simple terms, is that where a belief can be justified or verified, it may be accepted as knowledge. The question is, then, how can one justify a belief? There are a range of different philosophies, each with its own approach, but three main schools of thought are of interest to us here: *empiricism*, *rationalism* and *pragmatism*. All were developed most significantly during a period of history called the Period of Enlightenment (in the eighteenth century) in which philosophers from different disciplines argued passionately about the nature of knowledge. While it is not necessary for us to explore each of these schools in great detail, it is important to have a basic understanding of the key principles involved because they each form the basis of the various different strategies available to a criminological researcher. It is also important to recognize that although there are clear differences between them, they are not necessarily mutually exclusive. We offer a very brief summary of the key points here, but the interested reader is referred to the Further Reading section at the end of the chapter.

Empiricism has a long history in philosophy and its roots can be traced back to Aristotle, but it was first explicitly formulated by John Locke in the seventeenth century. Empiricists argue that the only way to acquire knowledge is through objective sensory perception. Thus, we acquire knowledge about the world through experience; that is by seeing, hearing, smelling or feeling phenomena. Through such experience, we are able to make *a posteriori* statements about the world, for example 'water boils at 100 degrees centigrade' or, to use a crime example, 'crime rates are highest in inner city areas'. Anything which cannot be verified through experience cannot be accepted as a truth. For the empiricist, then, the aim of research is to formulate 'laws' which are based on observations of patterns or recurring relationships, using *inductive reasoning*. This is the process of reasoning which moves in a logical manner from an observation to the drawing of more general conclusions. So, for example, we might find that all the inner cities in England have high crime rates and conclude that all inner cities have high crime rates. The point is that the process of reasoning does not start with a theory – the theory is derived from the data. The problem is that, although there may very well be a high probability of the conclusion being true, we cannot be completely sure.

The school of rationalism also has a long history (Plato, for example, was a rationalist) but it was developed most notably in the seventeenth and eighteenth centuries. The two most commonly cited rationalists are René Descartes (who led the way in introducing mathematical methods into philosophy) and Immanuel Kant (who is well known for his work on moral reasoning). Rationalists take a different approach to knowledge. While they would accept that knowledge may be acquired through experience, as the empiricists suggest, they argue that this is not the only way in which knowledge can be derived. It is proposed that human reason can also be the source of knowledge; something can be held to be true at a purely conceptual level. Rationalists believe, then, that *a priori* knowledge is possible, i.e. knowledge that is gained and verified by reason alone and does not need to be justified through actual experience (as does *a posteriori* knowledge). An example might be the statement 'nothing is red and green all over'. We can arrive at this statement through logical deduction, it is not necessary to prove it empirically (Kant 1871). Rationalists argue, then, that we can begin with an intuitive general principle (a theory) and derive complete knowledge by building on that basic principle using the process of *deductive reasoning*. To achieve this, we undergo a logical process of designing hypotheses, collecting data to test those hypotheses and, depending on the results, refining our original theories and developing new hypotheses to test.

The third school we wish to raise here is pragmatism. The pragmatic approach has been overshadowed slightly by the conflict between empiricism and rationalism, but several pragmatists have made an interesting contribution to the epistemological debates (well-known names include Charles Sanders Peirce and John Dewey). Pragmatists do not believe that one true reality can be conceived by the human mind, instead truth is 'what works'. The key idea in pragmatism is that 'truth' changes over time and across different circumstances and, therefore, all principles should be viewed as 'working hypotheses' rather than absolute truths. As a result, it is accepted that any set of data is explicable by more than one theory. Importantly, priority is always given to the practical, over the theoretical, in inquiry and it is accepted that both inquiry and facts are value-laden. The pragmatic approach has suffered significant criticism in the past because it amounts to little more than empirical relativism and short-sighted practicalism (Bertrand Russell was a famous critic).

Epistemology in criminology

Let us now bring the discussion back to criminological research. It is true to say that a great deal of criminological work is empirical in nature, and by that we mean that research is conducted using a working hypothesis that is tested through experiment or observation, rather than work which is purely theoretical. The empirical approach is most commonly associated with the *positivist* school of criminology. Positivism developed in the second half of the nineteenth century, at a time when the natural sciences and engineering were thriving and scholars from a range of disciplines were inspired by the advocates of empiricism. The positivist criminologists rejected the methodology of Classicism[1] and developed instead scientific methods of measuring and quantifying criminal behaviour, producing biological (Lombroso), psychological (Freud) and social (Durkheim) theories of crime. However, these early positivistic approaches were heavily criticized on the grounds that, unlike in the natural sciences, it is not easy to create universal laws about the social world, nor is it desirable to exclude from study those things which empiricists would call 'soft' and unreliable such as people's motivations or reasoning. In response to such criticism, positivists developed their methods and adjusted their principles over time in order to adapt to the peculiarities of the social world, but at the same time retaining scientific principles.[2] Thus, you will see references to neo-positivist and post-positivist theories which seek to make it possible to measure 'soft' concepts as long as heavy emphasis is placed on the standardization of measurement procedures. In modern forms of positivism, the empiricist's requirement for the establishment of universal laws is replaced with probabilities that relationships between concepts will hold true across all circumstances (Fischer 1998 and see also Popper's work on falsification (1959)).

However, although positivism has had a significant role in criminological thinking, it is not the only approach to research. Indeed, a number of anti-positivistic schools have emerged that criticize the overly 'fixed' approach to researching the social world and advocate a different epistemological and methodological framework. These include ethnography, phenomenology, hermeneutics and critical research, all of which are commonly referred to as *interpretivistic* approaches and involve a wide range of methods including observation, textual analysis, life histories and interviews. These approaches are not obsessed with fixed methods or fidelity to the phenomenon, but instead are focused on studying a phenomenon as it occurs in its natural state, undisturbed by the researcher. The idea of a standardized approach to data collection is rejected and it is argued that the method of data collection should be determined by the nature and setting of the phenomenon under study. The focus for research is on extracting the meaning of action, rather than simply calculating the frequencies of actions or characteristics. This, of course, means that this type of research is particularly vulnerable to accusations of subjectivity and invalidity.

Additionally, an approach to research which has recently enjoyed increasing popularity, particularly in the development of evaluation studies in criminology, is *realism*. This is an approach that attempts to combine the strengths of the positivistic and interpretivistic schools. It places a heavy emphasis on the importance of context, following the 'paradigmatic' approach of the pragmatist school in epistemology. Thus, it has the respectability which scientific study carries with it, but at the same time allows for exploratory methods to be used and, importantly, context to be explored. We will discuss realism in more detail in Chapter 4 when we look at evaluation research, but it is important to recognize it now as a potential research strategy.

Using epistemology in a research strategy

It is possible, then, to see how the epistemological positions play a significant role in the development of criminological thinking. Think, for a moment, what the empiricist, rationalist and pragmatist might say about approaches to learning about crime. The empiricist would argue that in order to learn about crime we must conduct scientific, empirical studies to measure the phenomenon. In contrast, the rationalist would argue that we can legitimately draw conclusions about crime through reasoning alone. The pragmatist would argue that we can never achieve a universal understanding of crime – instead we must focus on studying crime-related phenomena in the contexts of specific cultures or within social groups. By understanding the tension which exists between these epistemological views, we can better understand the development of knowledge in our discipline and also determine how best to design our own research, taking into account the potential strengths and weaknesses of different approaches. Remember, a good researcher places a high priority on the production of research that is valid and reliable and the epistemological basis of a research strategy is key in achieving this. Each of the different epistemological approaches has its own idea of what is and what is not valid, and this has to be acknowledged in the design of the research strategy.

As we stated at the start of the chapter, it is quite rare for a researcher to state clearly his/her epistemological position in simple terms (for example 'this work is positivistic') and often it is left for the reader to work out the theoretical underpinnings of a piece of published research for him/herself. This is usually a relatively easy task if you can clearly identify the aims (description, exploration, explanation), the nature of the hypotheses (narrow or broad), the methods used (fixed or flexible), the type of data collected (quantitative or qualitative) and the way in which conclusions were drawn (inductive or deductive reasoning). Even if it is not possible to be 100 per cent certain, usually enough detail can be drawn to allow a sufficient assessment of the epistemological approach adopted. As a result, we can interpret other people's research more effectively because we are able to question the relationship between theory and method in the approach they adopt and ultimately assess the validity and reliability of their work. Similarly, our own work is open to similar analysis by others and we must be careful to ensure consistency in our strategy and to anticipate potential weaknesses in our approach and, wherever possible, incorporate safeguards into our methods. It is worth noting that, although there is always a link between epistemology and research strategy, it is not always a perfect relationship. Sometimes, researchers employ a multi-strategy approach to research, combining different epistemological approaches.

Let us pause a moment to look back on the discussion so far and review our position. We have said that all research begins with the development of a research question and the setting of aims and objectives. At this stage of the research, any number of explanatory theories may be relevant and it is important for the researcher to clearly identify the area of theory which s/he hopes to explore or clarify and the level of explanation at which s/he intends to operate. The next stage is for the researcher to adopt a research strategy and to build a theoretical framework upon which the whole project can be built. This framework will itself be built on a series of epistemological principles and sets some important limits within which the researcher must make the decisions about methods and data analysis. It is these decisions which we now move on to consider in more detail.

Method selection and data collection

Once a framework for the research has been provided through the selection of a strategy, the process of method design can begin. This process must be conducted with continual reference to the aims and objectives of the research and to the research strategy adopted. The important theoretical implications that have influenced the research process thus far will continue to have an important role to play. A detailed discussion of the various methods available to the criminological researcher is contained in the chapters that follow, but it is important for us to be aware of the theoretical underpinnings of the methodological choices which need to be made. The choices we discuss in this section relate to the type of data, the hypotheses, the sampling strategy and the role of the researcher.

Type of data

One of the first decisions to make is whether to take a quantitative and/or qualitative approach to the data collection. We have already referred to the difference between quantitative and qualitative research in Chapter 1. Quantitative research epitomizes a positivistic approach, promoting the objectivity and remoteness of the researcher, the testing of hypotheses in a formally structured methodology and the collection of hard, numerical data. In contrast, in qualitative research, the researcher is encouraged to become involved with the subjects, looking for meaning and developing emergent theories through the analysis of soft, non-numerical data (Hammersley 1992).

A multi-strategy approach is actually common in criminological research and we are strong advocates of such an approach. It is important, however, to recognize that this position is subject to some controversy. Bryman (2004) notes two different objections to multi-strategy approaches. On the one hand, proponents of the 'embedded methods argument' say that specific methods carry with them irrefutable epistemological commitments. So, for example, if you choose to carry out participant observation you must adopt an epistemology consistent with interpretivism (Smith 1983; Smith and Heshusius 1986). Since different epistemological principles are inconsistent, it makes no sense to attempt to combine methods. On the other hand, advocates of the 'paradigm argument' say that quantitative and qualitative research are paradigms which are simply inconsistent with each other because they have opposing assumptions and methods.

However, Bryman illustrates very effectively how the distinction between quantitative and qualitative research is less apparent (and indeed problematic) in practice. He notes the many examples of common ground between the two approaches, illustrating that research often includes both an inductive and deductive approach to analysis and a combination of quantitative and qualitative data. He concludes that the relationship between epistemology and method is a tendency, rather than fixed and that, although there are some differences between quantitative and qualitative approaches, it is important not to exaggerate them.

Nowadays, particularly in criminology, researchers combine methods, theories and data in a single study to improve validity (Denzin 1988). Such an approach is referred to as *triangulation* and the idea behind it is that it improves the quality and validity of research by taking into account the possible weaknesses found in any single method. There are four different forms of triangulation: theory, methodological, researcher and data (see also Denzin's kinds of triangulation on p.000). Theory triangulation involves the combination of two or more theoretical approaches. Methodological triangulation requires the combination of quantitative and qualitative approaches. Researcher (or observer) triangulation occurs where more than one researcher is used in the fieldwork. Data triangulation is the combination of different methods of data collection. It is possible to use any combination of these approaches in a research study and increasingly this is being recognized as a desirable feature in criminological research.

Hypotheses

Whether you adopt a quantitative and/or a qualitative approach, it is likely to be the case that hypotheses are developed. As we saw in Chapter 1, a hypothesis usually takes the form of a short statement which speculates a relationship between two variables and is most commonly used in positivistic research. However, it may be incorrect to assume that the development of hypotheses is not appropriate to a non-positivistic study, especially if the aim is to explore or describe something. Indeed, in interpretive studies it is often the aim to look for emergent hypotheses, as well as testing them. An example is Becker's (1958) participant observation in which he sought to discover hypotheses as well as to test them. If a positivistic approach is being adopted, it will be necessary for you to clearly define and operationalize the key concepts which build the hypotheses. The danger here is that you are imposing your own concepts and it is important to ensure as far as possible that your concepts are valid and reliable. If an interpretivistic approach is adopted, the key concepts will become defined as the research progresses. There are also problems of interpretation here and it is again important to remain as objective as possible. We will consider these issues in more detail in later chapters.

Sampling

We will go into the methods of sampling, which can be quite complicated, in Chapter 3. However, it is important to realize that the choice of sampling procedure will have theoretical underpinnings and must be justified in accordance with the aims of the project and the epistemological approach adopted. There are two main approaches to sampling – probability and non-probability sampling. Probability sampling is based on a major assumption – the assumption of homogeneity. The principle is that a sample drawn is representative of a whole and each element has an equal chance of being included in the sample. So, when a doctor takes a sample of your blood, the assumption is that that sample accurately represents the condition of your blood generally. The doctor could take another ten, or even one hundred samples and they would all be identical. Similarly, if I make a cup of coffee, I expect the spoon of coffee in my mug to represent the whole jar – each sample should result in a cup of coffee which tastes the same. The methods for conducting probability samples are strictly controlled and methodical, using procedures to ensure randomness. The strength of this kind of sampling is that claims of representativeness can be made by the researcher. This kind of sampling is most commonly used for survey research which *tends* to be positivistic and quantitative but is not exclusively so.

Non-probability sampling is different. There is no way of predicting the probability that different subjects will be drawn and the researcher is often prevented from generalizing or making claims of representativeness. The methods used are tailored very much to the boundaries of the research. These methods might be used for reasons of convenience or where access to a closed group of people is very difficult. Say, for example, I wish to conduct research into teenagers who use drugs – it would be very hard to locate the population as the subjects might not want to be open about their addictions, but if I were able to locate a small group, they might be able to facilitate meetings with their friends or acquaintances. This kind of sampling is most commonly used in non-positivistic, qualitative research but, again, may be used in different kinds of approach.

Role of the researcher

Once a sampling strategy has been devised, there is one final decision to be made by the researcher and that is what role will s/he play in the research. In some cases, the researcher will play an active role, for example, by acting as an interviewer or participant observer. In other cases, the researcher will adopt a more objective, scientific role, for example by administering a postal survey or by being a non-participant observer. Whichever role is selected, thought must be given to the epistemological framework of the study itself. The more positivistic a study is, the more detached and procedural the research must become.

Data analysis and inference

Recall that in Chapter 1 we warned against succumbing to the temptation to postpone the development of a data analysis strategy until after the data has been collected. It is, indeed, tempting to wait and see what you get, and then decide what to do with it but this approach is likely to result in disappointment and frustration for the researcher. If the data is quantitative, it may need to be analysed statistically and therefore consideration needs to be given to how it will be coded and analysed. Qualitative analysis involves continual codification and interpretation of emerging concepts and you need to decide in advance such things as whether you are going to use a computer-based package to analyse qualitative material, and whether the data needs to be transcribed verbatim. We will go into the principles and methods of data analysis in more detail in Chapter 8, but the point we wish to emphasize here is that it is important to know from the outset exactly how you wish to use your data to address your research question, test your hypotheses and/or develop your theory. Again, the decisions made here will relate closely to the original aims of the research. Whether you are seeking to describe, explain or explore a phenomenon will influence the type of analysis you conduct.

A distinction must be made between two different relationships between theory and data analysis: *deductive* and *inductive* reasoning (we mentioned these earlier in the discussion about epistemology). Deductive reasoning involves the testing of theory through the selection of key concepts and the testing of hypotheses. Inductive reasoning involves the generation of theory through analysis of data. Although the two approaches can be, and usually are, distinguished, it is important to note that most research contains elements of both approaches, to some extent (Bryman 2004).

If you are adopting a deductive approach (most likely if you are using a positivistic approach), hypotheses are deduced from existing theory and subjected to empirical testing. The process of hypothesis building starts with the identification of key concepts. These key concepts, then, can be seen as the building blocks of hypotheses which, in turn, come together to build theories. In order to measure these concepts, it is necessary to transform them into variables. This process is called operationalization and will be explained in more detail in the following section. Once the data has been collected, it will be possible to either confirm or reject the hypotheses. Finally, the researcher reflects on the implications of the results for the existing theory and feeds back into it (Bryman (2004), notes that this is actually a process of induction tacked onto the end of the deductive process).

The development of theory through induction is different and is most often found in non-positivistic studies (i.e. those adopting an exploratory approach). Once the research question has been posed, it is not necessary to develop hypotheses for rigid testing. Instead, data are collected and analysed and the theory is developed from the findings. It may then be necessary to go back and explore the theory more. Grounded theory is an approach to research which moves from the stage of research question design to sampling and data collection. Data is coded and categorized and the researcher begins at that stage to generate hypotheses and build theories. By continually repeating the process until the 'point of theoretical saturation' is reached (i.e. the point at which new data does not add anything new to the concepts which have been developed), the researcher eventually develops theory out of the data (Strauss and Corbin 1998).

Conclusion

It is hoped that this chapter has illustrated the various ways in which theory can (and must) play a part in the research process. From the early stages of research question design, through to the design of methodology and analysis of data, theory underpins the research process. It is extremely important, therefore, for a competent researcher to consider the theoretical context of an inquiry, even if s/he is not undertaking research directly associated with the investigation of a particular theory. Most commonly, we understand theories to consist of explanations which are developed to account for phenomena which we have observed or experienced. But we have seen that theory is also relevant in terms of the theoretical approach we take to the research strategy. Crucially, a good research study has a clear research strategy which can be justified by the researcher. As we move on now to consider the technicalities and finer details of research design and specific methodologies, it is hoped that the importance of these issues will be borne in mind and, indeed, that their relevance will be enforced.

Further reading

We have only been able to scratch the surface of the role of theory in research in this chapter and there are a number of texts which are useful in developing a more in-depth understanding of explanatory and epistemological theories. Bryman (2004) gives a good textbook-style overview of the epistemological positions in social science and Delanty and Strydom's (2003) collection of over sixty extracts from classic works on the philosophy of social science is an excellent resource for anyone interested in reading epistemological works in their original form. For the explanatory theories, there are many theory texts on the market but one of the most comprehensive (and, indeed, most popular among our students) is the book by Vold and Snipes, now in its 5th edition (2001). Bottoms (2000) also provides a relatively short and very interesting account of the relationship between theory and research in criminology, focusing on different categories of criminological theory and providing a useful worked-through example to illustrate his points. Finally, Garland's (2002) chapter on the development of criminology in Britain in *The Oxford Handbook of Criminology* gives an interesting historical overview of the role of theory in criminology.

3 Designing criminological research

In this chapter we look at what is involved in designing a research project. In terms of the research process outlined in Chapter 1, this is the stage between formulating a theoretically informed research question and collecting the data needed to investigate the question. It includes deciding on an appropriate research design, choosing an appropriate sampling technique, and considering the important issue of researching ethically. During the course of the chapter we will look at some of the more widely used kinds of research design.

As ever, we emphasize that although we are setting out the steps involved in researching criminology in a certain sequence, this is not intended to be a rigid rule. For those who have not done much research before, this will be a useful framework. The more experienced researcher may well adopt a more flexible approach which reflects the exigencies of a particular project.

What is research design and why is it important?

Social research is sometimes thought of in terms of particular methods such as questionnaires and interview schedules, participant observation, documentary analysis. Such methods are the *techniques* used in collecting and handling data. Research design concerns the overall research plan, within which such methods are to be employed. To use a military analogy, research design is about strategy, whereas selecting specific methods is about tactics.

For example, if you are studying how local authorities implement legislation concerning child care, first you have to decide how you are going to approach this. Are you going to do a survey of all local authorities, or look in some detail at just a few, or perhaps a combination of the two? You then need to decide what methods to use within this design: a questionnaire if you are doing a survey, interviews with key officials, an analysis of an authority's records, minutes of meetings, and so on. As we mentioned in Chapter 1, it is quite common to have research designs that use mixed methods, perhaps combining a survey with case studies.

Causal analysis

If you are hoping to find out what caused something, the research design is an important means of ensuring that you have the basis for determining causality.[1] Usually this means being able to 'control' for, or take account of, certain factors. If you are looking at the effects of new legislation, or the introduction of a new policy then it is important to have information about the situation *before* the new policy or legislation is introduced, in order to compare it with the situation subsequently. You therefore have to decide which measures need to be compared. You may also need to compare instances where changes have been made, with instances where they have not. For example, if you were looking at whether a crime reduction programme has had any effect, you would need to consider whether changes in recorded crime have been affected by changes in policing practices in some areas. In some studies you may need to look at what is happening in different parts of the country, or among different groups of people in order to control for such things as socio-economic differences. A simple way of envisaging causal relationships is shown in Figure 3.1, where the question being addressed is whether changes in unemployment rates have an impact on crime rates:

A **variable** is simply something that is measurable; that varies (see Glossary). A *dependent* variable is the outcome you are interested in (in the example below, the crime rate). An *independent* variable (or variables) is what you hypothesize might be responsible for variations in the dependent variable. *Intervening* or *extraneous* variables are those things that might influence the relationship between the independent and dependent variables.

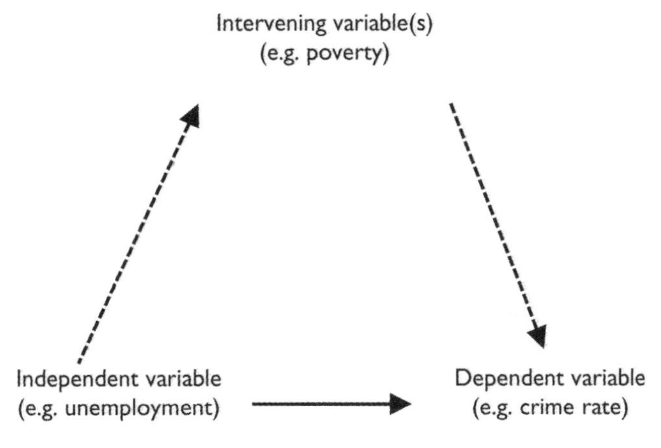

Figure 3.1 Causal analysis

In order to determine whether there is a causal relationship it is necessary to ascertain:

- whether there is a relationship between two factors (variables);
- whether the independent variable is logically and temporally prior to (i.e. comes before) the dependent variable;
- whether the relationship is true or spurious; can it be attributed to the presence of other factors (intervening variables)?

See also Bryman and Cramer (1990: 7 ff.).

To give an example, by choosing different geographical areas to study, we can 'control' for socio-economic variation to some extent by selecting a well-off area, and a not so well-off area.[2] The research design adopted is also critical for determining the basis for any sampling. In the example concerning local authority child-care practice, we may take a sample of local authorities and then select a sample of people within each authority to interview. We will come back to this shortly.

The main types of empirical inquiry

To enable us to work out what is causing a particular phenomenon (such as a change in the crime rate) we can employ several research strategies. In doing so, however, we need to be aware that there are certain ways of identifying how one variable might be affecting another. There are important distinctions between experimental research, quasi-experimental research, and non-experimental research. All three try to take account of the relevant variables in an effort to make a causal inference, but do so in different ways.

Experimental studies attempt to arrange a situation in which variables are controlled *prior to* the data being collected, often by allocating people, places (or whatever units are under investigation) to experimental and control groups. The best way to exercise control over extraneous variables is to allocate units randomly. Random assignment to 'experimental' and 'control' groups is crucial to avoid selecting groups that vary in some other way, such as friends choosing to be with each other. This is not easily achieved in criminological research in real life, but can be simulated in some situations. For example, magistrates could be randomly allocated to one of two groups. Those in Group A are given details of a case, and asked how they would deal with it. Those in Group B are given the same case, except that one piece of information is different, say, the defendant's race, or employment history, or the age of the victim, to see whether this has any effect.

As another example, is children's behaviour affected by watching violent films or television, or playing certain kinds of computer games? You could expose some children to such experiences ('experimentals') but not other children ('controls'), perhaps by showing them films which are either violent or non-violent in class, and measure or observe their behaviour during play time before and after watching the films. You would have to ensure that the controls are not accidentally or covertly exposed to such experiences and you will need to take account of the fact that other factors may also change over the time period concerned. You would then measure the dependent variable (such as the number of aggressive acts that each child displays) and determine whether any differences between the two groups are statistically significant. We have referred elsewhere to the importance of doing research ethically, and such a study would, of course raise ethical issues, including the need for parental consent. While the example above illustrates a methodological point, because of the ethical and practical problems involved, you are more likely to encounter other types of study in most criminological research.

Quasi-experimental studies, sometimes called correlational studies, include surveys. Here the variables frequently have to be manipulated statistically *after* the data has been collected in order to try to make inferences about the relationships between variables. It is more difficult to determine causality because there is less control over variables, and it may be difficult to determine the time order of variables. Taking the violent films and behaviour example used above, in a quasi-experimental design you might take a sample of school-children, ask them about their viewing, and their behaviour by means of a questionnaire, or see if they have been in trouble for behaving badly, and compare them, taking account of their age, gender, background and other factors.

Non-experimental studies make little or no attempt to control or manipulate variables. Their purpose might be to look in more depth at the mechanisms underlying a particular social process, and to gain insight into the interpretations and perceptions of actors, or other objects of study such as organizations. Ethnographic studies come under this heading. Applying this approach to the films/violence issue, you might spend time with children, watching how they spend their time, and talking to them in order to understand how their viewing habits and behaviour could be mediated by their social habits.

As a further example of the three types of study mentioned above, imagine that you are looking at whether the police are biased against certain groups of people. You could investigate this in the following ways:

1 by giving a random sample of police officers' descriptions of cases and asking them how they would proceed: would they caution or charge, and if so, with what offence? The details of the cases are exactly the same for all officers with one exception: for half the

group the race of the accused is white, and for the other half (determined randomly) the accused is black. This would be an experimental study.

2 Alternatively, you could go through a random selection of cases the police have dealt with over the last year and abstract information on variables such as what charges were brought and the race of the suspect, and any other variables that might be relevant. You then analyse this data to see whether black defendants are dealt with differently, using statistical tests to take account of such factors as the nature of the offence, previous criminal history, and so on. This would be a quasi-experimental study.
3 You could spend some time in a particular police force (or forces) learning about police culture and the way the police think, talk and act in relation to suspects from different ethnic backgrounds. This would be a non-experimental study.

You could also, if time and money allow, use a combination of the three approaches. Note that in all three instances you would need to make decisions about whether you are going to investigate one police force or many, and if several, should they be randomly selected, or selected on purpose to illustrate different parts of the country (e.g. the Metropolitan Police, one in the rest of the South of England, one in the North of England, and one in Wales).

Furthermore, all three approaches have ethical implications. These may be more apparent in the case of experimental designs because of the random allocation involved, but in all three instances there is the question of telling those involved what you are doing, and whether this is likely to affect the way they behave. We return to ethical issues shortly.

Some common kinds of research design

A thorough review of different kinds of research design would require a much longer discussion, but it is worth describing a few examples of different research strategies that are commonly used.

Prospective and retrospective studies

Studying what happens to people coming before the courts may be done either by sitting in court waiting for cases to come up (prospective), or going through court records to see what happened to people who *have* been through the court (retrospective).

In prospective studies, it is easier to ensure that the information you want is recorded, but they are very time-consuming. For example, there has been a lot of concern over the years about the way in which mentally disordered offenders are dealt with by the criminal justice system (e.g. Palmer and Hart 1996). But if you wanted to look at how mentally disordered people are dealt with in court, such cases are not that common compared to the total number of cases going through a court overall (for example, Browne et al. 1993). You might get much interesting information from such a sample, but it would involve spending a lot of time in court to get a viable sample, compared with doing a retrospective study of cases dealt with in the past by using court records.

Cross-sectional studies

These involve collecting information relating to a phenomenon at a particular point in time, usually in different locations. For example, does the rate of school exclusions vary in different parts of the country, and, if so, what are the differences and why? While such a design may be a useful basis for inquiries, it does mean that all kinds of other differences between areas have to be taken into consideration, and of course by excluding the time variable, it means you cannot consider how rates are changing.

Longitudinal studies

These are studies that involve collecting information over a period of time, on people, places, or events. They are usually a major undertaking, and there are some well-known national longitudinal studies which have collected information on a *cohort* of people over a number of years. For example, the National Child Development Study is a longitudinal birth cohort study of everyone born in a single week in 1958. It consists of data collected at intervals from birth to the present for some 17,000 individuals. One of the best-known examples of a longitudinal study in criminology is the Cambridge Study of Delinquent Development, in which a sample of about 500 boys, aged 8 to 9, was drawn from six primary schools in a working-class urban area in the UK. Longitudinal cohorts like these have been used to study the development of criminal careers, and the kinds of factors that affect whether and when people offend, and when they cease to offend.

Evaluation studies

There is one particular and very important kind of research design in criminology that we have not mentioned so far. This is the kind that involves evaluating the impact of various interventions. We mention it now because logically a chapter on research design is where it rightfully belongs. However, it has played such an important role in criminological research that it needs a chapter to itself, so it is discussed in more detail in Chapter 4.

Choosing a research design: an example

To illustrate the possibilities for choosing and developing an appropriate research design, take the following question as an example: 'Does an increase in unemployment lead to an increase in crime?'

Studies on the relationship between unemployment and crime tend to occur when unemployment is high. When the rate declines, such research goes out of fashion – until the next downturn in the economy. Perhaps in itself this says something about the relationship? Notice that the way the problem is defined is important. The question could have been phrased differently, such as 'does unemployment cause crime?'. This would involve approaching the matter in a different way, requiring a much more fundamental investigation of the relationship. The question here is more amenable to investigation, but more limited in scope – which for present purposes will suffice.

In order to investigate such a question, there are several preliminary considerations:

- *Measuring unemployment*: This has always been difficult, and the way such matters are measured is liable to change (see Chapter 5 on using other people's data).
- *Measuring crime*: Crime figures have several shortcomings, and are far from being a measure of true crime. Which crimes? All offences OR should we restrict ourselves to looking at those that one might theoretically expect to be susceptible to changes in levels of employment, such as theft?
- *Inference*: What is causing what?
  - It is important to compare like with like. If you are comparing employed with unemployed people, are they similar in other respects?
  - Rises in unemployment must be prior to rises in crime rate.
  - It is no good pointing to the fact that a lot of offenders are unemployed. Many alcoholics drink tea, but how many tea drinkers become alcoholics?
- *Generalization*: Be wary of drawing global conclusions based on limited studies. Researchers may have done a study of the unemployment–crime relationship in a particular area. For example, Gormally et al. (1981) studied the relationship in Northern Ireland, but how far can their results be used to draw inferences about the relationship in general?

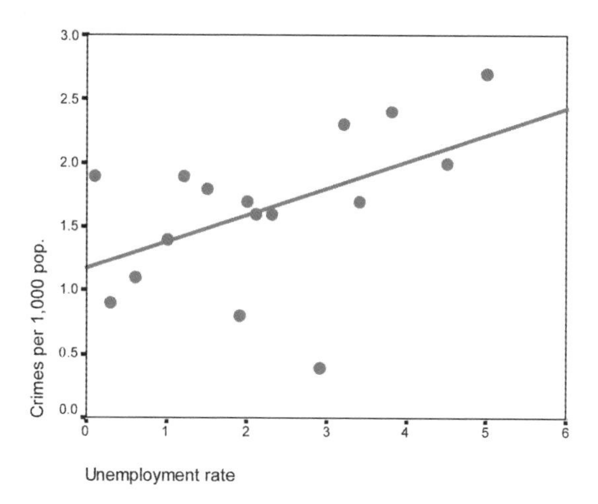

Figure 3.2 Crimes per 1000 population for police force areas by unemployment rate by travel-to-work area

In investigating this question, there are two main kinds of study that can be considered: studies of aggregate data and studies of individuals. Aggregate data are collections of statistics, such as the overall crime rate or the unemployment rate.

Aggregate studies

Cross-sectional

These compare areas with varying rates of unemployment to see whether crime is higher in areas with high unemployment rates. There may be problems matching the boundaries for police force areas for crime statistics with the travel-to-work areas used for compiling employment statistics. There may also be other differences between high and low unemployment areas which cause any differences. Look at the scatter diagram in Figure 3.2, for instance.

Figure 3.2 does show a correlation between crime rates and unemployment rates, but this does not take us very far. Even supposing that police force areas coincide with travel-to-work areas, it leaves us wanting to know much more about the areas concerned. Take the case at the bottom with a crime rate of less than 0.5 per 1000 population. It has a fairly average level of unemployment, but the lowest crime rate. Why is it so exceptional? As it happens, this represents an area in rural Wales, so one might hypothesize that it has a strong community identity which helps to protect it from the worst ravages of unemployment. One might want to investigate this area in more detail. In passing, it is worth noting that this also demonstrates the value of not just looking at overall trends, but also examining individual instances within them.

Time series analysis

In contrast to the cross-sectional design, time series designs look at the same variables over a period of time. To address our question, we might therefore look at trends to see whether crime goes up when unemployment goes up and vice versa. This has been studied by economists (e.g. Brenner 1976), but the period of time chosen may be important because there may be a relationship over some periods but not others (Tarling 1982), and this warrants further examination. It is also necessary to take account of underlying trends in economic indicators and lag effects – the impact of rising or decreasing employment levels may not become apparent for a while after they occur.

In both types of aggregate study it is necessary to control statistically for other factors which may explain any co-variation. Such aggregate studies are often based on econometric models, and tell us little about the people involved, the impact unemployment has on them and the way in which it affects their options and behaviour as individuals, hence a second kind of study taking individuals rather than aggregate measures is useful.

Individual studies

Matching groups

This design compares groups of employed and unemployed people to see whether the latter have committed more crimes than the former. The main problem here is comparing like with like (matching). We could follow a cohort of school leavers, comparing those who get jobs and those who didn't. What problems might be encountered here? Perhaps the kinds of people who don't get jobs are also the kind of people who get into trouble, either because they have a particular kind of personality or because they come from a particular background. If the latter, they may simply be more likely to be apprehended by the police but not necessarily be more delinquent.

Longitudinal studies

This design looks at a single group of people, comparing the extent of their offending when they are out of work with when they are in work. In this instance they 'act as their own controls'. One such study was undertaken using the Cambridge Study of Delinquent

Development cohort referred to earlier for a period during the 1970s (Farrington et al. 1986), and another in the early 1980s looked at young people in Northern Ireland (Gormally et al. 1981).

Studies based on individuals are preferable to aggregate studies in many ways, but have some disadvantages:

1 It is more time-consuming and expensive to study groups of people than to examine the statistics on unemployment and crime which are already available.
2 They are more limited in coverage, and therefore less generalizable.

As you can see, there is no easy, simple solution to the question of which research design to adopt, and this is often the case in criminological research. Researching such questions often involves finding the best option given the circumstances and resources available, while acknowledging its limitations. This does not mean that we cannot answer such questions, but it may mean that it is necessary to look at what emerges from a number of studies using different approaches in order to get the full picture, and this is the case with the unemployment and crime question (for a further consideration of such studies see Crow et al. 1989).

Sampling

Whatever kind of design is adopted, it is likely to involve looking at only a proportion of the cases, people, places, events, etc. that you are studying. Consequently, sampling is an integral part of any research design.

What is sampling?

A sample is part of a population, which is studied in order to obtain estimates about the population (e.g. the proportion of a population who are the victims of theft). A population is a set of all the units about which an inference is to be made. Consequently a sample has to be selected in such a way that the conclusions drawn are valid, i.e. it must be representative of the population. Sampling is done because it is often not possible to study the whole population.

It is important to bear in mind that beyond the population from which the sample is drawn there may be a wider universe about which generalizations are being explicitly or implicitly made. For example, in selecting a sample of schoolchildren from a school in Nitherington, are you seeking to draw conclusions about that particular school, about schools in Nitherington, or about the educational system? If anything other than the first (that particular school), then clearly a sample from one school, while it may be suggestive and illuminating, is not sufficient in itself.

Sampling what?

We referred above to 'units'. This is because a sample can consist of almost anything: people, organizations, places, objects or events (e.g. a study of fights in a town centre), or a combination of these. It is necessary to say what your sampling unit is.

Sampling frame

It is also necessary to identify a sampling frame. This is the list of all the units in the population from which the sample is to be selected (e.g. an electoral roll, a list of firms of solicitors, a list of all the magistrates courts in the country). However, be warned that sampling frames can be less than perfect. For example, if we are to take a sample of students from those registered at a particular university, despite everyone's best endeavours, the university's register may be less than 100 per cent accurate. Similarly, if we are hoping to sample from all the arrests made by a police force in a particular year, the force's records may contain errors.

Sampling fraction

The sampling fraction (f) indicates what proportion the sample (n) is of the population (N). Thus, $f = n \div N$. For example, if there are 400 students in the first year of a criminology course and we sample 40 of them, the sampling fraction is $40 \div 400$, or one in ten.

Size of sample

There is no hard and fast rule stating what size a sample should be. The best rule is the bigger the better, because the bigger a sample is, the closer it gets to the size of the population it represents. But clearly if you are trying to make inferences on a large scale about the population of whole towns, or countries, the proportion you can realistically sample is not going to be anywhere near the size of the population. This makes it all the more important to ensure that your sample isn't biased.

In practice, the size of a sample depends on several things. One of them is simply the resources you have at your disposal. With lots of money it is possible to acquire larger samples, but most research depends on limited resources. So the next thing is to consider the nature of your population (is it very diverse, so that you have to

Table 3.1 Cell frequencies in a cross-tabulation

	Black	*White*	*Asian*	*Other*	*Total*
Fine	5	5	5	5	20
Community Sentence	5	5	5	5	20
Custodial Sentence	5	5	5	5	20
Other	5	5	5	5	20
Total	**20**	**20**	**20**	**20**	**80**

cover lots of different groups, or relatively homogeneous?), and what do you hope to do with your data? If you are using quantitative analysis, then you are likely to want to break your sample down into sub-groups (e.g. men and women, young offenders and adult offenders, type of offence committed), and examine those sub-groups in relation to various dependent variables (such as what kind of sentence they get). Let's suppose you want to see whether people from different ethnic backgrounds receive different sentences, you would have a cross-tabulation[3] of ethnicity with sentence (keeping the categories as simple as possible) as shown in Table 3.1.

As a general rule, in order to carry out the necessary statistical tests, you need to have at least five cases in each cell (no pun intended) of the grid, and there is a convention in statistics that the ideal should be 30 per cell or more. As you can see, even at the lowest and simplest level you need a sample of 80 for this analysis. If you are analysing your data in various ways, perhaps differentiating between age groups, gender, and so on, then even with a sample of several hundred, you can quickly end up with quite small numbers in each cell of the cross-tabulation. This is particularly likely to happen in criminology, where certain groups in the population, such as women and those from ethnic minorities, tend to be less frequently represented than in the population as a whole. Consequently it is necessary to think backwards from the kind of results that you anticipate needing.

Sampling, error and inference

In itself size is no guarantee that the sample is representative. An important aspect of sampling concerns the extent to which your sample can be said to reflect the population being studied. If you are studying victimization, can the characteristics of the sample interviewed be said to hold for the population from which the sample is drawn?

Two concepts are relevant when considering representativeness. One is *bias*. All samples are liable to various sources of error, for example, as a result of interviewers not selecting people properly. Another source of bias is *non-response*, which occurs as a result of some people or organizations not taking part in the study for various reasons, such as choosing not to, or by an oversight get missed out. Those who should form part of a sample according to the selection criteria, but do not for whatever reason, may well be different in some systematic way from those who are included. For example, if you were trying to study a sample of ex-prisoners to see how well they managed to settle back into society, the ones most difficult to include may well be the ones with most problems who are most likely to re-offend. The sample is biased, and therefore not truly representative of the population you are interested in. The important thing to note about this is that bias is not reduced by having a larger sample. Indeed, if the bias is systematic, a larger sample will only make things worse, and increasing the size of the sample may be misleading because it makes it appear as if the sample is convincing when it isn't.

The other concept is *accuracy*. Accuracy can be increased by increasing the sample size, because increasing sample size causes the sampling distribution of the mean of a variable to approach a normal distribution.[4] However carefully done, a sample will rarely be like the population from which it was drawn in every particular. No one will expect it to be exactly the same. The important thing is to be clear and open when reporting a study about how it was done, and how any sources of bias or inaccuracy may have arisen.

Wherever possible (i.e. where the parameters of the population are known), then you should check to see whether your sample is representative of the population. Inferential statistics are used to determine whether a sample came from a particular population. For example, if you were doing a study of some aspect of youth offending and took a random sample of young offenders from one or more Youth Offending Teams, then we would hope that the principle of random selection would lead to your sample being typical of all the young people being dealt with by the YOT. However, it is prudent to check to see whether this is in fact the case. In such an example, the YOT is likely to have certain information about the characteristics of those on its caseload, such as their ages, the proportion of males and females. If we just take mean age as an example, then by calculating the standard error of the mean of the sample it is possible to say whether the mean age of the population (in this instance, the YOT caseload) falls within the confidence limits of your sample. More is said about analysis in Chapter 8.

Types of sample

There are two main kinds of sample: random or non-random. These are also referred to in some references as probability and non-probability samples. The distinction is an important one because true random samples are by nature representative of a population, and enable you to make statements of probability about the populations from which they are drawn, whereas non-random ones, however carefully selected, are not, and this affects the extent to which one can generalize from the sample to a population.

Random samples

These are also known as *probability* samples because the essence of a random sample is that every unit in the population has an equal probability of being selected, i.e. there is no bias in the selection process. This is what makes it representative of the population. Even so, statements made about the population based on a random sample are statements of probability, not certainties, because error can creep in. So we can say that there is a 95 per cent probability that the sample mean for a particular variable such as age is within a certain range of the true (population) mean, but because there is always the possibility of error, we can never be 100 per cent certain.

Random samples can take various forms:

- *Simple random sample* – This consists of picking a sample at random by, for example, choosing every tenth person on a list (the starting point being selected randomly), or by using a table of random numbers.
- *Stratified random sample* – This consists of dividing the population into identifiable groups, or strata, and then sampling randomly within strata in order to ensure adequate representation of the strata. For example, if choosing a sample of students, you may want to divide them into 1st, 2nd and 3rd year students and sample each year. Other examples of strata are race, gender or social class. Women are much less likely to be charged with offences than men, so in criminology if you want to ensure adequate representation of women in your study, it is usually necessary to stratify the sample in order to make sure that you have an adequate sample of women from which to make generalizations, as shown below.

A stratified random sample with a *constant* sampling fraction is one where the same proportion of each stratum is selected, irrespective of the size of the stratum. For example, there may be 200 first year criminology students, 400 second years, and 300 third years in the population of a university. If we take one in ten of each (a constant sampling fraction), we get 20 first years, 40 second years and 30 third years in a sample of 90 students out of a total population of 900

$$[f = \frac{90}{900} = \frac{1}{10}].$$

A stratified random sample with a *variable* sampling fraction is one where the proportion selected from each stratum is different, usually in order to obtain roughly equal numbers of each stratum in the sample regardless of the number of each stratum in the population. We may, for example, want to compare the way in which men and women are dealt with by the courts, but because females only comprise a small proportion of those coming before the courts, a simple random sample might yield insufficient numbers of females to make any statistical inference possible. Thus, if there are 6000 male defendants and 2000 female defendants, and we want 50 of each, we might take 1 in 120 males

$$[f = \frac{50}{6000} = \frac{1}{120}], \text{ and 1 in 40 females } [f = \frac{50}{2000} = \frac{1}{40}]$$

- *Multistage, or cluster, sample* – This is where there is first a sample of large units, chosen at random, then in each of these a random sample of smaller units is taken. So rather than try to sample all students in the country, we might first take a sample of universities, then take a sample of students within these universities. Several stages may be used, such as constituency, ward, street, and household. The British Crime Survey uses this kind of sampling technique. The approach is more economical than trying to sample the whole population as one group, but is less accurate for a given size of sample because error is liable to occur at each stage of the sampling process.

In addition, a sample may be weighted to take account of the fact that certain categories are likely to be more or less numerous in a population. Again, the British Crime Survey has done this in order to increase the proportion of black people in the sample to ascertain the level of victimization among ethnic minorities. To take another example, when carrying out a study of sentenced offenders, the researcher may sample one out of every two people fined, because a large majority of those sentenced at magistrates courts are dealt with by means of a fine; it is more economical to allow for this. When analysing the results it is necessary to take account of this weighting.

Non-random samples

These are *not* selected at random, with each unit having an equal chance of inclusion. This means that probability statements cannot be made, and it cannot be assumed that they are representative of the population. Nonetheless, they may be the best that is possible in certain circumstances. This is true of many studies of problematic social issues, where a sampling frame may be impossible. Consider trying to do a study of homeless people, or problem drug users, or people with debt problems. Criminology is particularly likely to encounter such situations because it is by nature concerned with deviant groups. When offenders come into contact with the law and end up on police files, in the courts, on probation caseloads, or in prison, then they can be sampled randomly as a sample of court cases appearing before a court, or as part of a prison population. Even then, as every criminologist knows, the offenders who end up in these situations are the ones who get caught, so they are not representative of offenders generally. This does not mean that non-random samples are not worth considering, but it does mean that any generalizations based on them need to be qualified. There are various kinds of non-random sample:

- *Quota sample* – is one chosen in order to obtain a certain balance of the population in the sample: so many men, so many women, a certain number of people from each social class, or each racial group. It is representative with respect to these determining variables, but not others, and thus the sample may not be typical of the population as a whole. Researchers debate the merits of quota sampling[5], but it is widely used in political polls and market research.
- *Snowballing* – this is sometimes done when you can gain access to certain members of a population but not others. For example, you might interview all the drug misusers coming to a treatment centre for help, then ask if they will introduce you to friends of theirs who have not come to the centre. In this way you can find out why some people seek treatment and others don't.[6]
- Other kinds of non-random sample sometimes referred to are *availability*, *judgemental* and *accidental* samples. As their names suggest, these are variations on the theme of using whatever you can get.

Most considerations of sampling tend to centre on quantitative studies. However, it is worth noting that qualitative methods of inquiry also usually involve sampling in some way, in that they 'dip into' the phenomena they are investigating. Here also some consideration needs to be given to how the units of study are chosen, and what they are intended to tell us. Such is the predominance of the survey based on probability sampling that it is easy to overlook the significance of the atypical and the different. A survey may reflect the 'average' family with its 2.4 children, but an extreme example can also tell us a lot. Take, for instance, the correlation between recorded crime, based on a sample of police force areas, and the level of unemployment in an area referred to earlier. This may show that the trend is for those areas with higher levels of unemployment to have higher crime rates, but as mentioned previously, the interesting case may be the area which has high unemployment, but low crime rates. Why is this? Can it be explained in terms of the special characteristics of such an area, which may have important lessons for how other places can protect themselves from the effects of unemployment?

A valuable contribution has been made to social research by the case study, whether it is of individuals, organizations or places, where one or a very few cases are selected for study. They may be selected on the basis of their special characteristics, or because they typify the kind of issues being investigated. Whether the aim is to provide an accurate picture of the whole population, or to study particular examples, whatever technique is employed, it is important that the researcher describes how the sample was acquired (even if it is a sample of one) so that readers know exactly what its strengths and limitations are, and the extent of its applicability.

Researching criminology ethically

Ethical principles

Awareness of ethical issues has been increasing in recent years. This has taken a variety of forms, including among other things, the ways in which countries and organizations do business with each other, and an acute awareness of medical ethics in the aftermath of organ retention scandals. The principles that should govern ethical behaviour generally also apply to criminological research, but when applied in this context they have particular characteristics, and raise specific issues. We cannot do justice to the full depth of these issues here, but aim to discuss some of the main considerations.

Guidance on ethical research is set out in several places. Most academic disciplines and organizations have ethical guidance, and the first place to go for any criminologist is the British Society of Criminology (BSC), whose guidance can be found on their website.[7] Universities and other bodies engaged in research will also (or should have) ethical procedures in place, as will funding bodies, such as the Economic and Social Research Council (ESRC), which has produced a Research Ethics Framework.[8]

Important though they are, just pointing to such guidelines is not the whole answer. One problem is the question of enforceability.

Membership of the BSC is entirely voluntary, and while a member who flouted the society's ethical guidelines could be expelled, this does not have the same effect that it does if someone is struck off as a doctor. Nor does the BSC vet research proposals. While there is provision at UK universities and other bodies employing researchers to vet proposals, it is nonetheless a good idea when planning your research to consider the ethical aspects, rather than wait for an ethics approvals committee to return your application. In order to do this it is necessary to have an appreciation of the issues involved.

First, it is important to understand *why* researching ethically is important. The reasons may appear to be self-evident, but it is necessary to appreciate the basis on which ethical research is founded. Research involves a transfer of information, usually to the researcher and whoever is paying for the research. Thus, research is a form of power. Information is taken from someone (perhaps in an interview or questionnaire), and may then be used by the researcher and others in ways over which the owner of the information has no control. Research can also empower people. For example, action research, a methodology in which the research is done in conjunction with certain groups, can give people more power over their lives and their options. This is because they can exert a certain amount of control over the research process and its results. So the key issue is control, and since research depends on resources, those who have most resources will be able to better control research and its results. This means that when research is undertaken, it should normally only be done with the express permission of those involved. However, this can lead to problems.

Research ethics are informed by various philosophical and theoretical positions. For example, some theorists give individual rights pre-eminence (e.g. Gewirth 1996), while others stress the need for community values to take priority (e.g. Sandel 1982). We cannot do justice to the range and depth of argument here, and more comprehensive reviews can be found elsewhere (Beauchamp and Childress 2001). However, (and to oversimplify) one of the main distinctions in ethical theory is that between consequentialist and deontological theories of morality. The consequentialist view, derived from the work of Jeremy Bentham and John Stuart Mill, has a utilitarian focus. This position would argue that even though research may sometimes have adverse features, such as invading someone's privacy, these should be outweighed by the beneficial consequences for certain groups or society as a whole. The problem with this view is who judges what is in people's best interests, and this raises the issue of the accountability of research. The deontological view, on the other hand, has its origins in the writings of Immanuel Kant. This tells us that certain things must be done or not done for moral reasons, irrespective of what we wish to be the case (what Kant referred to as the categorical imperative), and that no one should be treated as a means to an end. Thus, certain actions are not permissible regardless of the consequences. So while consequentialists seek to maximize the best possible outcomes, deontologists argue that an ethical person should act independently of the consequences. In recent years a rights-based position based on liberal individualism has been the more persuasive, and measures to protect individual human rights have tended to prevail. Although theoretical positions may differ and have different emphases, Beauchamp and Childress suggest that, when it comes to framing practical ethics, the distinctions are not as great as they may appear (ibid.: 376–7).

As a result, ethical research needs to be based on clearly defined principles:[9]

1 The right to self-determination: people have the right to decide whether or not to take part in research. This is usually referred to as informed consent.
2 We should not knowingly cause harm, or expose people to unacceptable risks.
3 We should not put people at a disadvantage: our research should be governed by fairness and equality.
4 We should be honest and truthful: we should not deceive people. We should keep our promises. We should avoid fraud and plagiarism.
5 We should respect people's privacy.
6 We should preserve confidentiality.

Ethical dilemmas and criminological research

These principles are high ideals, and not surprisingly they are not as simple to observe as they may appear. Thus, for example, not exposing people to unacceptable risks can be problematic because risk is a relative concept, based on the probability of something occurring. However, the main problems arise from ethical dilemmas. One kind of dilemma is whether research should proceed if it compromises any of the above principles. For example, there is a particular problem regarding covert research, which by definition means that informed consent is unlikely to be obtained. The ESRC's guidelines recognize that:

> Covert research may be undertaken when it may provide unique forms of evidence or where overt observation might alter the phenomenon being studied. The broad principle should be that covert research must not be undertaken lightly or routinely. It is only justified if important issues are being

> addressed and if matters of social significance which cannot be uncovered in other ways are likely to be discovered. (para. 2.1.4)

It is also noted that:

> As is recognized elsewhere (see Tri-Council of Canada, 2002. http://www.pre.ethics.gc.ca/English/policystatement/introduction.cfm) Research may be 'deliberately and legitimately opposed to the interests of the research subjects' in cases where the objectives of the research are to reveal and critique fundamental economic, political or cultural disadvantage or exploitation .... Much social science research has a critical role to play in exploring and questioning social, cultural and economic structures and processes. (para. 2.1.7)

The ESRC guidelines also recognize that:

> Informed consent may be impracticable or meaningless in some research, such as research on crowd behaviour, or may be contrary to the research design, as is often the case in psychological experiments where consent would compromise the objective of the research. In some circumstances – such as users of illegal drugs – written consent might also create unnecessary risks for research subjects. Even in this last case, however, a researcher should seek informed consent where possible to secure the trust and confidence of those involved. In some contexts consent may need to be managed at a point beyond the completion of research fieldwork, for example, where covert observation is necessary and warranted. This might apply to research in the field of deviance especially where it involves illegal or immoral behaviour. (para. 2.1.4)

Another kind of dilemma arises when one of the principles comes into conflict with another. This can happen when the requirement of confidentiality conflicts with the avoidance of harm: what should be done when, having given an undertaking of confidentiality to respondents, it is discovered that one of them is likely to cause harm to other people?

As may be deduced from the quotations from the ESRC guidelines above, criminology is particularly susceptible to ethical dilemmas because of the nature of its subject matter. The criminological researcher is likely to be dealing with illegal activities, with people who have committed and have been the victims of crime, and inquiring about difficult topics, such as substance misuse, physical and sexual abuse, mental disorder, and many other things requiring care and sensitivity. Perhaps some indication is best conveyed by referring to a few examples, which are taken from actual situations.

Box 3.1 Example 1

You are undertaking a study of people addicted to drugs, which involves in-depth interviews with addicts. You have given assurances of confidentiality. During the course of one interview a female respondent discloses that her partner sometimes hits her young child. She begs you not to tell anyone, because being a known addict she already has problems with the Social Services Department, and is afraid that her child will be taken away from her.

Box 3.2 Example 2

You are undertaking an ethnographic study of attempts to rehabilitate offenders who are in a hostel for ex-prisoners. The success of your study depends on gaining the trust of the hostel residents, and on them being able to confide in you. During the course of your studies you learn that one of the residents has a firearm hidden in his room. What should you do?

Comment: Both these examples illustrate a conflict between confidentiality and preventing harm. In the first example, in Box 3.1 most people would agree that the interests of the child come first, but there are various things that could be done. The first is that situations like these might have been anticipated when planning the research, and prepared for. It could be that the undertaking of confidentiality should be modified from the outset by making it clear to respondents that there are circumstances in which you would have to do something. It is also worth noting that the young woman addict has put the researcher in a difficult position, and may well be expressing her anxieties in a 'cry for help'. This raises the issue of the limits of a researcher's competence: researchers are not counsellors, and should not try to be so. However, it is possible that the researcher could refer the respondent to a suitable agency or individual for help.

Box 3.3 Example 3

Another situation might arise if you were looking at the relationship between race and sentencing. The most direct way of doing this is to look at the sentences given by magistrates and judges, but if you tell the courts that this is what you are doing, then you alert sentencers, and this will influence their behaviour, at least for the duration of the study. Should you therefore effectively deceive the courts, perhaps by a less than truthful claim that you are looking at the 'factors that play a role in sentencing'?

Comment: Some might argue that in this instance deception is justified because your research is investigating a potential injustice (a consequentialist argument), especially since sentencers are in positions of power. But are the more powerful subjects of research less entitled to be treated in an ethical way than the less powerful?

Earlier in this chapter, and in the next, we make reference to the ethical issues that arise in criminological research when considering random allocation. This can be illustrated by an experiment that took place some years ago in a juvenile court in the north of England. This adopted a system whereby delinquents who had been truanting from school were not dealt with by the court immediately, but had their cases adjourned for a number of months, during which time their school attendance was monitored. What happened to them subsequently depended on their behaviour during the period of adjournment. This was nicknamed the Damocles experiment, and in order to test its efficacy, juveniles were randomly allocated either to be given the Damocles treatment, or to be dealt with in the normal way (Hullin 1985). The procedure was controversial and was eventually discontinued.

Conclusion

There are undoubtedly further aspects of these scenarios that might be considered, and this is only a brief review of research ethics and the moral theory on which it is based. The aim here is to ensure that those researching criminology are aware of the duty that they have towards those who take part in their endeavours. It is also worth noting that, in accordance with one of the themes that underlies this book, ethical practice should be regarded as an integral part of the research process, and the kinds of ethical issue that arise will reflect the kind of research being undertaken. Thus, surveys most often raise issues of confidentiality; qualitative methods, such as participant observation, raise more acutely such matters as informed consent, and random controlled trials may mean that some of those taking part are put at a disadvantage. Evaluative studies can have significant implications for the futures not only of those who are the subject of an intervention, but of the staff involved in an intervention.

Having indicated some of the problems that can arise, what can be done about them? Can criminologists not do any research that involves observing other people's behaviour without telling them, or never get involved in any research where they might encounter illegal behaviour because they cannot give undertakings of confidentiality? Some might think so, but an alternative is to ensure that there are adequate safeguards.

There are two main ways of doing this. One is careful planning and preparation prior to the start of any research. While you can never anticipate all the situations that might arise, as the examples above illustrate, it is not too difficult to see how problems might occur. The planning and preparation should involve consultation with colleagues or supervisors, and with any agencies that might be involved. Careful scrutiny of ethical guidelines is also important, and of course any reputable project will need to be reviewed by a research ethics committee. But this should not be the end of any ethical concerns. The other main way of responding to ethical problems is continued monitoring and review of the research as it progresses. This can be done through formal advisory committees, or it may be that arrangements can be made with others to see where problems might arise. This is particularly important in the case of ethnographic research, where the researcher can become caught up in events, and not realize that they are stepping over the lines of what is acceptable professional behaviour.

Further reading

Bryman (2004) has chapters on research design and sampling, and qualitative, quantitative and mixed method approaches to research design are considered by Creswell (2002), who also has a section on ethical issues in Chapter 3.

Regarding research ethics, Beauchamp and Childress's book is largely concerned with medical ethics, but Chapters 1 and 8 contain useful discussions of ethical theories and the general principles. The guidelines produced by the British Society of Criminology and the Economic and Social Research Council should also be consulted.

4 Criminological evaluation

Defining terms

One particular, and very important kind of research design in criminology is that which involves evaluating the impact of various initiatives and interventions. The term 'intervention' can refer to a variety of things. It could mean:

- the way that individual offenders are dealt with, either by sentence or by participation in a treatment programme;
- an initiative designed to reduce crime, such as putting on more police officers, or more surveillance technology, in an area;
- new legislation;
- social policies intended to affect crime, such as more drug treatment or education programmes.

Evaluation designs are significant in two main respects. The first is the way in which they fit into criminological and methodological theory. Evaluation should not just be seen as a technique, but as a way of theorizing about what is happening. The second is their political and policy implications; most evaluations are likely to have come about as a result of some practical or policy initiative, and their results are therefore likely to have very real consequences.[1] In this section we will start by looking at the nature of evaluation, and then go on to consider the practical aspects of doing evaluation.

Before doing so, however, it is useful to start by defining some terms.

- *Evaluation* is the process of examining whether interventions achieve their desired outcomes. However, the simplicity of this definition conceals a world of complexity. It is also important to define some other terms commonly used in association with evaluation (and not infrequently confused with it).
- *Aims* are the goals which an initiative or organization is striving to achieve.

- *Monitoring* is the process of checking what is happening in relation to what an initiative or organization planned to do.
- *Inputs* are what are put into an initiative, such as time, money, and activities.
- *Processes* are what happen in order to make an initiative occur (also referred to as implementation).
- *Outputs* are the direct results of inputs, such as the number of people who have been involved in the intervention.
- *Outcomes* are the desired and specific results, such as a reduction in offending, a reduction in the amount of burglary, reduced fear of crime, reduced incarceration, reduced costs, and so on. Outcomes should be directly related to aims, and should be based on measurable criteria.

We will give an example later of how these terms might apply to a particular project.

The evaluation paradigm

When considering an evaluation design we come back to the model of causality that was referred to in the previous chapter (see Figure 3.1, p. 41). Here, however, the dependent variable(s) are the intended outcome(s) and the independent variable is the intervention itself (Figure 4.1).

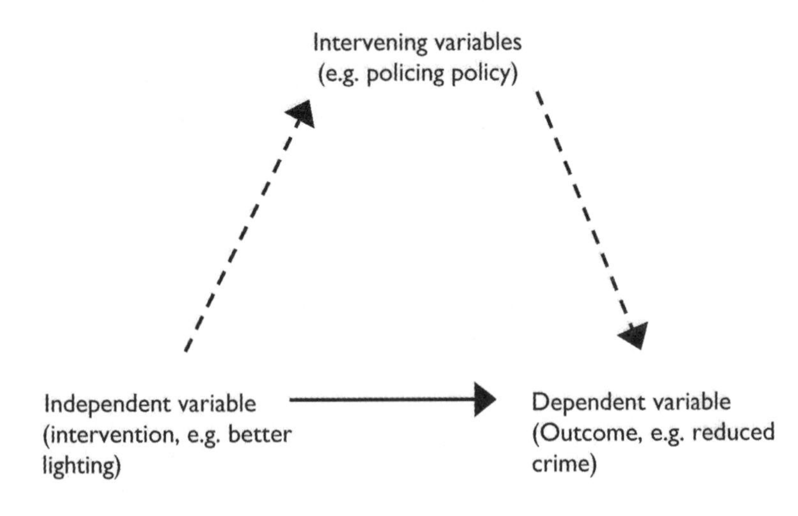

Figure 4.1 Causal analysis in evaluation

	Before Intervention	Intervention	After Intervention
Intervention Situation	O_1	X	O_2
Non-Intervention Situation	O_1		O_2

Figure 4.2 The OXO Model

The critical bit is the intervening variables. In evaluation it is important to compare like with like, so that the only thing that varies is the intervention. The reasoning is that it is only when all other factors have been controlled that the effect of the intervention can be seen. The traditional way of doing this is by applying the intervention to one situation or group of people, but not to another situation or group, which is like the first in all other respects. This is sometimes referred to as the OXO model (Figure 4.2).

This model is similar to that employed in clinical trials in medicine when a new drug or other form of treatment is being developed. The ideal situation is one where those who get the treatment are randomly allocated to the intervention or non-intervention situation – the random controlled trial (RCT). Those allocated to the non-intervention situation usually get something, such as an inert substance, known as a placebo, which mimics a situation where nothing happens.

However, when it comes to applying the model to criminology problems arise. First, there are difficulties in applying the model in its pure form in real life. It is difficult enough if one is trying to see whether a particular sentence or programme for offenders is more effective than another, but even more difficult if you are looking at whether, for example, initiatives that affect a whole community are effective. To some extent these can be overcome by what is referred to as quasi-experimental designs (see Chapter 3; Cook and Campbell 1979), where statistics are used to take account of possible intervening variables when comparing intervention with non-intervention situations, but this is not as effective as RCT. For a start you have less control over what has happening in the non-intervention situation. Rarely will nothing be happening; individuals and communities that are not receiving an intervention are quite likely to be experiencing something, and researchers need to document what this is. There are also ethical concerns about the use of random allocation, which involves subjecting one group of people to something while denying it to another group.[2]

In recent years American researchers have produced a more highly developed version of the OXO model. As a result of reviewing evaluations of crime prevention projects Sherman et al. (1998) developed the Maryland Scale of Scientific Methods as a way of determining how strong the internal validity of each study was.[3] The scale ranked each evaluation study on internal validity, from 1 (weakest) to 5 (strongest). Rating was based primarily on three factors:

1 *Control of other variables* in the analysis that might have been the true causes of any connection between a programme and crime prevention.
2 *Measurement error* from such things as subjects lost over time, or low response rates.
3 *Statistical capability* to detect programme effects (as a result of things like sample size, and the base rate of crime at the outset).

Table 4.1 summarizes the key elements in the scoring of various evaluation research designs (*where X = present and O = not present*). 'Before-After' refers to whether measures of outcome variables were taken before and after implementation of an initiative. 'Control' refers to whether there were any control groups, or control situations, where intervention did not occur. 'Multiple units' refers to whether there were a number of units involved (such as people, communities, or agencies). 'Randomization' refers to whether there was randomization in the allocation of units to intervention or non-intervention situations. The levels can be further explained as follows (with our comments in italics):

Table 4.1 The Maryland Scale of Scientific Methods (a)

Methods score	*Before-After*	*Control*	*Multiple units*	*Randomization*
Level 1	O	O	O	O
Level 2	X	O	O	O
Level 3	X	X	O	O
Level 4	X	X	X	O
Level 5	X	X	X	X

Level 1 corresponds to a study where there is a correlation between, for example, a crime prevention programme and a measure of crime or risk of crime at a single point of time (*which cannot give very much, if any, indication that the programme has an effect on crime*).

Level 2 shows that there is a temporal sequence between the programme occurring and the outcome measure of crime (*i.e. following implementation of a programme, crime levels change, but it cannot be shown that this is due to the intervention*). At this level there may be a comparison group or area, but it cannot be demonstrated that it is truly comparable with the intervention group or area.

Level 3 indicates that there is a comparison between two units (e.g. neighbourhoods) one of which has had the programme and the other hasn't (*more indicative that if there is any change that it was the programme that was responsible*).

Level 4 compares multiple units or groups with and without the programme, controlling for other factors, or using comparison units that show only minor differences from the intervention units (*e.g. taking several places where programmes were implemented and comparing them with several other comparable areas where they were not*).

Level 5 Random assignment of comparable units of analysis to intervention or comparison group (*e.g. take a couple of dozen comparable neighbourhoods, give half of them, randomly chosen, a programme, and the other half not: the most powerful way of evaluating impact, but difficult to do in practice*).

Table 4.2 illustrates the importance of these elements, showing the extent to which each level controls for various threats to internal validity.

The threats are:

Table 4.2 The Maryland Scale of Scientific Methods (b)

Methods score	*Before-After*	*Control*	*Multiple units*	*Randomization*
Level 1	X	X	X	X
Level 2	O	X	X	X
Level 3	O	O	X	X
Level 4	O	O	O	X
Level 5	O	O	O	O

- *Causal direction*: whether the intervention caused the observed level of crime or the level of crime brought about the intervention.
- *History*: The passage of time causing any change rather than the intervention.
- *Chance factors*: Unforeseen events such as a police operation, or an outbreak of disturbances.
- *Selection bias*: Characteristics of the unit of intervention (*e.g. a neighbourhood*) which influence the chances of it being selected for intervention.

It can be seen that Table 4.2 is almost a mirror image of Table 4.1. The removal of each threat to internal validity increases the likelihood of a causal link between intervention and crime reduction.

While the Maryland Scale has refined the basic OXO model, it still considers the random controlled trial to be what is referred to as the 'gold standard' for programme evaluation. Other researchers have criticized such a purely outcome-oriented approach, and here we need to more fully explore the relationship between evaluation and theory.

Evaluation and theory

In Chapter 2 we looked at two different kinds of theory, criminological theories and epistemology. The same applies in relation to evaluation: there is evaluation as a way of examining theories about crime, and there are also theories about evaluation as a methodology.

Looking at evaluation as a methodology, the OXO model and the Maryland Scale can be seen as essentially positivist in nature (see Chapter 2), in attempting to apply the methods of the physical sciences in a criminological context. Other researchers (and we would include ourselves in this) have criticized such a purely outcome-oriented approach. One criticism is that such a model is 'black box' research. That is, it is principally interested in the end products, paying little attention to the processes that take place during the course of intervention which make the relationship between intervention and outcome comprehensible. There is more to it than whether something 'works' or not. We also need to know *how* and *why* something has the effects that it does in order to generalize the results, otherwise we are disregarding the theoretical basis for intervention, which also requires explanation. Two criminological researchers in particular, Ray Pawson and Nick Tilley, have gone even further and during the 1990s mounted a wholesale assault on the OXO model, advancing a different model based on scientific realism. This became known as the 'paradigm wars', involving exchanges in academic journals between Pawson and Tilley, on the one hand, and Trevor Bennett and David Farrington of the Institute of Criminology in Cambridge, on the other.

In an article in the *British Journal of Criminology* Pawson and Tilley (1994) argued that the traditional OXO model had resulted in moribund evaluation. Although they claimed to be raising fundamental objections to the traditional model, their main criticism was essentially the familiar criticism that such an approach fails to comprehend *how* a programme works (ibid.: 294), and they submitted to critical scrutiny an evaluation by Trevor Bennett of a police initiative for reducing fear of crime (Bennett 1991). Pawson and Tilley recognized this to be a well-executed study in OXO terms, but said that it failed to explain how police activities might bring about change in a community (Pawson and Tilley 1994: 297). It was suggested that what was needed was to understand a programme's *mechanisms* and the *context* in which it takes place. Pawson and Tilley then put forward their solution, citing a study by Nick Tilley of the operation of closed circuit television in car parks as a model of such an approach. This approach is what they term a 'scientific realist' evaluation. It is explained that for a realist evaluator,

> Outcomes (O) are understood and investigated by bringing to the centre of investigation certain hypotheses about the mechanisms (M) through which the programme seeks to bring about change, as well as considering the contextual conditions (C), which are most conducive to that change. (Pawson and Tilley 1994: 300)

The original article was the subject of subsequent exchanges in the *British Journal of Criminology* between Pawson and Tilley and Trevor Bennett (Bennett 1996 and Pawson and Tilley 1996). Bennett disputed that researchers who use quasi-experimental designs 'overlook … mechanisms and contexts' (Bennett 1996: 568), citing Cook and Campbell's work on quasi-experimentation in support (Cook and Campbell 1979). He also denied that competent evaluators merely seek associations between treatments and outcomes. In defence of his own work, Bennett said that he did consider causal mechanisms and the areas in which the research took place. He suggested that, although there is a need to refine evaluation methods, Pawson and Tilley offer 'little that is new and nothing that is useful in moving towards this goal' (Bennett 1996: 572).

The debate continued in the pages of the journal *Evaluation* where it focused on a community safety programme developed initially in the United States, but since implemented in the UK and elsewhere, Communities That Care (CTC; see Crow et al. 2004 and Chapter 11 of this book). Farrington recommended the comparison of experimental and control communities, and taking measures of key outcome variables (crime, delinquency, substance abuse and adolescent problem behaviour) before and after the intervention package (Farrington 1997). Pawson and Tilley responded by criticizing Farrington's design for not sufficiently taking account of the complexity of the Communities That Care programmes. They suggested that the design favoured by Farrington would miss the opportunity to look at 'what works for whom in what circumstances' (Pawson and Tilley 1999: 83). Instead they stressed the importance of studying the theories that underlie a programme such as CTC, and suggest that a 'scientific realist' study would transform the evaluation 'so that the test of the programme becomes a test of whether its theories come to pass' (ibid.: 85). Accompanying Pawson and Tilley's article was a response from Farrington in the same issue of the journal (1998) suggesting that the main difference was that whereas he had seen CTC as a 'well-developed technology waiting to be tested', Pawson and Tilley assumed it to be an 'iterative, evolving, ill-defined, highly variable procedure that essentially required further exploratory and developmental work'.

One of the reasons why the debate between Pawson and Tilley, on the one hand, and Bennett and Farrington, on the other, became such a prolonged, and indeed heated, one is because it concerns different philosophical approaches to evaluation, hence the reference in one of the articles to the 'paradigm wars' (Pawson and Tilley 1999: 73). Pawson and Tilley make a distinction between two modes of causative explanation:

1 'successionist' causal thinking (more frequently referred to as deterministic causality), which describes a constant conjunction between events ('the action of billiard balls is archetypally describable in these terms'; Pawson and Tilley 1994: 293). This is the approach, they say, of quasi-experimentation.
2 the 'generative' conception of causation, which they explain as describing the transformative potential of phenomena, rather like gunpowder whose potential to explode inheres in its chemical composition. This is the approach of the school of thought that they espouse, 'scientific realism'.

In his response to the original Pawson and Tilley article, Bennett denied that quasi-experimentation is necessarily deterministic, and said that in the social sciences probabilistic causality is generally accepted to be more appropriate. In their response to Bennett's criticism of their article, Pawson and Tilley said that Bennett had failed to grasp the basic difference between the principles of successionist and generative causation (Pawson and Tilley 1996: 574), and that while Bennett's own research may have incorporated some attempts to describe what was happening alongside his outcome evaluation, these did not constitute a realist approach to evaluation (Pawson and Tilley 1996: 576).

A key passage in the exchanges occurred when David Farrington referred to Pawson and Tilley's contention that mechanisms provide the 'reasons and resources' to change behaviour. Farrington's comment is that it is not clear how reasons could be investigated:

> Many psychologists are reluctant to ask people to give reasons for their behaviour, because of the widespread belief that people have little or no introspective access to their complex mental processes ... Hence, it is not clear that reasons in particular and verbal reports in general have any validity, which is why psychologists emphasize observation, experiments, validity checks, causes, and the scientific study of behaviour. (Farrington 1998: 207)

This passage epitomizes the difference between the positivist approach to inquiry, and the interpretive approach. It is therefore not surprising to find that Pawson and Tilley take issue with this in their rejoinder:

> Suppose a woman locks a door and is asked why she is doing so. If she says that it is a precaution against intruders, there seems no reason to us not to take her reply seriously. To be sure, and as we have argued repeatedly, such reasoning may have unacknowledged conditions and unintended consequences, but these do not place the ideas beyond investigation. (Pawson and Tilley 1998b: 211)

Pawson and Tilley's approach has been set out in more detail in their book *Realistic Evaluation* (1997), which is recommended for further reading.

These exchanges give the impression of a polarization of views on evaluation models. There are, however, other perspectives, which are not so extreme. For example, it has been suggested that the danger with the OXO model is that it becomes reduced to a purely technical exercise focused on outcomes, forgetting that evaluation needs to be seen in a theoretical context (Crow 2000). The OXO model represents only a small part of the research process referred to in Chapter 1 (Figure 1.2). What is missing is the fact that all interventions are essentially a test of a theory. For example, if one is evaluating an employment training programme for offenders with the aim of reducing their likelihood of re-offending, then implicit within this is a theoretical position about the relationship between employment and criminality. Similarly, a project for drug users designed to reduce drug-related offending is based on assumptions about the relationship between drug misuse and crime. Not to labour the point too much, but a third example might be a project designed to provide sporting activities for young people at risk of getting into trouble, which is likely to encapsulate theories about youthful behaviour and offending. It is worth noting that in referring to theory we are not necessarily envisaging anything profound about the nature of crime and criminality; it is more a case of unravelling the thinking that is informing action. It is also worth noting that medical trials are also based on theories. Quite often such theories are not made explicit by the programme itself, or are poorly articulated, and part of the task of the researcher is to explore the theoretical assumptions implicit in any initiative. Seen in this context, therefore, an evaluation is an empirical test of a theoretical proposition, and the results of any evaluation should be seen not simply in terms of 'does it work?', but 'what does this tell us about the theory underpinning the initiative?' Thus:

Theory ⇒ Intervention ⇒ Outcome ⇒ Modified Theory

The OXO model referred to above should therefore really be located within the broader research process, outlined in Chapter 1, as shown in Figure 4.3. Similar observations have been made by Carol Weiss, who refers to a programme's 'theories of change' (Weiss 1998). She describes the theory of change as having two components: programme theory and implementation theory. Programme theory refers

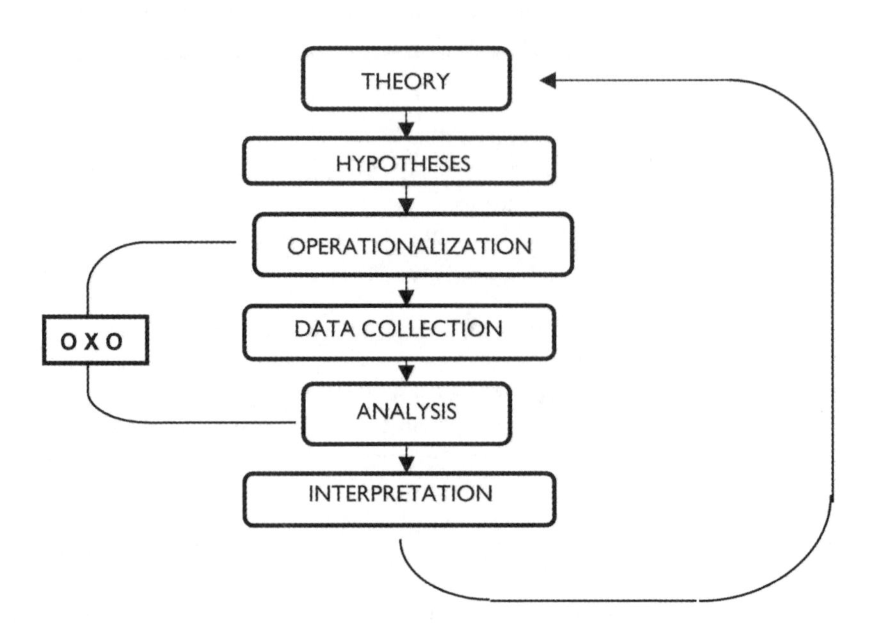

Figure 4.3 The research process and the OXO model

to 'the mechanisms that mediate between the delivery (and receipt) of the program and the emergence of the outcomes of interest' (ibid.: 57). It is a set of hypotheses on which people build their plans for a programme, and one of the jobs of the evaluator is to find out ('surface') what these hypotheses are. Note that in referring to mechanisms Weiss echoes the views of Pawson and Tilley. Implementation theory refers to the fact that if the programme does the things it intends to do, then the desired outcomes should occur: 'Implementation implicitly incorporates a theory about what is required to translate objectives into ongoing service delivery and program operation' (ibid.: 58).

One feature that Pawson and Tilley and others have in common is their insistence on evaluation consisting of both process and outcome research, the process research being likely to incorporate qualitative components intended to explore programme theories and how programmes are implemented. In an attempt to bring together the various perspectives on evaluation that developed between 1994 and 2004 Home Office researchers have produced what they consider to be an integrated model of evaluation for criminal justice interventions (Friendship et al. 2004) (Figure 4.4). This is primarily concerned with the treatment of individual offenders.

Friendship et al.'s model incorporates some quite specific suggestions for what needs to be done in relation to the various components of the model, and at this point, having looked at some of the principles underlying evaluation designs we go on to consider what criminological evaluation needs to involve in practice.

Doing criminological evaluation

Identifying the aims

From what has been said above it should be apparent that a first priority for the evaluator is to find out what the aims of any intervention are. This is important in order to understand what theories, explicitly or implicitly, underlie the initiative, and to determine what outcome criteria are relevant. Identifying the aims of a project may at first appear to be fairlystraightforward, but this is not always the case. In criminology it is quite likely that an initiative will feature crime reduction as one of its aims in some form or other. But this may not be the only objective. For example, training and education programmes for offenders may hope to reduce the chances of re-offending, but perhaps the first aim is to get people qualifications and jobs. It may be that a programme is directed at individuals, such as drug users, where the initial concern is to reduce drug consumption, but that the main concern is with reducing levels

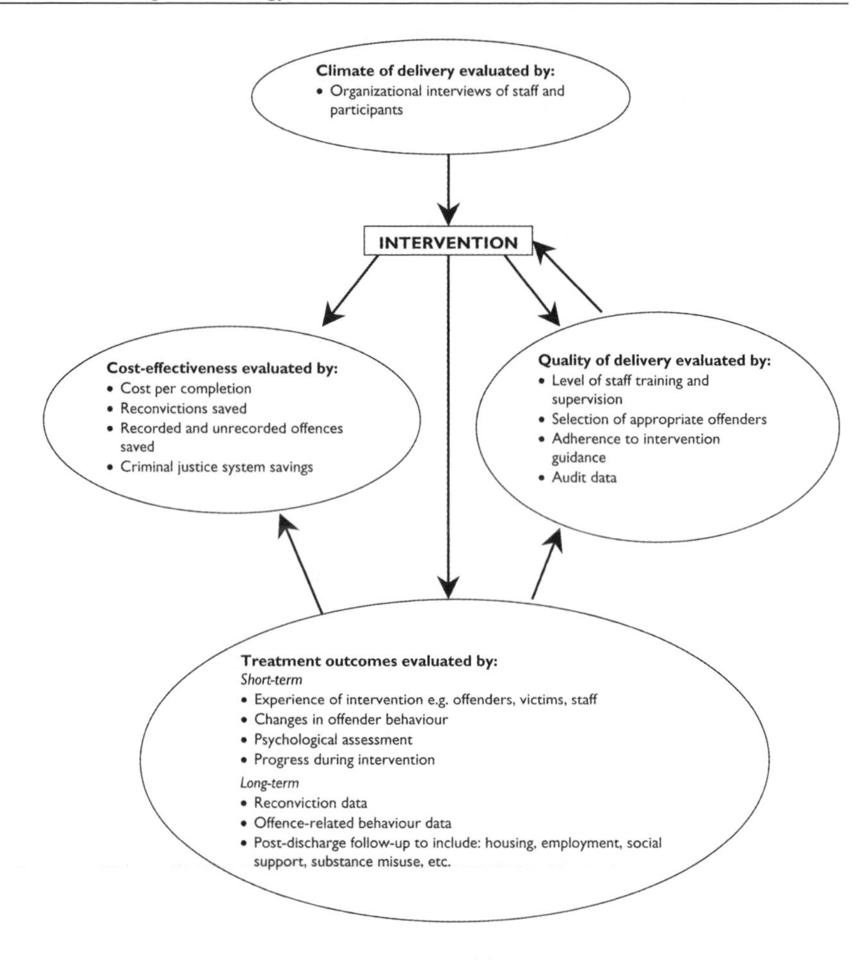

Source: Harper and Chitty (2004: 15)

Figure 4.4 Friendship et al.s' integrated model to evaluate the impact of interventions

of crime in an area. Some types of evaluation cover developments with quite complex aims: if you were seeking to evaluate the impact of a new Criminal Justice Act, then a variety of ideas may have gone into framing the legislation at various stages.

It may also be the case that there are differing views about what the aims are. For example, a sponsoring agency or management board may have set out what the aims of a project are in formal terms, but when you talk to the staff delivering the service on the ground, they see things quite differently. This is even more likely to be the case where, as often happens, more than one agency is involved. One agency may have one agenda, while another agency is more concerned with other goals. The eventual aims of a programme may be a compromise that has come about as a result of a series of negotiations.

What all this says is that the researcher should take nothing for granted. Evaluation should start with a careful consideration of where the initiative has come from, who is involved and what each party hopes to get out of it. This is likely to involve the use of interviews, and where a large number of parties or people are involved, the use of questionnaires may be justified. For example, if a new initiative is being brought in that will affect the way courts work, then in addition to interviewing key players it may be instructive to do a survey of the magistrates who sit in a court (or courts), which asks them what they think the initiative is about (see Chapter 10 for an example of such a project). It may also be relevant to identify primary, secondary, and even tertiary aims. Thus, if a programme of sporting activities has *as one of its aims* reducing the likelihood of young people getting into trouble, is this its primary aim, or something that depends on other things being achieved that are more important to the project?

Implementation and when to evaluate

Another key element of any evaluation is to determine whether an initiative is in fact doing what it sets out to do; this is known as 'programme integrity'. A programme may end up doing something different from what was intended. It may be that the original intentions were found to be too ambitious, or could not be implemented in their original form. This raises the question of *when* to evaluate. It is often assumed that evaluation should commence when an initiative first starts. This certainly has advantages because the researcher can then observe how the intervention is put into operation. But the early months, or even years, of a new initiative can also be a time when it is settling down and finding the best ways of operating. If outcome evaluation starts too early, it may not reflect what the programme eventually becomes.

However, another kind of change in implementation can occur when an initiative has been going for some time, and there is 'programme drift'. This can come about as a result of changes in the external environment in which the programme is operating, or because the key people who originally set up a project have moved on and new people want to bring in their own ideas – or just through tedium. New projects attract a lot of attention (not least from researchers), but after a while what the programme was originally supposed to do becomes lost.

It is when examining implementation that researchers are most likely to get drawn into an initiative. They may then influence what happens because initiatives are modified as a result of their enquiries. Views vary about how acceptable this is. Should the evaluator stand aloof while possibly holding information about how an important and expensive project is failing disastrously? This illustrates the difference between natural and social sciences, since most researchers would regard doing nothing as both unethical and prejudicing the likelihood of learning from the results of the intervention. Evaluators will often provide feedback at certain stages in the investigation, and this is defensible. What is most important is being transparent about the role the researcher plays.

Another aspect of evaluating programme implementation may be to consider whether the initiative was delivered to an appropriate target group. It is all too easy for a training project, for example, to take people who are most likely to boost its success rates rather than those most in need. Is a programme aimed at young people at risk of getting into trouble actually getting those most at risk, or is it getting young people who might not otherwise get into trouble anyway? This is likely to be particularly important if the initiative involves referrals being made by other agencies or individuals. It may be that those agencies are referring to the project those who they don't want to deal with themselves, rather than the people at whom the initiative was aimed.

Outcome criteria

In criminological evaluation the outcome criteria are likely to centre around a reduction in re-offending in the case of individuals, and a reduction in crime rates in the case of geographical areas or collections of people. However, care should be taken to check whether these are necessarily the appropriate criteria given what an intervention is trying to do, and what it is actually doing. Many initiatives, such as employment schemes, community programmes, or leisure activities have other criteria by which they might be judged (and on which their funding is based). Even where re-offending or crime reduction is a relevant criterion, there may be other outcomes that need to be measured, such as cost, whether the intervention has reduced the likelihood of imprisonment, or a reduction in concern about crime in the local community.

It is also worth considering who will be the parties to any outcomes. It may be offenders, or communities, or perhaps the victims of crime. A good example of the last outcome criterion comes from restorative justice interventions. Here an important outcome measure might be the degree of satisfaction felt by victims.

The criteria by which an intervention is to be evaluated are largely determined by its aims. But it is not unusual for the criteria to be redefined by the project so that they are more achievable. For example, having failed to reduce offending a project may be tempted to fall back on 'softer' outcome measures based on changes in attitudes or perceptions rather than behaviour. This may occur because of the need to be seen to achieve something in order to secure continued funding, or simply because those involved feel their credibility is on the line. Researchers should be on the look-out for such outcome shifts.

Crime and offending as an outcome

While the possible outcome criteria for an intervention should be considered with an open mind, crime reduction or reduced offending is likely to feature as one of the main measures. Re-offending is usually measured by reconviction information. This is often done by comparing actual reconvictions with the expected rate of reconviction for a given group of offenders using the Offender Group Reconviction Scale (OGRS), which uses known predictors of re-offending to produce a predicted probability of reconviction. The problems of measuring crime and re-offending are one of the main issues in criminology but we will not discuss the difficulties at length here. However, we will briefly highlight some of the main considerations as far as evaluation research is concerned (for broad-based discussions, see Lloyd et al. 1994; Friendship et al. 2002).

First, reconviction information, and crime rates can be unreliable, depending on factors such as detection and successful conviction. They can be affected by variations in reporting, and in police practices and policy, and by recording errors. The use of OGRS for evaluating reconviction has its limitations because it depends on prediction data which may be unreliable or not appropriate for certain groups (Kershaw 1998).

However, simply measuring whether or not offenders are reconvicted, or crimes rates go up or down are, by themselves, very crude measures. Looking first at reconvictions, there can be relative success. Following intervention, offenders who have frequently re-offended in the past may go for a longer period than they have previously before being reconvicted. This suggests that the intervention may have had some effect, even if its influence was only temporary. Someone may also be reconvicted for a less serious offence than previously, indicating at least a shift from violent robbery perhaps to shoplifting. The same can be true if you are looking at whether or not crime has gone down following a crime prevention initiative; patterns of crime might become less worrying to residents or businesses if they involve less violence or damage.

Another consideration is the length of follow-up. Where individual offenders are concerned, a two-year follow-up period has traditionally been used. However, this may need to be adjusted to take account of particular circumstances. For example, young people in their teens tend to re-offend more rapidly than older people, so changes over six months or a year may need to be examined. Research on sex offenders has shown that such offenders need to be followed up for much longer periods than the usual two years (Ditchfield and Marshall 1990; Marshall 1994; Hedderman and Sugg 1996). Where you are dealing with crime rates, rather than measures of reconviction of individual offenders, it is also relevant to consider over what period changes in offence patterns should be studied. This is because it is possible that more than one follow-up is needed in order to see whether an initial reduction in crime rates has been maintained in the long term.

It is also necessary when using reconvictions as a measure to take account of 'false positives': convictions for offences committed prior to intervention, which occur following the offence that led to intervention. In the same way, it is necessary to take account of the custodial and non-custodial periods 'at risk'. Periods when someone is in prison do not count for follow-up purposes.

Because of the difficulties posed by actual reconvictions and crime data, some researchers have resorted to secondary 'offence-related' measures to supplement crime data. In the case of individual offenders this might include whether or not someone's general behaviour or attitudes change, referred to as 'non-reconviction benefits' (Friendship et al. 2004: 13). It might also include the use of unofficial sources of data such as police intelligence, and information from probation, social and health services (e.g. Falshaw et al. 2003). The problem with such measures is that they may be unreliable indicators of potential behaviour, or based on the subjective judgements of others. In situations where changes in crime rates cannot be demonstrated, then changes in measures such as the fear of crime might be substituted (Ditton, 2000, is a useful discussion of the 'fear of crime' as a crime survey measurement). The use of such measures can be controversial. On the one hand, it might be argued that these are not true measures of outcome, and rely on subjective perceptions to obtain a less satisfactory (and perhaps more amenable) result than it is reasonable to expect. On the other hand they could be defended on the basis that more objective measures cannot be obtained, or are also likely to be unreliable, and that more qualitative measures do have value in their own right. Whether they are justified is likely to depend on the circumstances of a particular evaluation.

Where interventions with individuals are concerned, it is important to consider completion rates. It is not unusual for participants in a programme to drop out before the end. To take one instance, this has been found to be the case for Drug Treatment and Testing Orders (DTTOs; Hough et al. 2003). What is important here is that those who drop out may be different from those who complete the programme in certain ways. For example, they may be the most recalcitrant individuals who are most likely to re-offend, and therefore the results are not a true test of the programme. The best that can be said is that the intervention works with the kind of people who complete it – which rather limits its applicability.

Finally, do we know *what* happened – why a project did or did not work? This is especially important where a programme consists of several different kinds of intervention, which we consider next.

Complex evaluations

We have been concerned so far with the evaluation of a single intervention, which might be a single treatment programme, a crime prevention initiative in one area, or a community-based project. However, evaluation can be more complex than this. For a start, an intervention might be what is referred to as 'multi-modal', consisting of several components. Schemes for ex-prisoners may need to address several needs, such as accommodation, literacy and social re-integration. Research has suggested that reducing re-offending is best done, not by addressing offenders needs one by one, but by looking at the ways in which their needs are inter-related, requiring an integrated approach which may involve several agencies (Harper and Chitty 2004).

Sometimes there may be a number of interventions which are part of a broader programme. This was the case with the UK Safer Cities Programme which ran from 1988 to 1995, costing £30 million. Just over 500 schemes were set up to prevent domestic burglary. Most schemes upgraded physical security in British cities, although some mounted community-oriented initiatives as well. The schemes usually centred on local neighbourhoods or estates, and an evaluation of the programme reported results based on nearly 300 schemes (Ekblom et al. 1996).

The evaluation strategy involved comparing changes in the risk of burglary in a number of areas with differing levels of anti-burglary action, against areas with no action. The data collection operation was large-scale and complex. The amount of input ('scheme intensity') was measured by the amount spent per household in the scheme area. Outcome was measured by means of before and after surveys in 400 high crime neighbourhoods, and local police statistics before and after implementation. Evidence from the surveys and police figures showed that Safer Cities reduced the risk of burglary in the areas covered (Table 4.3).

The researchers then had to consider whether there were explanations other than the impact of Safer Cities intervention that might be responsible for the observed results. These included selection effects (whether areas with temporarily high crime levels

Table 4.3 Burglary prevalence by intensity of burglary action

	Safer cities				*Comparison cities*
Amount of burglary action	*none*	*low*	*medium*	*high*	*None*
Percentage of households burgled once or more in previous year.					
Before (1990)	8.9	10.3	12.7	13.4	12
After (1992)	10.2	9.3	9.9	7.6	12.4
% change	**+15**	**–10**	**–22**	**–43**	**+3**
No. of EDs	163	58	36	23	126
No. schemes	–	34	40	41	–

Source: Ekblom et al. (1996: 13). Note: EDs = Enumeration Districts

had been targeted, which would have resulted in a downturn in crime regardless of whether the action itself worked), the influence of other Safer Cities activities going on to tackle other problems in the areas, and the influence of action other than the Safer Cities programme in the areas. A statistical technique known as multi-level modelling[4] was used to analyse the effect of background trends in crime and demographic differences across the areas and between survey respondents. The study also took account of cost-effectiveness and displacement effects.

As a result of these further analyses it was concluded that the schemes' impact had two distinct components:

- setting up *any* action reduced burglary risks;
- the more *intense* the action, the greater the additional decrease in burglary risk.

In a different way a number of evaluation studies have been generated by the UK Government's programme to discover 'What Works?' in reducing offending. The 'What Works?' movement developed in the late 1980s and 1990s as a reaction to the 'Nothing Works' doctrine which had dominated criminology and criminal justice since the mid-1970s. The 'What Works?' agenda was taken up by an incoming Labour administration after 1997, resulting in numerous evaluation studies. Although these studies were not part of a single co-ordinated piece of research, their findings have been cumulative and have tended to focus on the use of cognitive behavioural therapy (CBT) as a means of changing offenders' behaviour. This illustrates the way in which evaluations add to, and become part of, developing ideas and practice in criminology, again making the point that evaluation is about examining the theories that underlie interventions. (For further information about the 'What Works?' programme see Crow 2001, Chapter 4; Mair 2004, especially the first couple of chapters; and Raynor and Robinson 2005, Chapter 6.)

The politics of evaluation

Evaluation often takes place in a political context, of which the researcher needs to be aware. This can range from 'politics' on a small scale, to the larger-scale politics of government programmes. Even when you are evaluating a local community-based project, its future is of great importance to a number of people and the community itself, and this means that the evaluator may be conscious of the aspirations and the jobs that might depend on him or her. When evaluating larger-scale programmes there is a danger that evaluation may be used to justify policies. In both instances there can be pressure on evaluators. It is therefore worth noting that however 'scientific' and 'objective' evaluation research is supposed to be, power relationships are involved, and the evaluator is part of this. It is not just a matter of producing the desired results. Practitioners and policy-makers work to demanding time frames, whereas a final evaluation is likely to take some time for many of the reasons outlined earlier (allowing time for an intervention to settle down, doing follow-up, etc.). The result may be that by the time the results are produced the political agenda has shifted, or the environment in which the intervention was introduced has changed.

Evaluation research can also affect the way criminological research progresses. Evaluation is one of the main sources of funding available to criminologists. This means that while criminologists have the opportunity to influence social policy, the criminological agenda can be affected by what needs to be evaluated. The arrival of a new government in the UK in 1997 had a big impact on the amount of funding available for criminological research. However, it was of a particular kind. The Government was particularly keen to promote its 'evidence-led', 'What Works?' programme (referred to above), and this meant that from the late 1990s into the early years of the twenty-first century much of the funding available from the Home Office was for the investigation of programmes for treating individual offenders, and in particular leant towards psychologically-based initiatives such as CBT. Criminological researchers needing to think about getting funds in order to satisfy the needs of their university's Research Assessment Exercise (RAE) rating may be more inclined to take up such funding than pursue studies in other

Box 4.1 The Future for Youth Project

Among many of the problems faced by Youngtown is how to counteract the reputation that the area has for being a focus of drug dealing. Whether this is true or not, the fact remains that for many young people being part of this culture is irresistible. For many it begins as an adventure and excitement, with little awareness of the dangers.

The project has targeted a core group of such young people and has a room in a local community centre which is being converted into an open school forum area. The objective will be to create a space where workers can work with the young people in a personalized and intensive way. The project has links with local statutory and voluntary agencies.

Central to the project's way of working is linking the young people with a group of volunteers who are themselves part of the community. The volunteers will act as mentors, and will have received training to enable them to fulfil this role. Some of the volunteers are ex-offenders and ex-drug users.

The key features of the project are:

- it focuses on an area of poverty;
- it involves the local community and other agencies in developing a community-based approach to community safety;
- it attempts to reduce crime and the fear of crime in the area;
- it promotes an alternative lifestyle for young people;
- it lays the foundation for further developments;
- it targets young people who are vulnerable to becoming part of an ever-growing drug scene in Youngtown.

criminological areas, which might be more questioning of current policy initiatives. All this makes evaluation one of the most difficult and demanding kinds of research design that a criminologist is likely to encounter.

We will end this chapter by giving an example of the issues raised by the evaluation of a fairly small-scale project. It is based on a real-life project proposal, which we will call the 'Future for Youth Project'. The proposal reads as follows:

Faced with such a project being implemented, how might one set about evaluating it? First, what are the aims? Well, there seem to be two main aims. One is to reduce the likelihood of young people becoming involved in drug misuse and the other is, as a result, to reduce drug dealing in the area, so there are aims relating to individuals and to the community as a whole. However, this interpretation needs to be checked with those running the project. If one were proposing to evaluate the project, one would want to talk to those running the project about what they are doing. The very act of doing this is likely to result in some things being changed. Perhaps as a result of asking about the project's aims, the organizers decide to clarify or modify them.

The inputs are likely to include the resources needed to staff and run the project, the volunteers, and the activities that are carried out. As far as the processes are concerned, 'The objective will be to create a space where workers can work with the young people in a personalized and intensive way'. However, exactly what these activities are, and how they are supposed to affect involvement in drug use are unclear. Will they divert young people from drug use by providing them with something more interesting to do? Will they occupy time that might otherwise be taken up hanging around locations where drugs are dealt? Will the volunteers act as potential role models for young people? Or perhaps there is some idea that all these things will happen? These are all hypotheses waiting to be explored. One might also want to know more about the young people themselves. How are they to be identified and recruited to the project? Furthermore, the implementation of the project needs to be monitored by collecting information of various kinds regarding both the inputs, and the outputs, such as the number of young people attending, and how frequently, and what activities take place when. The involvement, recruitment and monitoring of volunteers may also need some consideration.

However, none of this constitutes evaluation. In addition, outcome measures also need to be identified. What criteria are relevant? Drug arrests? Other crimes? Residents' perceptions and fear of crime? These might involve interviews with young people regarding their activities, police data on drug arrests, and before and after surveys of local residents about their perceptions. In order to attribute any changes in these measures to the project, some comparisons need to be made. These might involve comparisons with other young people and/or with another area. We are not saying that there is a single 'right' way of doing such an evaluation; much will depend on the specific circumstances. But the proposal above is not dissimilar to many others that have been developed, and we have highlighted some of the issues that need to be considered, and would once again make the point that research is often a case of balancing a number of factors.

Further reading

The literature on evaluation has become a big market in recent years, but most of it deals with evaluation designs in general.

Regarding its use in criminology, we have already mentioned Pawson and Tilley's (1997) book, *Realistic Evaluation*. Chapter 1 of the book is entitled 'A History of Evaluation in 28$^{1}/_{2}$ Pages', and it is just that, although it has to be said, reflecting their perspective. It is also worth reading Chapter 1 of the Home Office Research Study 291, *The Impact of Corrections on Re-Offending: A Review of 'What Works'* (Friendship et al. 2004). Although primarily concerned with the substantive issue of what policies and practices are most effective in dealing with offenders, the first chapter looks at the methods used for assessing that evidence, with a particular Home Office approach to such matters. There is also a good collection edited by George Mair on *Evaluating the Effectiveness of Community Penalties* (1997). Carol Weiss's book, *Evaluation: Methods for Studying Programs and Policies* (1998), on theories of change is also recommended; Chapter 3 is a useful summary of her model.

Part II

Collecting and analysing material

5 Researching by reading

Introduction

We gain our knowledge about crime through the processes of acquiring and interpreting different types of information from a range of different sources including personal experience, gossip, political rhetoric, scientific evidence and the media – this is as true for ordinary members of the public as it is for us as researchers!

In Part II of the book, we will be exploring the different methods we use to build knowledge about crime and we will do this by focusing separately on how information is gathered and analysed by researchers through 'reading', 'seeing' and 'talking/listening' about crime. When we begin our work as researchers, a lot of our authoritative knowledge about crime is derived from things we have read, and that is an obvious starting point for this section of the book. In this chapter, we are going to consider methods of research which involve the use of research material that has been documented and made available by other people. This material might be produced expressly for the purpose of building knowledge about crime (for example, studies, reports, statistics, and books produced by academics or government departments) but we also wish to consider how we might use material which is produced for other purposes (e.g. news, entertainment) which may, nevertheless, contribute to our understanding of crime.

There are three different approaches to research by reading that we cover in this chapter. We begin the chapter by thinking about how we utilize the material that has been produced expressly for the purpose of building knowledge about crime. First, the process of reviewing the literature in an area of study. Second, the process of reading and using other people's research data. Finally, we will conclude the chapter by considering how documents which have not been specifically produced for research purposes, such as newspaper reports or historical documents, may be analysed through a method called content analysis.

Reading and reviewing the literature critically

It could be said that the most important part of any research project is the literature review. Indeed, it would not be too strong for us to state from the outset that it is the *responsibility* of any researcher to have a very good understanding of the literature which exists in his/her field of study before embarking on a research project. However, although the literature review is the essential first step in most research projects, it is important to recognize that it is not merely a preliminary exercise in research design. It may very well be necessary to consult and expand the literature review at various points in the research process – before a topic is selected, during the process of designing a research question, at the stage of methodology design and during data analysis. As researchers, we also need to be mindful of the possibility that new material may be published during the life of a project which overlaps, contradicts or steers the direction of the work in progress.

Perhaps it is worth pausing a moment to consider what exactly we mean by 'literature' in the research context? Put very simply, most of the work used by researchers is published in the form of books, reports and articles in academic journals. However, there is an additional type of source which O'Leary (2004) calls 'grey literature' and includes sources such as unpublished conference papers, newspaper articles, and student theses. For the criminological researcher, the literature base is particularly broad due to the multi-disciplinary and policy-driven nature of our discipline. We must become familiar with relevant research produced by a range of people including academic researchers, government departments, public and private sector agencies and interest groups and it is also often necessary to delve into literature from other disciplines such as sociology, psychology, law and geography.

The potential range of sources, then, is extremely wide and the process of searching for and reviewing the literature can be a particularly challenging and time-consuming one. A researcher will have to invest a significant amount of time and effort in reading and critically analysing the work of other researchers in the field and this must be factored into the research design. It is worth pointing out that this can be an isolating task as a lot of time is spent working alone in libraries and/or at a computer and so it is important to work some variety into the working day and to make efforts to talk to colleagues about recent discoveries or research problems. It also requires a good level of organization as several different lines of enquiry will need to be followed simultaneously in order to build a complete picture of the work in an area.

There are different ways of approaching a literature review and it is important to have a clear strategy from the outset. Often, the most difficult part is getting started, but once you have identified some initial sources, new sources will start to emerge and accumulate (rather like a snowball effect). It may be necessary to adopt several different search strategies to start the ball rolling. For example, a good way to identify journal articles is to use a bibliographical database (examples include the ISI Web of Knowledge and the Social Sciences Citation Index), many of which are now available online, whereas for books, it may be better to search library catalogues and bookshop databases for books in the area. Furthermore, in order to find reports and studies which are published by public and private sector agencies and interest groups, the best approach might be to search the online sites of these organizations or, if necessary, to use an internet search engine. The key to success in all of these approaches to searching is to develop a good set of search terms which can be derived from the topic, subtopics, key concepts, theories and named authors. So, for example, if you were to be searching for literature relating to methods used by credit card fraudsters, your search terms might start very simply: 'fraud' and 'credit card'. Then, as you get to know the literature in the area, you would discover that the terms 'payment card' and 'plastic card' are often used and you would repeat your searches using these new terms. As the search continues, yet more search terms will emerge – continuing our example here, the concepts of 'identity fraud', 'card-not-present fraud', 'skimming' and 'counterfeit' will become apparent as methods of credit card fraud. It may also be the case that theories can be identified or that authors' names can be used as search terms (for example 'opportunity theory' or 'Levi').

Once each item of literature has been identified and found, the researcher must manage and evaluate the information. As we said earlier, it is usual for the researcher to accumulate a large literature collection for a project and there are two issues to resolve – first, how to catalogue the sources and, second, how to record the information contained within them.

In years past, it was necessary to use manual filing systems and card indexes to build a catalogue or bibliographic database but this task is made easier now by the use of a computer. There are a number of good bibliographic computer programmes (such as *Endnote* and *Reference Manager*) which are particularly useful because they are automatically formated and particularly easy to search, but many people prefer to use their own personal system of cataloguing. Whichever approach you use, the most important thing to remember is that you should ensure that you record a *full* reference for each item at the time of acquisition – there is nothing worse than discovering that you have not recorded a reference and you cannot remember where or how you found the item (probably many months ago!). You will need to decide which details are important to record (such as author name(s), year of publication, title of article/book, journal title, page numbers, ISBN/ISSN, http address, date source was recorded, where it was found/how it was acquired and whether a copy is held on file) and choose which category of information you will use to organize the materials (for example, chronologically by date or alphabetically by author).

Having located and accurately recorded an item in the catalogue, you can finally sit down and read it! This is perhaps the most challenging part of the literature review process because it requires *critical analysis*. It is, of course, impossible to commit everything which has been read to memory and therefore it is necessary to keep some kind of record of what is contained within each source. But it is neither efficient nor productive to record a simple description of the content of the source – such descriptions tend to be lengthy yet mean little when utilized later in time. Instead, it is better to critically analyse a source and distil its 'contribution to the field'. By doing so, the researcher is able to build a meaningful picture of knowledge in a particular topic and identify gaps or inconsistencies which can be developed into research questions. However, the process of critical analysis is not easy and requires confidence and practice. We do not intend to give any lengthy instructions here on how to conduct analysis but O'Leary (2004) provides some excellent guidance, especially for those who are new to research. We also include at the end of this chapter, a 'Guide to Dissecting Articles' which we use when teaching our own students how to critically evaluate published research, (Appendix on p. 112).

We also think it is necessary to make one final point about context, which is particularly important for those of us who research in the areas of crime and crime policy. It is important to step back sometimes and consider the contexts in which the literature has evolved. As researchers in crime, we are usually dealing with contemporary social problems which have arisen from specific political, economic and legal contexts. An example would be the debates surrounding ASBOs: the emergent literature in this area is best understood in the context of the public debates taking place surrounding binge drinking, knife possession and the 'respect agenda'. Similarly, the controversial proposals to introduce identity cards are best understood in the context of post-9/11 concerns about terrorism and the situation regarding illegal immigration. We can imagine that researchers looking back on today's literature on anti-social behaviour or identity cards in ten years time might not fully understand the *meaning* of its conclusions and fully appreciate its contribution to criminology *and* policy if they were not aware of the wider context.

To conclude, then, the process of finding and reviewing the literature in an area can be onerous and time-consuming. It should, however, be an interesting, stimulating, thought provoking, challenging and forward-looking exercise. If you find yourself struggling, Hart (1998) gives excellent guidance on maintaining momentum and helping to make the process a positive experience.

Analysing other people's data

In the preceding section, we discussed how published research (articles, books, reports, etc.) should be analysed in order to build a critically informed picture of the proposed area of research. Often, you will be reading and reviewing data which has been analysed by researchers and presented in a summarized form (there is, after all, a restriction on the number of points which can be made in a single publication!). There will be times when you wish that you had access to the data. Perhaps you want to know more about the relationships between sets of variables which are of interest to you, or perhaps you can think of different avenues for analysis than those which are presented. If the latter case is true, you may be able to envisage an entire research study which could be carried out using data which has already been collected by somebody else! In some situations, for example where the data presented comes from a government department, major survey series (see below) or a project funded by a Research Council, it may be possible to get access to other people's datasets and actually conduct fresh analysis on the raw data. This approach is referred to as *secondary analysis* and is a common method in criminological research.

Put simply then, secondary analysis involves an 'independent' researcher (i.e. who has not been involved in the data collection or who was not originally envisaged as a primary 'user' of the data) conducting analysis on the data and drawing conclusions from that data. Usually, the secondary analysis involves a new interpretation of the data and thus can be a novel and exciting approach to researching. It is also attractive as a research method for a number of practical reasons (for a good overview, see Dale et al. 1988). First, the process of collecting and analysing empirical data is often time-consuming and expensive, so there is a clear incentive to utilize data which has already been collected by someone else. More time can be spent on analysing data, a luxury not always available in empirical work. Good quality datasets are also increasingly easy to access. This is certainly the case in the UK, but access to international data is also becoming easier. In the UK, we are fortunate to have the UK Data Archive (based at Essex University) which acts as 'curator' of the largest collection of digital data in the social sciences and humanities in the UK. The archive can be accessed freely by researchers through its webpages (http://www.data-archive.ac.uk/)

and both qualitative and quantitative datasets are available for download (sometimes there is a small administrative fee and some special conditions may be imposed on publication rights).

Secondary analysis of qualitative data

Secondary analysis of qualitative data is becoming more popular, especially as data is being made more widely available through the Economic and Social Data Service (ESDS) provided by the UK Data Archive (UKDA) at Essex University.[1] The service holds digital data collections from purely qualitative and mixed methods contemporary research, including all relevant studies funded by the ESRC. General guidance and a dedicated advisory service for data creators and depositors on research project management, issues of confidentiality and consent, and data documentation of data for archiving are provided.

It can be difficult to analyse qualitative data which has been collected by someone else. As we shall see later (in Chapter 8), qualitative analysis is not governed by as clear a set of rules and procedures as is quantitative analysis. Thus, it is essential for the researcher to develop an analytic strategy of his/her own, ensuring high standards of reliability and validity throughout the process. This requires an in-depth knowledge of the project's methodology and an understanding of the contexts in which the data were collected. It is, indeed, argued that secondary analysis of qualitative data is simply not feasible because it is impossible for someone who was not part of, say, the interview or observation to understand the data fully. However, the possibility that a new analyst may bring a valuable objective perspective to the data, combined with the very fact that there is so much room for exploration and conceptual development, seems to outweigh the potential pitfalls (Bryman 2004).

Secondary analysis of quantitative data

The range of quantitative datasets available to the secondary analyst are more plentiful and consist of both major survey series conducted by research organizations and official statistics collected and produced by government agencies. A large proportion of these quantitative datasets are held by the UKDA and are available for secondary analysis but some are administered by dedicated research institutions (see below). The data tends to be of particularly high quality, drawn using well-developed sampling procedures by large, well-established research organizations. Often, the datasets are repeated (annually or less often) and may then be suitable for longitudinal analysis or the analysis of trends.

There are, however, a number of disadvantages too. Because you have not been involved in the operationalization of the measures, the collection of the data and the preparation of the dataset, you have to spend a lot of time understanding the data before you can begin to analyse it. This is particularly problematic in the case of large datasets such as the British Crime Survey (see Chapter 12 for an illustration). There will also be a number of restrictions on what you can do with the data. You may, for example, have data which operates at only the individual level (rather than the household, local or national level). There may also be some key variables missing, either because they were not originally included or they have been removed for the purposes of anonymizing the data (for example, the postcode variables are sometimes removed from datasets which can be frustrating when you are intending to attempt area-level analysis). Finally, Arber (2001) makes the excellent point that secondary analysis requires both sociological imagination and the construction of theoretically informed research questions.

There are two types of quantitative data which will be of use to you as a criminological researcher. First, we will briefly consider the major survey series which are available. Although these are not dedicated 'crime surveys', they tend to contain information about social characteristics and indicators of social change that criminologists are interested in (for example, poverty, unemployment, health and political attitudes). Next, we move on to consider the series of data collected by the government, information that we usually refer to as Official Statistics.

Major survey series

There are a number of major surveys and longitudinal studies which have been carried out for a period of years, which provide a fuller and more detailed picture on various topics. Some of these are government surveys and some are funded and carried out by independent agencies. They include:

- *The OPCS Longitudinal Study* – based on records of vital events relating to 1 per cent of the population of England and Wales born on each of four dates each year, starting in 1971 (about 500,000 people). It represents a continuous sample of the population rather than a sample taken at a single point in time. More information is available through the Office of National Statistics (ONS): http://www.statistics.gov.uk/about/data/methodology/specific/population/LS/
- *The National Child Development Study* (NCDS) – a longitudinal study of all those living in Great Britain born between 3rd and 9th of March 1958 (17,000 people). Originally designed to investigate perinatal mortality and infant health. To date, there

have been seven main follow-ups to monitor the sample's development, the latest in 2004 carried out by the Social Statistics Research Unit (now known as the Centre for Longitudinal Studies (CLS)), when the sample was 46 years old. More information is available at: http://www.cls.ioe.ac.uk/

- *The 1970 British Cohort Study* – similar to the NCDS, based on a cohort of 17,000 people born in the UK between 5th and 11th April 1970. Also being carried out by SSRU and was last followed up in 1999/2000. More information is available at: http://www.cls.ioe.ac.uk/
- *The Millennium Cohort Study* – The sample population for the study was drawn from all live births in the UK over 12 months from 1 September 2000 in England and Wales and 1 December 2000 in Scotland and Northern Ireland. The focus is to study the all-important first year of life and potentially resolve many of the issues about its long-term impact. These include issues of central policy interest such as the foundations of social capital and cohesion. There have been three sweeps of the survey to date, the most recent occurring in 2006 when the children started primary school. More information is available at: http://www.cls.ioe.ac.uk/
- *Labour Force Survey* – a quarterly survey comprising 80,000 people which mainly focus on employment and training activity. Unlike the monthly claimant count, its definition of unemployment is based on an internationally recognized definition of unemployment, and its results are often compared with the claimant count. More information is available through the Office of National Statistics at: http://www.statistics.gov.uk/STATBASE/Source.asp?vlnk=358&More=Y
- *General Household Survey* – an annual survey started in 1971 covering about 10,000 households used to monitor the effect of various areas of government policy over time. More information is available through the Office of National Statistics at: http://www.statistics.gov.uk/ssd/surveys/general_household_survey.asp
- *British Social Attitudes Survey* – an annual survey charting continuity and change in British social, economic, political and moral values in relation to other changes in society. Topics include newspaper readership, political parties and trust, public spending, welfare benefits, health care, child care, poverty, the labour market and the workplace, education, charitable giving, the countryside, transport and the environment, Europe, economic prospects, race, religion, civil liberties, immigration, sentencing and prisons. More information is available through the National Centre for Social Research at http://www.natcen.ac.uk/natcen/pages/or_socialattitudes.htm

Official Statistics

When we talk about Official Statistics, we are referring to a wide range of statistics which are produced by government departments and agencies. The government collects a vast amount of data relating to its citizens and, if you think about it, most of the major events and activities in a person's lifetime are recorded by government agencies. From the moment a birth is registered, an individual's interactions with state agencies such as the NHS, Benefits Agency, Passport Office, HM Revenue and Customs, Land Registry and criminal justice system are recorded. This, of course, is increasingly true in the modern era of powerful electronic data storage and exchange systems. Each government department collects and produces statistics on areas within its remit, but since 1996 the Office for National Statistics (ONS) has been the central government agency responsible for co-ordinating government statistics. There is an ONS website (http://www.statistics.gov.uk/) which gives access to a wide range of government statistics, but it is often better to go to the website of a particular department to seek out published information.

It is, of course, the Crime Statistics (a sub-set of the Official Statistics) which are of most interest to the criminological researcher. As we saw earlier in this chapter, when you begin to investigate a specific topic or research idea, it is necessary to build a picture of what is already known about that issue. It is common to include an overview of the relevant official statistics in the literature review and this can be particularly useful for developing the context and theoretical framework. You might be interested in establishing answers to the following questions: How much crime is there? Is crime going up or going down? Are the police doing their job? How do criminals get punished for their crimes? These are the kinds of questions of interest to policy-makers, the public, the media and researchers and the data has been used as a kind of barometer of the moral health of the nation for more than a century (Maguire 2007). It is also possible for researchers to gain access to the datasets and conduct secondary analysis on the data. The British Crime Survey, for example, is made available through the UKDA and the Criminal Statistics through the Home Office (http://www.homeoffice.gov.uk/rds).

The Home Office is currently responsible for the collection and publication of crime statistics for England and Wales (data for Scotland and Northern Ireland are collected independently by the Scottish Executive and the Police Service of Northern Ireland respectively). The statistics have traditionally been published in three main statistical series/reports and the strengths and weaknesses of all three are well documented (for a good overview, see Maguire 2007). We present a summary here, highlighting the key points of interest.

- *The Criminal Statistics*: The Criminal Statistics have been produced for more than 150 years by the government. They are a national compilation of records produced at a local level by the police and the courts, focusing on notifiable offences recorded by the police, the number of cautions given and the number of offenders found guilty of specific offences. The main reports and accompanying data spread sheets are available through the Home Office webpages (the most up-to-date at the time of writing are for 2004; http://www.homeoffice.gov.uk/rds/crimstats04.html). For many decades, the Criminal Statistics were the key measures used to monitor crime change in the country. In the 1970s, however, a change in criminological thinking prompted demands for new kinds of information. Police and court records were heavily criticized for not being a neutral set of facts about crime but more of an indicator of institutional needs, and new interests in victims and situational crime prevention sparked off a whole new range of empirical studies. Whereas it was once the case that the Criminal Statistics provided the one official picture of crime, now they are simply part of a whole 'kaleidoscope' (Maguire 2007).
- *The Recorded Crime Statistics*: The Recorded Crime Statistics (RCS) are a national compilation of crimes recorded by the police which has been administered since 1876. The Home Office lays down a set of rules which determine how and when crimes are recorded and are responsible for collating and publishing the results provided by individual forces. The statistics are useful in providing overall totals of all crime which is recorded and can highlight changes in crime problems through trends and comparisons of crime types (so, for example, we can see whether auto crime is on the rise or whether property crime is more common than violent crime, etc.). However, the RCS have received significant criticism regarding validity and reliability and you therefore have to interpret the data with great caution. Maguire notes that there are three main factors which need to be taken into consideration:
  - *Conceptual consistency*: As new legislation and policies are introduced over the years, definitions of offences are subject to change. You have to be careful, therefore, that the crime you are examining now meant the same to people working in, say, the 1950s. The last major changes were made in 1998 in an attempt to bring consistency between police forces, implementing a whole new range of recordable offences and changing the rules for recording multiple offences. The effect was to drastically boost the recorded crime figures and this has made comparisons across time very difficult.

  - *Consistency in recording practice*: Although the Home Office provides rules which govern the practice of recording (the National Crime Recording Standard was introduced in 2002), there is still room for police discretion and therefore a risk of discrepancies between the approaches taken by individual forces. It is often argued that police attitudes and practices can significantly influence the statistics.[2] Although changes have been made to help ensure consistency, it is still a concern that the police have the ability and, in a growing culture of performance and managerialism, the incentive to hide some offences and/or over-record others. It is still the case, then, that you have to be wary of possible variations within and between forces.
  - *Reporting of crime by the public*: We know that people choose whether to report crimes or not to the police for a range of reasons including trust, apathy, access or ignorance. The RCS then are subject to any changes in reporting behaviour and you should always keep this in mind when interpreting the statistics.
- *The British Crime Survey:* The British Crime Survey (BCS) was introduced in 1982 at a time when official statistics based on the work of the police and the courts were receiving heavy criticism and criminologists were becoming increasingly interested in the victim perspective. The BCS is a national household survey which seeks to establish whether anyone in the household has been a victim of crime and, where a victimization has occurred, to gather information about that experience. Thus it is said to provide a more accurate picture of crime because it picks up all crimes which are not reported to the police and/or end up in the courts. It also includes questions which measure attitudes to the police and the Criminal Justice System, as well as self-completion questionnaires for drug taking and domestic violence. In its early years it was conducted on a four-year cycle, but now is based on a continuous annual cycle with a sample size of 40,000 respondents per year. The questionnaire has not changed a great deal since its original format and great emphasis is placed on maintaining its content to allow for accurate trends analysis. However, this has actually led to considerable criticism because it has prevented changes being made to some measures which have been recognized as poorly constructed or in need of conceptual development (see Chapter 12 for an illustration). The BCS is also limited to a relatively small range of crimes and this makes comparisons with the RCS data quite difficult (according to Patterson and Thorpe 2006, only 3/4 of BCS crimes are comparable with 1/2 of the RCS crimes).

For the past two decades, the RCS and BCS statistics have been the figures most often cited by both researchers and the media as indicators of crime. Traditionally, they were published separately as distinct but complementary sources of data, but recently the Home Office took the decision to merge the two in an annual report called 'Crime in England and Wales'. This decision has been heavily criticized because it has resulted in what appears to be 'analysis with political spin' and not a neutral presentation of factual data (Maguire 2007). Perhaps the most damning criticism came in the 2006 review of crime statistics conducted by the Statistics Commission (Statistics Commission 2006) in which it was recommended that the distinction between BCS data and Recorded Crime Statistics is reintroduced as soon as possible.

Despite the obvious flaws in all three approaches, the Criminal Statistics, the British Crime Survey and the Recorded Crime Statistics are still arguably three of the most important sources of information for criminological researchers. However, the crime statistics are reviewed periodically, and it is important for those involved in criminological research to stay abreast of the changes being implemented. Changes occur in terms of the volume and range of data collected and the ways in which analysis is conducted and disseminated. Indeed, Maguire (2007) refers to a 'data explosion' which has occurred in the field of crime statistics in recent years, propelled in part by significant technological advances which have transformed the ways in which we can store and analyse electronic data but also by a new culture of managerialism and performance management in government departments and agencies. He observes that there is now more data (quantitative and qualitative) being collected in a range of new areas including unreported and unrecorded offences, the circumstances of the offence, the geographical distribution of offences, better development of concepts (such as street crime), more on hidden crimes and hidden offenders and on victims and public perceptions. It also seems that there is now a willingness to think more imaginatively about how crime is counted, and a move away from 'legal definitions' of crime in favour of seeing crime as a socially constructed phenomenon. The Simmons Report proposed a 'national index' of crime which would focus on the most serious and high volume crimes, for example. However, it would appear that we are some way from developing a meaningful 'index' of crime.

It is clear, then, that it is possible to become confused when working with the official crime statistics. Indeed, there has been growing criticism that the statistics are presented to the public in a confusing way and it has been suggested that the widespread misunderstanding about rates and distributions of crime is eroding public trust (Statistics Commission 2006). How these issues are resolved remains to be seen but it is perhaps worth concluding by reflecting on the six key recommendations made by the Statistics Commission aimed at improving the availability, usability and accuracy of official crime statistics:

1 The structure of the Home Office should be changed to separate the policy-making and information provision/publication functions.[3]
2 Improved communication with users.
3 Better data at the small area level.
4 Furthering of research opportunities.
5 Improvements to the comparability of data (especially with Scotland and Northern Ireland).
6 Further work on index measures of 'total crime'.

Criminological research, policy and politics

Before leaving the topic of official crime statistics, we think it is important to say something about the relationship between criminological research and politics. Crime statistics are actually used by a variety of different people acting in different roles. The government and local delivery organizations, for example, use statistics to develop policy on criminal justice and crime reduction and to manage performance and to communicate about crime with the public. The public use crime statistics to understand the rationale for government policy, to hold local delivery organizations to account and to build knowledge about other people's experiences and perceptions of crime and disorder, and to use this information to assess risk in their everyday lives. Consequently, there is a close relationship between public concern about crime, the position of crime on the political agenda and government investment in data collection (Maguire 2007) and this relationship is one which always needs to be considered in the context of research.

It is hard to think of a time when criminological research would not have had some political implications. During the 1970s, for example, *The New Criminology* (Taylor et al. 1973) epitomized a radical critique of a criminology that had previously been seen as an extension of a criminal justice establishment. Nonetheless, there was a time, prior to the 1980s when crime and the treatment of offenders were not a party political issue (see Cavadino et al. 2000 for a fuller history). However, criminal justice policy, and consequently criminological research have become increasingly politicized in recent decades. Concomitant with this (we do not necessarily suggest a direct causal link) criminological research has seen debates emerging about its methods and their relationship to policy. These have covered two main areas of criminological endeavour: evaluation and criminal statistics. During the 1990s there was a debate about the nature of evaluation, the so-called 'paradigm wars' (see Chapter 4). However, this was mainly an argument about different models of evaluation, and not overtly political. The significance of evaluation was, however, boosted in the late 1990s when the Labour Government declared itself committed to 'evidence-based' research. This commitment later became doubtful when it seemed that some of the evidence did not provide what the Government desired, leading the President of the British Society of Criminology, Tim Newburn, to refer to 'the rise and fall of evidence-based research' (address to The University of East London's Crime Research Conference, Royal Statistical Society, 27 November 2006).

One of the most trenchant critics of the Home Office has been Tim Hope, once a Home Office researcher himself. In the context of a controversial project in which he was involved, Hope discusses the role of 'scientific' evidence in politics (Hope 2004). The traditional Enlightenment model, he notes, sees science as something separate from policy. However, more recent thinkers, notably Beck in his discussion of the Risk Society (1992), have argued that as scientific evidence becomes the basis for policy decisions, so 'science becomes itself a site for politics. ... The value of science ceases to be derived from its methodology alone and is now also to be derived from its promise of applicability and utility' (Hope 2004: 290–1). This promise has been augmented in recent years by the appearance of what is claimed to be a new 'crime science', which seeks to apply techniques in ways that might enhance the work of criminal justice agencies, and sees research as essentially something that is intended for policy utilization (ibid.: 291). This 'reflexive' role of science is different from the previously accepted view that criminology is concerned with understanding and explaining crime and criminality, and that policy relevance is incidental.

Another element in the way that research links in with politics is the role played by the Treasury. HM Treasury requires that Government departments demonstrate the cost effectiveness of their programmes, based on guidance issued by the Treasury in the form of *The Green Book*, which sets out a framework for project appraisal. This is supplemented in the context of Government social research by the *Magenta Book* of guidance for policy evaluation and analysis. It is not surprising that a Government should want to demonstrate value for the money it spends, but it can constrain research in terms of both scope and timescale. Raynor and Robinson have argued that

> The policy of recruiting as many offenders as possible to programmes to meet Treasury targets has probably tended to undermine the fit between offenders' needs and programmes and contributed to increasing attrition and non-completion, which in turn reduces the overall impact of the programmes if non-completers reconvict more. (2005: 116)

In addition, one of the most common complaints among researchers is that programmes which need careful planning and development are rushed in order to produce results before they have really had time to bed in.

To conclude, then, while the Home Office is not the only arbiter of criminological research, it does play an important role in both setting a research agenda and providing a significant amount of funding. The point we wish to make here is that these matters should make the criminological researcher aware that research does take place in a context where values, disagreements and politics occur, and these need to be considered when research is undertaken.

Analysing documents

The final approach to research through reading that we want to mention in this chapter is the method of analysing documents known as content analysis. Content analysis is often used as a supplementary method in a multi-method strategy. It can involve the collection and analysis of both quantitative data (for example, the number of relevant words or paragraphs) and qualitative data (the nature of language or style of pictures). In the criminological context, most studies using a content analysis approach have focused on printed news media and official policy documents.

We do not wish to discuss the technicalities of the process of content analysis in depth here because we do so later in Chapter 8. We should, however, say a little about content analysis here as a method of research by reading. The process begins with the identification of a focused research question and, where suitable, developed hypotheses. The next stage is to develop a sampling strategy. The sampling frame will depend entirely on the nature of the research question, for example, if the aim is to test the relationship between crime reporting in the news and perceptions of crime rates, the sampling frame would be constructed of relevant national and local newspapers and/or news programmes on television and/or radio. The sample can be drawn according to a number of different elements, for example, time, publication, author and reference to particular events; again, this will be determined by the nature of the research question. Once the sample has been drawn, the analysis can begin and the process of development of categories for analysis and the definition of recording units is described further in Chapter 8.

Like all methods of research, content analysis has its strengths and weaknesses. On the plus side, the documents under scrutiny have usually been produced for another purpose (i.e. not for the purpose of the research) and content analysis has a clear strength in being unobtrusive and non-reactive. However, this can also cause problems for the researcher as the document can be structured in an unhelpful way, leaving the researcher the tough task of organizing the material. One of the major challenges is to ensure validity in the research, especially where the analyst must distinguish between 'witting evidence' (information which the author of the document intended to convey) and 'unwitting evidence' (any additional information which the analyst can glean through his/her reading of the document). Finally, content analysis is renowned for being a rather laborious and time-consuming process although it is true that computers have eased the labour to some extent.

Conclusion

In this chapter we have introduced a range of different approaches to research in which you might use documents, publications and other people's data. We hope to have illustrated the vast amount of information available to the criminological researcher and opened your eyes to the opportunities for incorporating this information into a research strategy. We have discussed how we utilize material that has been produced expressly for the purpose of building knowledge about crime, and considered how we might conduct original analysis on other people's data. Also, we have considered the use of documents which have not been specifically produced for research purposes, such as newspaper reports or historical documents. What we hope to have illustrated is that criminological research is not simply about going out and harvesting new data. In the majority of research projects, you will need to spend a lot of time reading and it is important to recognize that this element of research requires a range of skills and awareness of the wider contexts in which information about crime is published.

Further reading

O'Leary's (2004) book, although not specifically tailored to the criminological researcher, provides some useful information about the role of the literature review in the research process for students. Hart's text (1998) is more detailed and perhaps more appropriate for practitioners or those conducting more advanced research projects.

In terms of the datasets available for secondary analysis, we would recommend that you use the weblinks we have provided to gain access to the most up-to-date information about the major survey series and official statistics. The UKDA also has a great deal of useful documents on its website. For those looking for a more general text, both Bryman (2004) and Arber (2001) provide good discussions of the secondary analysis of survey data. Dale et al. (1988) is also a useful text, but a little dated. Maguire's chapter on crime statistics in the fourth edition of the *Oxford Handbook of Criminology* (2007) is perhaps the most comprehensive overview of the current state of crime statistics in England and Wales. It is a 'must-read' for anyone intending to use crime statistics in research. Another useful document for anyone interested in the current debate about the relationship between science and politics is the report by the House of Commons Science and Technology Committee (2006).

Content analysis is discussed further in Chapter 8, but a comprehensive discussion is given by Holsti (1969).

Appendix: A Guide to Dissecting Research Publications

What is the point of the study?

The researcher should convey to the reader concisely why the study was undertaken, what the field of study was, what the key questions were which the study was trying to answer. Evaluate whether the way the study is written up easily enables you to work out its purpose and summarize it.

The objectives of the research could include:

- the development of a particular area of theory
- the collection or accumulation of a new body of information or data
- the development of research methods or techniques
- a contribution to knowledge or understanding
- a contribution to policy and practice in a particular area
- a product such as computer software, patents or research facilities.

What kind of theoretical explanation is it using?

Describe briefly the kind of theoretical explanation which underlies the study. This may be a particular school of criminology or well-known theory (for example, positivism or subcultural theory) or it may be a set of ideas or way of viewing the subject of the empirical work. Remember that not all authors set out clearly what their theoretical basis is. You will need to evaluate how clearly you are able to understand the author's theoretical position and how well this is set out in the article. Remember that there is always a theoretical underpinning to empirical work – if only the unstated predisposition or ideological position of the researcher.

Evaluate as well whether the type of theoretical explanation is suited to the purpose of the study. What other levels or types of explanation would be possible or have been used in previous research cited in the article? Would any of these have been more suitable than what the author actually used?

What methodological possibilities present themselves?

Given the purpose of the study and the kind of explanation, think through for yourself what methods the researchers could have used (for example, think through the different types of methods covered in the course and see whether each one could have been helpful for the topic being researched). Is the method the author actually chose the most sensible? Why/why not? Do the researchers make it plain why they chose this method?

How appropriate were the methodological choices related to doing the research?

Given the choice of that particular method, you need to work through the methodological choices which the researchers have then made, at each point (briefly) setting out what the researchers did, whether that was the most sensible choice and why/why not. If they don't tell you what they did, why they did it – and it's not obvious – then that's a negative mark for them; you should comment upon any lack of information as much as upon what is said in the article.

The particular questions you should ask yourself will vary with the method chosen, but some likely ones are:

- What key concepts are being used, are their definitions and operationalization clear?
- Was there just one method, or was there method/theoretical triangulation?
- What role is the researcher taking (scientist, 'disinterested' observer, participant observer, action researcher, analyst of previous data, etc.)?
- What population was chosen on which to do the research and how were people/records sampled? Was the site for the research the most appropriate/practically feasible one?
- What are the likely biases leading from those sampling choices of population, sample and site?
- How was access achieved?
- What ethical/legal considerations are involved and how were they dealt with (particularly focusing on confidentiality, disclosure of purpose of research, learning about illicit behaviour)?
- If an interview/questionnaire, were the questions appropriately phrased? Does it look as though any precautions were taken to guard against leading questions, socially desirable answers, etc?

- Hence, how reliable and valid were the research method(s) chosen?

How effective were the methods of data analysis?

- Is it clear how the data were analysed (whether a qualitative or quantitative approach was used, the kinds of statistics used, etc.)?
- Is the overall decision on which kind of data analysis was used appropriate for the research method chosen?
- Are the variables/topics analysed clearly defined and suitable for the theoretical questions being asked in the study (for example, how variables analysed emerged from open-ended questioning)?

The conclusions of the study and its presentation

Describe briefly the conclusions of the study. To what extent do you think the conclusions drawn fit the results of the analysis (are there any unjustified leaps of guesswork)?

Do the study's conclusions relate in the way you would expect to the original purpose and aims of the study? Has it managed to create theoretical insights/test its hypotheses, etc?

How effective was the presentation of the study to the reader? How could it be improved?

6 Researching by looking

Introduction: watch and learn

If you think about it, the process of observation is one which we all use instinctively. Every day we are learning about the world around us by looking at our surroundings and interpreting our observations. You might, for example, notice a sudden increase in traffic around mid-afternoon and conclude that the problem is caused by parents collecting their children from a nearby school. Or, you might observe that two friends are acting frostily towards each other and realize that they have had an argument. A lot of the time we are making these kinds of observations subconsciously and using our interpretations to inform our own decisions or actions.

It is possible to formalize these skills and utilize them in research, either as a stand-alone method or in combination with other methods such as those covered in the chapters on 'talking' and 'reading'. Observation is a particularly useful approach in criminological research because we are so often concerned with understanding behaviour, interactions and processes which both drive criminal behaviour and facilitate the dispensation of justice. Often, observing the actions of individuals or a group dynamic is a far better indication of how people are feeling than asking them to try and explain it themselves.

Observation is used in criminological research studies but there are a number of issues which require careful consideration before it is adopted as an approach. It is extremely time consuming and there are a number of ethical and philosophical problems to be overcome. We will discuss these issues in this chapter.

The science of observation? Epistemology and research design

Natural scientists who adhere to the principles of positivism (see Chapter 2) accept that knowledge about the natural world is best gathered through systematic, objective and repeated observations of naturally occurring phenomena. So, for example, we might gain knowledge about the physical properties of glass through a series of experiments in which we heat a piece of glass to different temperatures and record observed changes in colour and texture. Observational methods in this context, then, would be formal, structured and objective and we would control the experiment using tools such as a stopwatch, a thermometer and a pre-designed table for recording results. But can such methods be used to study social phenomena?

Social observation methods were originally developed during the colonial period of the British Empire. British anthropologists were keen to study and understand the 'exotic' cultures which existed in the newly established colonies and so developed an approach to research which incorporated methods of observation, the collection of documents and interviews. This approach became known as ethnography. Although early anthropologists actually accompanied scientific expeditions into new territories, an 'armchair approach' was more typical as it became an established procedure. Rather than working in the field, they would work from their libraries in London constructing a picture of life in the colonies from notes sent back by the teams of colonial administrators. The colonial administrators were instructed what to do by a guidebook, initially published in 1874 (BAAS 1874), which provided the local district commissioners with a set of questions to put to native informants.

After the colonial period, ethnographic methods were taken in a new direction by the Chicago School of sociologists working in the 1920s and 1930s in the USA. Importantly, the Chicago School scholars developed two key elements which added to the British anthropological approach. First, they introduced an element of pragmatism to what had previously been a very positivistic approach. They accepted the view that social life is not a fixed, unalterable phenomenon (the sort of thing that positivists like to study with their fixed measuring instruments) but instead was dynamic and changing. The second element was formalism. This is the idea that although social relationships will always differ in content from each other, they nevertheless represent underlying forms which can have similarities. So the focus in any social setting will be the interactions between people and not the people themselves.

Thus, the methods used by the Chicago School researchers were strikingly different from the anthropological approach. Having shunned the strict principles of positivism, they believed that understanding cannot be derived from a formal process of testing hypotheses. Instead, they argued that one must undertake meticulous and detailed observations, and then generate understanding from the data. The researchers were, then, encouraged to go out and plot the contours of the city streets – not with clipboards and questionnaires (as these asked static, fixed questions) but with empty notebooks. Their aim was to attempt to record and understand change in the city.

Crucially, the Chicago researchers did not start with a specific theory which they wanted to test. Instead, they ended up with a theory after the data had been collected and analysed. This is one of the key features of ethnography – the theory is generated from data (rather than collecting data to illustrate a theory). It is usual then for the researcher to re-formulate the research question as the research progresses. Hammersley and Atkinson (1983) note, however, that there is a constant interplay between 'substantive' or 'topical' theory (i.e. theory which is developed for specific empirical inquiries) and 'formal' or 'generic' theory (i.e. broader conceptual theory). An ethnographic study may move from the formal to the substantive (see the study of classroom deviance by Hargreaves et al. (1975) in which labelling theory was taken as a starting point and transformed into a 'shopping list' of issues directly relevant to schools), or the opposite way (a good example of this is Atkinson's study of industrial training units (1981) in which topical, concrete research questions were related to generic concepts such as labelling and stigma).

It is important for anyone considering an ethnographic approach to realize that ethnography and observation are different – it is possible to carry out an observation study without it being an ethnography. It is perhaps most helpful to think of ethnography as a research *strategy* and observation as a research *method*. An ethnographic study, then, may incorporate a number of different methods, including observation, documentary research and interviews. For example, look at a study by Tomsen (1997) in which the researcher combined observations in pubs/bars, interviews with bouncers and the analysis of police data in his study of the culture of drinking violence in Newcastle, Australia. The defining features of an ethnography are its theoretical/epistemological grounding (the generation of theory from data) and the 'immersion' of the researcher into the social setting for an extended period of time. It is the case then that a 'grounded theory' approach is adopted in which the observer enters the environment completely open-minded as to what might emerge. This kind of approach is particularly well suited to cases in which the researcher intends to explore and understand an unknown phenomenon or situation. By adopting an open observation approach, the observer assumes a neutral starting point and opens his/her mind to the environment and relationships which evolve in front of him/her. There is no need to make a list of concepts for observation, nor to construct hypotheses in advance of the observation. Instead, the concepts, hypotheses and theories emerge as the process unfolds. The observer is able to determine what information is noted and recorded from the outset and has complete freedom to allow the observation process to evolve.

However, as we emphasized earlier, observation is a research method in its own right and does not have to be carried out as part of an ethnography. An observation can be integrated into different types of research strategies, including those with a strong positivistic leaning. There are, indeed, research contexts which are suited to a more prescriptive and structured approach to observation. If, for example, the aims of a research project included the testing of specific hypotheses and measurement of pre-identified concepts, it would be necessary for the observer to pre-determine the concepts which are to be measured and to develop a research tool or instrument to be used in the observation process. In these kinds of studies, it is common for the observer to take on the role of a detached/non-participant observer (see later) and there are a number of good examples of this approach in criminology, including a street observation study by Shapland et al. (1994) (discussed later in this chapter) and observation of the Youth Court by Allen et al. (2000) (discussed in detail in Chapter 10).

While there is a clear contrast between the open style of observation found in ethnographic work and studies which use a structured observation approach, an important feature common to both approaches is the process of analytic induction. If you recall from the discussion in Chapter 2, this process begins with the development of a theoretical framework (in a grounded theory approach the theoretical framework will emerge as the study progresses, rather than being constructed at the start). Using this framework, hypotheses are constructed and are then tested, and usually redefined as the observation process progresses (Denzin (1978), see also Cressey's study of embezzlers (1950)).

Methodological decisions

Sampling

The three main sampling dimensions in observational research are time, people and setting or context (Hammersley and Atkinson 1983). In terms of time, you have to decide when observations are most appropriate – what time of day, which days of the week, which months of the year, which seasons (taking into account events like Christmas or Bank Holidays), and so on, as well as how long the period of observation should last (a couple of hours, a whole day or the duration of an event such as a meeting). When it comes to people, you have to think in terms of sociological demographics (gender, age, ethnicity, etc.) but also about the roles or categories one has identified as existing in the observed group (so, for example, workers, middle managers and executives). Importantly, roles can be 'member identified' or 'observer identified' (Loftland 1973). You also need to consider the different settings or cultural contexts in which the phenomena under examination might occur. For example, there may be a difference between the way police officers act when in public and when in the work's canteen. Finally, it might be the case that the phenomenon can be studied from any number of theoretical angles and you must decide which of these angles to take.

An example may help to illustrate the kinds of sampling decisions which are necessary in observational studies. Suppose that a research team studying the experiences of witnesses in the Crown Court plan to conduct an observation as part of the study. You can imagine that the sampling design discussions might include consideration of the following questions:

- *How long should the overall period of observation be?*
  Weeks, months? What time of year (if it is over Christmas, for example, how will the holiday period affect the court timetable)?
- *How often will the observer go to court and how long will s/he spend there?*
  How many times a week? Which days? Should it be the same days each week or different days? On Mondays, are the majority of cases likely to be alcohol-related incidents from the weekend – how will this be dealt with? Should the observer attend all cases during the day, or only some? If cases are adjourned, should the observer return to hear the rest of the case on another day?
- *Which types of witnesses should be selected for observation?*
  Are we interested in distinguishing between witnesses of different genders, ages and socio-economic status? If so, how many of each demographic group should we aim to include? Are there any other characteristics which might be of interest (perhaps the legal teams tend to distinguish between reliable and unreliable witnesses or perhaps between confident and nervous/reluctant witnesses)?
- *Where will the observations take place?*
  Should the observer focus simply on the role of the witness during the formal proceedings in the courtroom or should s/he also examine the ways in which other members of the courtroom behave towards the witness? Should s/he also observe the activities and interactions outside of the courtroom (for example, in the waiting area, in interactions with the Witness Service or when being briefed by the lawyers for the prosecution)?

The answers to many of these questions will, of course, depend upon the research questions which have been identified previously. Also, a lot will depend upon the time and resources available to the researcher.

Access

As we have seen in previous chapters, one of the major challenges in criminological research is getting access to the site of interest. This is especially true for observation studies because it requires a significant level of intrusion on the part of the researcher – it is not just like having someone dropping in to do a few interviews and leaving again, it is a much more invasive process. So, the researcher must have excellent communication and negotiation skills and must be able to strike up good relationships with research subjects.

Generally, there are two kinds of setting to which the researcher can seek access. The first kind of setting is a group or institution which has a clear organizational structure. This may be an official organization (such as a prison or a school) or it may be an informal group (such as a street gang or criminal network). It may be the case that the observer already has access to this group/organization due to an existing position (for example, Holdaway, in his (1983) study of the police, was already in position as a police officer). It is more likely, however, that the observer will not already be part of the setting and needs to negotiate access. The second kind of setting is a public environment in which the observer can access freely. Usually it will not be necessary for the observer to seek permission to infiltrate but there may be practical and ethical issues to consider.

The process of gaining access to an organizational/group setting often involves seeking permission from 'gatekeepers'. Gatekeepers are individuals (or sometimes committees) who have a formal responsibility to control the boundaries of the setting, particularly where that setting is an organization or institution of some kind (for example, a police force, government department or a prison). Where the setting does not have an official organizational structure, an 'informal sponsor' may be used instead of a gatekeeper. A sponsor is usually someone who is part of the setting and who is prepared to brief, train and vouch for the observer (see, for example, Whyte's 1981 study of street corner society in an Italian slum in which a character called Doc famously coached the researcher in order to help him to blend in). This person should be contrasted with the 'gatekeeper' who is a more formal guardian of the boundaries (Hammersley and Atkinson 1983). Access can even be hard in public space settings because the observer still has to somehow account for his/her loitering. In some very closed situations, it may even be necessary for the researcher to negotiate access with the gatekeeper *and* to secure a relationship with an informal sponsor.

It is essential for the researcher to define a good working relationship with the gatekeeper. When approaching a gatekeeper, s/he needs to think carefully about how s/he describes the proposed hypotheses since the gatekeeper is likely to feel responsible for protecting his/her institution and having it portrayed positively. In addition to appropriately presenting the aims of the study, the researcher has to think also about how the gatekeeper perceives the role of the researcher him/herself. Depending on the situation, s/he will be perceived as either an 'expert' (who is able to sort a problem out) or a 'critic' (there to evaluate) and either perception needs careful management (Hammersley and Atkinson 1983).

Inevitably, though, however good the relationship between the gatekeeper and the researcher is, the gatekeeper will have a significant hold over the direction of the research and complete independence for the observer is unlikely. This may actually be a problem for some researchers, especially where the setting is closed or where the observer needs to uncover information which is particularly sensitive. There is, therefore, a possibility that the researcher may choose to avoid these problems by resorting to covert or secret research. Of course, this means that the researcher must deceive all gatekeepers and participants within the setting and, as well as raising obvious ethical questions, this kind of approach can be very stressful for the researcher. It is, however, an approach which has been adopted in criminological research but is not now common. Holdaway (1983), in his study of the police, opted to carry out covert research, arguing that to misrepresent his research would be dishonest and to seek permission would be unrealistic as it would be refused. A completely covert approach such as this is obviously highly controversial, especially in the modern climate of formalized research ethics procedures and not a decision to be taken lightly by the researcher. It does, however, lie at the extreme end of the deception scale and it is more common for the researcher to strive to achieve a balance between presenting any details which may be perceived as controversial or threatening in a positive light while avoiding any unjustifiable deception when negotiating with gatekeepers.

Once you have gained access, you then have to actually enter the setting. This can be difficult because you often have to immerse yourself into an already established group context. There are three main challenges to overcome in this regard. First, members of the group are likely to be wary of a stranger who they know to be 'researching' and you have to think carefully about disclosing the nature of the research being undertaken. If subjects are unfamiliar with the whole notion of social research, they are likely to see the researcher as an 'official' and behave accordingly. If they are, however, familiar with the research process, they may feel defensive (depending on the critic/expert roles described above). Second, the social characteristics of the observer, especially gender, age and ethnicity can also have an effect on the way in which s/he is perceived. Third, you must think carefully before interacting too 'honestly', it may be necessary to avoid sharing your personal beliefs.

The skilled observer, then, will be adept at what Hammersley and Atkinson (1983) call 'impression management' – dressing and carrying yourself like the subjects, without taking it so far that you appear completely uncomfortable and stand out like a 'sore thumb'.

To conclude, access is a serious practical issue in observational research and there are a number of important decisions to be made. Interestingly, the process of obtaining and negotiating access can give a valuable insight into the social organization of the group or setting and it should form part of the observational process (rather than being seen merely as a preliminary administrative procedure).

The role of the observer

Perhaps the most important decision you need to make in an observation study is what role the observer will take during the observation. Broadly speaking, there are two types of role: one where the observer is a participant in the group and setting and one where the observer is not a participant and is detached from the setting. Robson notes that the key difference between the two roles is that where the non-participant observer typically *uses* an observation instrument of some kind, or where the participant observer *is* the instrument (2002: 313).

The choice will depend upon a number of things including the nature of the research question and the epistemological approach adopted by the researcher. In ethnographic work, the participant role is the norm. In other situations, especially where the avoidance of 'observer effect' is paramount, a non-participant role is adopted. The observer will have decided whether to adopt a covert or overt role. As we saw earlier, the decision to adopt a covert role is not one to be taken lightly since there are clear ethical issues. The advantage is that no one knows they are being observed and are therefore more likely to act naturally.

Although it is common to see the simple distinction between participant and non-participant observation, in reality, there exists a spectrum of observational roles which lie between the two extremes of full participation and complete detachment. Gold's scheme of classification of participant observer roles is often cited in textbooks as the most useful analysis of observational roles (1958). Within it, he identifies four key roles:

1 *Complete participant*. The complete participant is a fully participating member of the setting and his/her role as an observer is not known to the other members of the group. This, of course, is easier where the observer has an existing role in the group. A good example is Holdaway's work referred to earlier in the chapter (Holdaway 1983). In his study, Holdaway was already a

police officer and was able to conduct his research without his colleagues knowing about it. The advantage here is that the observer is able to fully immerse him/herself in the 'true' social setting and does not have to worry about the effects that the research might have on the behaviour of group members. While, however, this might sound like the 'ideal' research environment, it does require a high level of deception and this can be an extremely stressful experience for the observer, both mentally and physically. There is also a danger of 'going native' – a term which is used to describe the situation where a researcher becomes *so* emotionally involved in the setting that s/he is unable to retain his/her sense of objectivity, thus threatening the validity of the research. Examples of this are not easy to find in the literature (after all, if the researcher has 'gone native' it is unlikely that the research would be published!) but examples can be found of researchers struggling to maintain their objectivity (see, for example, Hobbs' (1988) study in which he struggled to maintain his role as 'researcher' during pub visits with the entrepreneurs he was studying).

2. *Participant-as-observer.* In this role, the observer fully participates in the group in the same way as the complete participant but here the other group members *are* aware that s/he is carrying out research. It is not necessary for the group members to know what the researcher is studying, in fact, it is often preferable for the topic of observation to be kept secret. An example of this role can be found in Ditton's study of fiddling and pilfering in a bakery in which his co-workers knew he was a research student but they did not know that he was observing their dishonest behaviour specifically (Ditton 1977). Had they known, they may have changed their behaviour.
3. *Observer-as-participant.* The observer-as-participant does not actually participate in the group activities. S/he can be present in the setting but does not fully participate as a functioning group member. As Bryman (2004) notes, in this role the researcher is effectively acting as an interviewer. Since s/he does not have a role to play in the setting itself, s/he must ask people questions about why they act in certain ways or make certain decisions as those acts/decisions occur. An example is Punch's research on police work in Amsterdam. Since he was not a trained police officer, he was not able to participate fully in police activities, but he was able to accompany officers on their patrols and ask them questions (Punch 1979). However, Robson (2002) questions whether anyone who interacts with group members in this way can really be described as 'not taking part' in the setting, and therefore one must be careful to take this into account when assessing the validity of the results.

4 *Complete observer.* The complete observer lies at the opposite end of the spectrum to the complete participant. S/he is completely detached from the group and does not interact with the group members in any way. A classic example is Loftland's study of public behaviour in the street through a window (Loftland 1973). An interesting modern approach to this role was taken by Sampson and Raudenbush (1999) who observed disorder on the streets of Chicago by driving slowly and systematically through the streets, discreetly filming their surroundings with two cameras attached to each side of the car. They were able to collect and analyse their data without intruding into the settings under observation.

There are clearly advantages and disadvantages to all four roles and the researcher must consider these in detail when making the decision as to which role to adopt. Interestingly, Hammersley and Atkinson (1983) note that the complete participant and complete observer roles share some advantages and disadvantages, even though they lie at different ends of the spectrum. Both approaches minimize reactivity as the researcher does not interact with the subjects in his/her role as a researcher. Yet, direct questioning is improbable so the researcher must rely entirely upon his/her own interpretations of the observed behaviour, conversations and events. They conclude that it can be difficult to generate and test theory in a rigorous way when a role at the extreme ends of the spectrum is adopted. They also question, however, whether there is a meaningful distinction between the participant as observer and observer as participant and this is a valid concern.

Data collection

In the previous sections, we have discussed the various epistemological, methodological and ethical decisions which need to be made before an observation study is undertaken and highlighted the importance of a well-thought-out research strategy. Once these decisions have been made, the observation may finally begin. There is, however, one final issue to be resolved – how will the data be recorded and analysed? The answer to this question will depend upon the nature of the observation (structured or open) and the nature of the data (quantitative and/or qualitative). In all observational work, it is essential for the observer to regularly record his/her observations because it is extremely difficult to reflect back on an event days, weeks or months later and recall all of the important occurrences. But there are different methods of recording data and these are described below.

Open/unstructured observation studies

In unstructured, open observation studies, the observer's essential tool is the notebook. Note-taking is a skill which the observer must perfect and there is a careful balance to be struck between too many and too few notes. On the one hand, as Hammersley and Atkinson note, (1983: 146)

> [A] research project can be as well organised and as theoretically well informed as you like, but with inadequate note taking, the experience will be like using an expensive camera with poor quality film. In both cases, the resolution will prove unsatisfactory and the results will be poor. Only foggy pictures result.

It is, however, impossible to record *everything*. This might seem an obvious statement, but it is an important point. Try to conduct a 10-minute observation of a television programme (soap operas or dramas work best) in which you record *everything* you see – the setting, interactions, and events. Use a stopwatch to keep track of the time and aim to record your observations in a notebook. At the end of the 10-minute period, you are likely to feel exhausted and your notes are probably lengthy and confused. Ask yourself if your notes would make any sense to you six months from now.

Most experienced observers will agree that the best time to record events is as soon as possible after the action/event has occurred, even if things are not immediately understood, it is important to write them down. If the observation is covert, this is of course not easy to achieve as suspicions are sure to be raised by the incessant scribbler (unless writing is part of the role being adopted, perhaps). Although open note-taking is easier in an overt situation, it is still necessary to make sure that note-taking does not appear odd or distracting in the setting.

What should be recorded and what should be omitted from notes will depend upon the study in question, but there are general guidelines to follow. Broadly speaking, fieldnotes should contain concrete descriptions of both social processes and contexts. Robson (2002) suggests that in observation there are different types of question for the observer to raise: *what*, *how* and *why*. The *what* factors are simple facts and contexts which may be recorded during the observation but can also be found out from other evidence (e.g. documents). So, for example, if we were to conduct an observation in a courtroom, the *what* questions might include a description of the court personnel (the names of judges and barristers), what cases are listed to be heard that day or how many witnesses are called during a specific case. The *how* questions relate to interactions and events which occur during the observation process. To use the courtroom example again, we might then ask how the judge addresses the defendant (words used, tone adopted, facial expression) or how barristers present a legal argument (using cases and statutes to support their case). It is often necessary to take things a little further and explore the reasons for the behaviours being observed. The *why* questions are, perhaps, the more challenging since they require the observer to draw inferences from what is said/done. Where the observer has adopted a participatory role, s/he will be able to build on these inferences by actually asking the participants questions about the situation.

Structured observation studies

In a structured observation, it is usual for the researcher to use an observation schedule or coding scheme to record his/her observations. A coding scheme is simply a set of pre-determined factors which will be counted or rated during the observation. The coding scheme can involve simple counting of objects/events or more complex recording of sequences of behaviour. An example of a simple structured scheme for use in a Youth Court can be found in Chapter 10.

Coding schemes do need to be designed and used carefully in order to ensure validity/reliability. It is not unusual for researchers to adapt existing coding schemes which have been used in previous studies. The categories used should be focused, clearly defined, objective, exhaustive, mutually exclusive and easy to record. A good example is the street observation by Shapland et al. (1994) mentioned earlier in the chapter. In this study, the researchers wished to explore the crime patterns in different areas of a city. They wished to examine these patterns in the context of the physical environment in which they occur, thus they argue that it is important to establish how people use different parts of an area and what crime opportunities are present. So, in this study they used street observations in which an observation schedule was used. The results of the observation were used in conjunction with interviews and analysis of police data to target crime reduction initiatives.

In the first stage of the observation, the process of mapping an area allowed the observers to identify potential crime targets. They focused in particular on mapping residential, commercial and industrial property, public space/property, routes (pedestrian and vehicles), parking, possible crime hotspots (car parks, pubs, amusement arcades), possible problems (litter, roads in bad repair, unused buildings, graffiti) and crime prevention levels (burglar alarms, security lighting, CCTV, etc.). The next stage of the observation was a series of 10-minute observations of street activity which took place at different times of day. Before the observation began, observers were required to note the general environmental conditions: weather, lighting, general feel of the area, any activities happening, etc. During the 10-minute observation period, observers were required to note down everything that moved, including traffic flow and social use of the area (totals of each kind of vehicle and pedestrian counted). The observation schedule was designed so that each item of interest, be it vehicles (cars, taxis, buses or lorries) or pedestrians (women alone, families or groups of children), was clearly and individually logged.

In both stages of the research, then, carefully designed observation schedules were used and this allowed the collection of useful quantitative data. A coding scheme/schedule does not, however, necessarily collect purely quantitative data and can be useful in a range of different contexts. It is particularly useful for ensuring consistency between observations, especially where there are many different sample periods or where a team of observers are employed.

Alternatives to note-taking

The most effective way to keep an accurate record of situations where a lot of speech is used is to use a tape recorder. However, there are a number of disadvantages with tape recording. The presence of a tape recorder can make people feel uneasy; indeed, some people may not consent to it in the first place. This approach also produces a great deal of data which needs to be carefully filtered through at a later stage. If an observation study is likely to be carried out over long periods of time, it may be impractical to tape record and transcribe everything. It may be more appropriate to select only specific formal meetings or interviews for taping and select a different method of recording for other, more informal, situations (Hammersley and Atkinson 1983). Video-taping is another option and it has been used successfully in some research studies (see Sampson and Raudenbush (1999) in which the researchers drove through the streets of Chicago video-taping them as they went to develop scales of social disorder, and Shrum and Kilburn (1996) who video-taped the Mardi Gras festival in New Orleans to examine episodes of nudity and ritual exchange). It is also recommended by some researchers that a fieldwork journal is used as a way of recording the process of research. It enables the observer to record methodological problems and developmental ideas and can be used in 'de-briefing' sessions as a way of reducing stress (Johnson 1975).

Data analysis

Once the process of data collection has begun, you must then think carefully about the storing and cataloguing of that data. There are different ways of approaching this. For example, you could choose to catalogue data chronologically. However, it is often better to develop a system of cataloguing based on theoretical themes and concepts identified before (and during) the study. So, for example, you might organize according to people or places, or by events. There is also a decision to be made with regards to whether one keeps manual or computerized records. It will be necessary to create indexes, annotate files and sometimes (where observations fall into more than one category) duplicate entries. For some people, a manual system is easier to control; for others, a computerized approach makes it easier.

Unlike other methods, the process of analysis in observation studies is not a distinct stage. Instead, analysis takes place throughout the research process. The precise methods of data analysis in an observation study will vary, depending upon the amounts of quantitative and qualitative data collected, but there are some basic principles which should be followed. These are discussed in detail in Chapter 8 but it is appropriate to give a short overview here. All observation studies should start with the process of descriptive observation – a 'painting the picture' exercise (Robson 2002). We saw an example of this in the street observation study where the observers 'mapped' what they could see before the 10-minute observation period began. The next stage is to go beyond the descriptive and identify concepts and develop theoretical frameworks. To give an example, in a study of the ways in which the police deal with disputes, Kemp et al. (1992) identified a series of different concepts which together form an 'incident': the arrival of the police at the scene, contact (when the police physically restrain someone), information-gathering, decision-taking and implementation, the conclusion and the aftermath.

By thinking about how different concepts relate to each other and how emergent 'problems' might be defined, you should be able to draft some hypotheses. The next stage of analysis is to check on the frequency and distribution of these observed concepts and test the preliminary hypotheses. If the hypotheses are disproved (as they often will be), then they are reformulated and re-tested. The reformulation of hypotheses continues until successfully proven. The final analysis involves the more complex modelling of relationships (and relationships between relationships). This involves the construction of 'roles' and the creation of relations between roles which can finally be developed into full descriptions of lifestyles and social worlds.

The disadvantages of observation

Observational methods have received some significant criticisms over the years but still remain popular in criminological research. It is important, therefore, for you to be aware of the potential criticisms before undertaking any observational work. First and foremost, the process of observation is time- and resource extensive. Goffman said that the minimum period of time for a participant observation study should be one year (1961). We would not wish to set absolute maximum or minimum time frame here, but there is a careful balance to be struck between the need for adequate data collection and the limits placed by finite resources. Some commentators have also raised grave concerns about the ethical issues raised by both covert observation (Bulmer 1982) and overt observation (Norris 1993). Another common criticism is that observation can be highly subjective and so there is a significant risk that the researcher's own views may influence the outcome of the study. In the case of structured observations, this happens where a completely inappropriate conceptual framework is put onto the group or setting that you are observing. This is particularly problematic where the study is intended to be exploratory and uncover new material. Bryman (2004) suggests that a possible solution to this problem is to start with some unstructured observations and to use the results to develop the observation schedule. However, this is not to say that unstructured observations are more immune from subjectivity. It may be argued that, especially in the case of grounded theory studies, analytic induction serves as a useful tool in theoretical development, but we would join critics in questioning whether it is really possible for a researcher to approach a research study without bringing any theoretical ideas to it at all (for further discussion, see Chapters 2 and 8). Thus, we think it important to emphasize how crucial it is for the researcher to build validity checks into the research methodology wherever possible.

It is also important to recognize the limits of what can be understood through observation. One of the major restrictions with structured observation is that you are restricted to recording only the 'directly observable'. This means that you may overlook the context in which an event or interaction occurs and that you may not be able to extract much information about people's intentions or motivations. Participant observation in particular has been heavily criticized as, due to the significant access issues, it is mostly restricted to working-class settings and therefore cannot generate any real analysis of power relations. For the criminological researcher this is particularly frustrating because interesting avenues of research are closed off (for example, finding out how senior personnel in the criminal justice system do their jobs, or how crime and corruption are committed by executives in multinational corporations).

Conclusion

Ultimately, the decision whether to use observational methods will depend upon the nature of the proposed research questions. Hammersley and Atkinson (1983) emphasize the logic of the ethnographic approach and argue that its reflexivity eases the tension between positivism and naturalism. Yet, observation is not useful for understanding 'past or fast' events, nor is it possible to move beyond a local, restricted level of explanation and generalize our conclusions. Why, then, would anyone bother engaging in this kind of research? Well, the attraction lies in the ability to discover things which are new, often things which are deeply buried. Observation can reveal surprising phenomena and that is its major value.

Further reading

Both Robson (2002) and Bryman (2004) contain useful illustrations of schedules for structured observation and we provide our own example in the Appendix to Chapter 10. One of the most useful texts on ethnography is by Hammersley and Atkinson (1983) although it is now a little dated and might be best supplemented with a more modern text such as Coffey et al. (2007). We do believe, though, that in order to get a real feel for the advantages and disadvantages of participant observation, you really have to read one in its original form! These kinds of studies tend to be both accessible and engrossing to the novice researcher and we have found that our own students particularly enjoy reading Ditton's bakery study (1975), Holdaway's ethnography of the British police (1983) and Becker's classic, *Outsiders* (1963).

7 Researching by asking and listening

Introduction

The method that has produced probably more criminological research than any other is that of listening to what is said. We use the word listening here in a colloquial sense because we include questionnaires which may sometimes, but not always, produce non-verbal responses, but we think that using written responses to questionnaires is a way of listening to what you are being told. The three main types of listening covered here are semi-structured interviews, questionnaires and the kind of group interviews usually called focus groups. What they all have in common is that there is some form of interaction between researcher and participants. This is important because a two-way relationship is involved. It is easy for the researcher to be concerned only with the information that they require in order to pursue their studies, and to see the people they are relating to as passive partners who are there to provide what they want. This would be a serious mistake for several reasons. One is that it involves the objectification of participants, and once this occurs, unethical research practices can happen more easily. The second reason is a more pragmatic one: the more aware you are of how others respond, the more likely you are to gain reliable and meaningful insights.

It is also important to be aware of how participants might use researchers. This can happen in various ways. One is that the researcher can become an ad hoc, *and totally unqualified*, counsellor. Research gives people an opportunity to be listened to that they might not otherwise have, to say what they think, to say what they feel, perhaps to talk about some very personal matters. We have already referred, in Chapter 3, to the ethical concerns that such a situation can raise. A good and experienced researcher will acquire the skills to draw information out of people, sometimes victims, sometimes offenders, sometimes members of the public or the judiciary. A victim may be opening up to someone for the first time about what they have experienced. An offender might be revealing things that they have done that they wish they had not. It is in this sense that the researcher is being used as, almost literally, a listening post. This is perfectly reasonable, but it is important to remember, and remind respondents of, what your real role is, and what the limitations of that role are lest unrealistic expectations occur. When talking to people who represent various parts of the criminal justice system they may be using the researcher to get their views taken note of by the consumers of the research, whether that is the Home Office funding the project, or the wider readership of the research output. For example, if you interview court officials about the effects of new legislation or criminal justice procedures, you need to be aware that what you are getting may reflect the agency's 'party line' on the issue. It may be that you are happy to find out what the agency's 'party line' is, and accept it as such, or it may be that this is masking what is really happening. The skilled researcher has to make many judgements about the kind of information they receive, and how to interpret it in the light of their own intervention.

Listening can occur in different methodological contexts. Ethnography and participant observation are likely to involve the least structured kinds of research encounter, whereas a survey will usually be much more structured. A research project might use more than one kind of listening technique, combining structured questionnaires with semi-structured interviews. This might be because different techniques are appropriate to different situations, or it may be that different techniques feed into one another. For example, a study of patterns of crime and law enforcement in a particular area might start with some relatively unstructured discussions with various groups of people and key individuals. What emerges from these might be incorporated into a more structured questionnaire given to a larger number of people to see whether what came out of the small-scale explorations is reflected on a larger scale.

Interviewing

Interviewing can range from a very minimal structure to the much more highly structured interview conducted using a questionnaire (which we will return to in the next section). Denzin (1988, Ch. 6) defines three types of interview:

- the schedule standardized interview;
- the non-schedule standardized interview;

- the non-standardized interview.

The *schedule standardized* interview is characterized by being highly structured, the wording and order of all questions being the same for every respondent. However, careful preliminary investigation, development and pre-testing (probably involving less structured forms of interviewing initially), are required. The *non-schedule standardized* interview, also referred to as the focused interview, consists of a list of information required from each respondent, but the phrasing and order of questions may vary. It recognizes the special nature of each interviewee's contribution, and requires skilled interviewing. In the *non-standardized* interview, questions are not pre-specified. The interviewer probes various areas, and can explore a range of hypotheses as the interview progresses. It also means that the interviewee has the freedom to take the interview into areas that the researcher had not previously considered. Where unstructured, non-standardized interviews are used, the aim is usually to elicit material that comes from respondents with the minimum of input from the researcher. Even here, however, there is likely to be an agenda that the researcher will follow. The researcher will usually bring to a situation some expectations, and emergent hypotheses.

The three types of interview serve different functions. For example, the non-standardized interview is best for exploratory work, ascertaining the meanings and definitions used by respondents, whereas the standardized interview enables more generalizable hypothesis testing. It is important to be clear about which function is being used at different points in the investigation. Each interview type has shortcomings, and their use depends on the purpose for which they are intended, the expertise of the interviewers, and the time and resources available.

We have already considered the listening that takes place in the context of ethnographic research, so we focus first on semi-structured interviewing, which comes closest to Denzin's non-schedule standardized interview. This is an interview where there is an interview agenda, usually with certain pre-determined questions, but with a degree of flexibility in the way in which the interview proceeds. Following this, we consider group interviews and focus groups, and finally consider the most structured form, the questionnaire, which may be used in interviews, but may also be used as a self-completion tool.

Semi-structured interviews

When is semi-structured interviewing appropriate?

In our experience, this is a method that is popular in socio-legal research,[1] especially with those who do not have a background in social research training. It is appealing because it does not appear to be as demanding as designing a questionnaire, but it should be used for the right reasons – because it is appropriate rather than merely convenient. The decision to employ such a data collection technique should be primarily determined by the theoretical requirements of a study rather than just as a way of 'fishing' for information. You need to be knowledgeable enough about the topic as a result of preliminary investigation and informal enquiries to get the most out of an interview without appearing naïve. Don't rely on semi-structured interviews to enable you to get to know about an issue.

Semi-structured interviews may be used where depth of study is of foremost concern, especially where it is important to know what meaning certain things have for people, or where one wishes to explore a process or sequence of events. Semi-structured interviewing is likely to be particularly helpful where you are looking at complex phenomena that may have developed over a period of time. For example, if you were attempting to unravel the relationship between employment and offending, it might be useful to take people through a period of time, since they left school, for example, and ask them what they were doing at particular periods in time (this was done in a study in Northern Ireland: Gormally et al. 1981). In a similar way, a study of how fine default is related to people's other debt problems may need to help respondents recall their debt situation by means of a patient and careful reconstruction of their circumstances (Crow et al. 1993). Another example of the use of semi-structured interviews might be to examine the experiences that people from ethnic minorities have of the criminal justice process with which they have been involved. In this instance it may be valuable to take people through various stages of the process (see Smellie and Crow 1991).

Another example of situations where semi-structured interviews are appropriate is when you are doing what are referred to as 'elite' studies (Moyser and Wagstaffe 1987). Much social research is directed at 'ordinary' people, or at the least well-off and least powerful in society. Elite studies involve the more powerful members of society, such as judges, magistrates, senior police officers, and senior members of organizations. Such people, if you gain access to them at all, are likely to regard filling in a questionnaire as not for them. It is both a matter of making the most of an opportunity to engage with powerful elites, and of them wanting to be accorded some status in the research process. These are likely to be situations requiring careful handling by the researcher.

Another situation where semi-structured interviewing is applicable is where you are studying sensitive issues – something that is quite common in criminology. These may include both offending and victimization experiences, situations of abuse and mental ill health.

This is not an exhaustive list of circumstances where semi-structured interviewing is likely to be advantageous, but gives an indication of some of the circumstances where it can be appropriate.

The interview schedule

We will come on to question construction in the context of questionnaire design shortly, but the significant feature of the semi-structured interview is that questions, and the order in which they are asked, are not completely pre-determined. Thus, primary questions may be followed by pre-determined 'prompts', or the interviewee may encourage the respondent to develop his or her thoughts on a matter with such general prompts as, 'Can you tell me what you mean by that?' or 'Could you tell me more about that?'. This does not mean that semi-structured interviews are completely free-flowing. The interview will be shaped by the hypotheses that have been developed as a result of the research process outlined in Chapter 1, but the interview is likely to contribute to hypothesis development as much as hypothesis testing. The extent to which this takes place depends on the generalizability of the interviews. In some situations, the interviewees may be part of a wider group of people, a bench of magistrates, for example, and the interviews tell you something about the group. But unless the interviewees constitute a reliable sample then they will not enable you to determine whether what you hear from interviewees is true generally. A more systematic process of data collection, such as a questionnaire to all magistrates, may be a necessary further stage for this to happen. If, on the other hand, you were interviewing individuals who play a pivotal role in the issue being researched, such as a chief constable, a Crown Court judge, or a senior civil servant responsible for an area of criminal justice policy, then what they say may be more definitive.

When working on the questions to go in a semi-structured interview, it is a good idea to frame them in such a way as to encourage the respondent to open up, rather than something that will simply elicit a 'yes' or 'no'. So rather than ask a probation officer 'Do you think the proposals for a new sentence for offenders are a good idea?', ask, 'What do you think of the new sentencing proposals?'. The studies of the unemployment and offenders described in Chapter 9, and the Youth Court (Chapter 10) also used semi-structured interviews.

Conducting the interview

The way the interview is conducted will vary depending on circumstances. If the interviewee is a member of a criminal justice agency, or some other organization, then the interview is likely to be in his or her office. If they are a member of the public, a victim, or an offender, then it might be in their home, in your office, or it might be in some mutually agreed public space. Whatever the setting, it is important to try to arrange for privacy, and for the interview to be uninterrupted (e.g. by telephone calls). Bars and cafés are not a good idea. The interviewee needs to be told things in advance, such as how long the interview is likely to last. The length of interview will depend on circumstances, and there may be situations where more than one interview with the same person is desirable and possible (if trying to reconstruct someone's life history, for example). If interviewing a busy criminal justice practitioner, then 45 minutes to an hour may be as much as you can expect. If the respondent is a teenager who has been to court, then one might be lucky to get 20–30 minutes. While people don't like the prospect of an interview lasting too long, it is not unusual for the interviewee to become involved in the topic and talk for longer than intended, so be patient and be prepared to listen to some things that may subsequently prove to be irrelevant.

An important consideration is how the interview is to be recorded. Ideally a recorder will be used, but this will depend very much on the interviewee's agreement and, if possible, ask for permission in advance rather than put them on the spot at the time of the interview. If a recorder is being used, then ensure the recording will be clear and free from background noise. Check that batteries are topped up (or that a mains supply is available), and that whatever recording medium is being used, there is enough tape, disc or memory for each interview. These may all appear to be obvious, but good interviews have been spoiled by batteries running down or tapes running out.

If the interview is not being electronically recorded, then taking notes is the next best option, but it is difficult to handle the rapport needed to conduct an interview, listen carefully to answers, and write notes at the same time. Respondents are unlikely to open up if they have to keep waiting for you to write things down, so some very brief *aide-mémoires* may be best, and if you don't know shorthand, try to develop your own shorthand codes. It is sometimes possible to do an interview with a fellow researcher in attendance, which makes it easier to share the tasks of interviewing and writing notes, and to compare notes afterwards. In certain situations even note taking is not possible and the best you can do is write down as much as possible as quickly as possible after an interview. This has happened to one of us when doing research involving drug users and dealers. Even when notes have been taken and the interview recorded, it is still a good idea to write it up as soon as possible – certainly the same day. Straight after an interview phrases and ideas remain in the mind which fade after a night's sleep. When a series of interviews are being conducted it is also worthwhile drafting a synopsis of the results of a group of interviews at regular intervals, and it is important to reflect on what you are learning and its relevance to the hypotheses you are investigating.

Your design may require that the interview agenda or schedule remains the same on each occasion. This enables you to make generalizable statements covering all respondents, but equally this can be frustrating because after you have interviewed a few people you may think of further questions that you would like to ask, but if you keep altering the interview, then you have no way of knowing how earlier interviewees might have responded.

Analytic induction

There is an alternative option and this is the technique known as analytic induction (also mentioned in Chapter 8 in relation to the analysis of qualitative data). Using this approach, instead of covering the same or similar questions for all respondents, the aim is to progressively develop your knowledge and ideas from one respondent to the next. To do this you start with a preliminary hypothesis and interview the first respondent on the basis of this hypothesis. You then consider what has been learned from this respondent, and modify your hypothesis accordingly. The next respondent is interviewed on the basis of this modified hypothesis and the second interview is used to refine the hypothesis further so that it can apply to both respondents. This process is repeated until diminishing returns are achieved. Analytic induction is put forward by Denzin as participant observation's way of demonstrating causality (Denzin 1988: 194–9). While quantitative analysis using survey techniques can manipulate variables statistically to control factors that might affect the relationship between the dependent variable and independent variables, the participant observer seeks to disprove a hypothesis until all the cases in the study can be explained.

The technique was used by Lindesmith in explaining the onset of opiate addiction in 1947. As an example, one of us used this technique some years ago when doing some exploratory investigations into why some people were having bad experiences when using certain illegal drugs such as cannabis and LSD. An initial hypothesis might be that the drug was contaminated in some way. The first interview reveals that while the respondent had a bad experience, friends who had taken the same drug had not. Thus the first hypothesis was rejected, and this led to the hypothesis that it was some of the friends he was with who had made the experience a difficult one. Further interviews revealed a series of other factors, including the setting in which the drug was taken, and personal problems being experienced at the time. After a couple of dozen interviews it emerged that the bad drug experience could result from a particular combination of factors which might vary from individual to individual, enabling advice to be given to users about how to reduce the risk of harm occurring.

While analytic induction can be a useful method, it is important to bear its limitations in mind. The first concerns the selection of cases, and as ever in social research the question is how far one can generalize from the cases interviewed. Denzin suggests that the principle covering the selection of cases to test a theory is that the chances of discovering a decisive negative case should be maximized (1988: 194). One case is sufficient to refute or modify a hypothesis. However, this depends very much on the context in which one's study is taking place. Analytic induction can be very useful for developing and refining hypotheses which are then validated on a larger and more generalizable sample. It also has the advantage of enabling the researcher to understand the processes that shape the relationships between variables in a way that purely correlational analysis does not.

Writing up

As mentioned above, once completed, interviews should be written up as soon as possible afterwards, preferably the same day while words and phrases are still fresh. How this is done will depend on the circumstances and recording medium, but even an interview that has been recorded and is to be typed out verbatim should be summarized in order to distil the key issues. Where a series of interviews, perhaps comprising different groups of respondents are involved, it is worth reflecting on how each interview adds to the overall picture that is emerging. We discuss the analysis of material further in Chapter 8.

Group interviews and focus groups

The second method for collecting material by asking and listening is that which involves groups of people. This takes two main forms. One is using *group interviews*, and the other is *focus groups*, so it is useful to start by defining the difference.

Put at its most simplistic, group interviewing is a way of doing interviews with people more than one at a time. You can use the kind of schedule that one might use for a semi-structured interview, responses can be recorded on the basis of what each individual said, and the results can be analysed both quantitatively and qualitatively. It is more complex than doing interviews one by one, but the key features are:

- group interviews are a way of saving time and resources;

- several topics are usually discussed;
- the researcher is interested in the responses of the individuals involved.

Focus groups, on the other hand, are usually used to explore a specific topic in some depth, with the main interest being in the interaction between group members. The use of the two methods is similar in some respects, but we will concentrate mainly on focus groups, referring to group interviews where appropriate.

When are focus groups appropriate?

Focus groups were developed by the sociologist Robert Merton in the 1940s as a way of evaluating the effects of wartime propaganda (Merton et al. 1956). They came into prominence again during the 1990s both as a research method, and as a tool of social and political policy (Morgan 1992; Morgan and Krueger 1993). Questionnaires and semi-structured or unstructured interviews involve asking and listening to individuals. But people's views and perceptions, and what occurs in organizations, don't happen in isolation from others; they develop in a social context. Even people's most personal experiences are often interpreted by them in relation to others. What people think, and how they frame their thoughts, takes place in interactions with their neighbours, work colleagues, family and friends. Therefore if we want to understand how people feel about crime and safety in their neighbourhood, for example, one way of doing this is to get a group of them together. This enables you to get closer to the to-and-fro social exchanges that take place in everyday life. You also get a more dynamic picture. One-to-one interviews produce static results, as though this is what a person has always done or thought, but people's knowledge, interpretations and conclusions change through exchange. In a (non-scientific) way people are constantly producing their own hypotheses and testing them out in relation to the world around them. Focus groups are a way of getting some insight into this process, albeit a limited one. Focus groups are therefore useful when we are interested in finding out how people reason through problems or make decisions about things. They help us to understand why people feel the way they do, and they enable us to find out how groups of people interpret a phenomenon and construct meaning.

Limitations of focus groups

On the other hand, the views that people might express by themselves are liable to be challenged when mentioned in a group, and if the topic is particularly sensitive, people may feel uncomfortable. One of the drawbacks of collecting material from groups of people is that they may not say what they really think in front of others, and they may not want to talk about experiences, such as victimization, with other people present. As another example, if we were wanting to explore how people's views and experiences of the way the criminal justice system deals with people from different ethnic backgrounds, then it is less likely that people will be honest if they are in a mixed race group. Similarly, there are things that women and men may be less likely to want to talk about in a mixed sex group.

Furthermore, the dynamics of a group and the way they interact can affect how the discussion goes. If ten people are allocated to two groups on the basis of the first ten in one group and the second ten in another group, we might get a very different picture to that which would emerge if the first, third, fifth, seventh and ninth people were in one group, and the second, fourth, sixth, eighth and tenth people were in another group.

Interviewing in groups, whether focus groups or group interviews, is an altogether more complex undertaking than one-to-one data collection. The researcher has less control than s/he would have over a single interview and has to have good interpersonal skills. There is a delicate balance to be maintained between having enough control to ensure the group doesn't take over and stray away from the topic, and exerting too much control on the other. If the latter happens, then the group's responses may be dictated too much by the researcher's influence. The material is also more difficult to record and analyse when several people are involved.

Forming the groups

It is usually necessary to do more than one focus group because you have to be sure that the discussions emerging are not unique to that group. How many groups you do will depend on the resources available, but there is a general rule that you should keep running groups until you think you can predict what kind of things a group is going to say, known as 'category saturation'. Typically, a group will consist of 6–8 members. A common problem is predicting the number of people who actually turn up on the day. How people are selected will depend on the topic. In theory, the same principles of sampling apply to focus groups as to any other form of social research: you try to ensure that they are as representative as possible for the topic being studied. However, one of the great strengths of focus groups is that they engage people in discussing common interests (e.g. magistrates talking about sentencing or sex workers talking about things they would not want to discuss with others). Sometimes it is necessary to sample very purposively, such as asking a group of young offenders about their experiences of the criminal justice process. Indeed, Morgan (2006: 121) argues in favour of homogeneous group composition because such groups can discuss topics that would be considered taboo in other contexts.

Running the groups

As mentioned already, listening to what people have to say can come from using a structured set of questions, or from having just a few broad questions as a starting point, which can then be followed up with subsidiary questions and prompts ('What do you mean when you say that?', 'Can you give me any examples?'). The same is true of focus groups. Even if the questions are not structured, it is important to have an agenda, both to ensure that participants don't stray too far from what you need to cover, and to ensure that you cover the same ground when several groups are being used.

The role of the *moderator* is crucial. He or she may be a researcher, but if resources permit, it may also be worth having someone whose role is purely to facilitate. This leaves the researcher(s) free to concentrate on what is going on, both verbally and visually. The down-side of this is that a non-researcher facilitator may not be so well attuned to the requirements of the research, and less likely to steer participants in the desired direction. If there is no independent facilitator, it is desirable to have two researchers present – one to moderate and one to record, although this is less crucial if the session is being filmed.

The moderator should not be too intrusive, achieving a balance between enabling discussion and keeping focused on those matters which will permit the research hypotheses to be explored. He or she should introduce the participants, explain the purpose of the research, and tell participants about the format of the session, recording techniques, and of course about confidentiality and what people can do if they have any concerns. The moderator will also conclude the session, thanking people, and explaining what will happen to the data. One of the biggest concerns about focus groups is ensuring an adequate balance of participation, so that more assertive people don't become too dominant, and bringing more retiring members into the discussion. However, there may be situations when sensitive topics are being discussed (e.g. domestic abuse) when it is proper to give participants the option to remain silent.

It is also worth commenting on the fact that a focus group may, whether intentionally or not, affect participants in some way, especially since criminological research is liable to deal with uncomfortable issues relating to victimization and offending. Sessions may evoke changes in attitude and perception, or re-awaken memories.

As a matter of good ethical practice there should be some provision for dealing with this by following through any consequences, and referring participants for help if appropriate.

Focus groups should ideally be recorded using a voice recorder, and if possible filmed. It is important to remember that in addition to what people say, a lot can be learned from visual responses and reactions. Do people look angry, concerned, disgusted? Eye contact and body language can also be revealing. This is particularly important where groups of a particular type are being used. For example, if you were bringing together a group of criminal justice personnel such as magistrates, police and probation officers to talk about how crime problems in an area are being dealt with, do some members appear more confident than others? Similarly if the focus group was young people, then it may be interesting to see whether some of the group are more assertive than others. This may tell you a lot about peer group influences.

We deal with the analysis of data in Chapter 8, but it is worth noting here that the analysis of group interviews and focus groups is likely to be more complex than other, one-to-one forms of data collection. But it is the very richness of the material that gives such group data collection methods their value to researchers.

Illustrative examples

Having written about focus groups in the abstract, it is probably useful to end with some examples. A good example can be found in an article by Överlein et al. (2005), which discusses the focus group as a method for engaging young women aged 15–20 at a detention home in talking about sexuality. They show how the focus group approach can enable a quite troubled group to engage in discussing a 'high involvement' topic with their peers in a way that might not happen if they were just responding to a researcher. In this study, articles from popular magazines for young women were used as discussion material in five one-hour long focus groups. The use of some kind of presentation, video, or reference to material is helpful in focus groups, since it acts as a stimulus to discussion. They explored topics such as femininity and body image, starting with less sensitive topics such as 'female role models' before moving on to more sensitive topics such as 'when to say no to sex'. The researchers found that participants provided mutual support to each other and concluded that the method had provided a rich and varied set of data that could not have been obtained by individual interviews. They also found that the groups enabled the young women to pursue matters that they had been concerned about previously, but not felt able to discuss, and to this extent focus groups can also act as a form of action research.

Another example is a study that was done by one of us concerning the ways in which magistrates and social workers respond to youth crime. Eight group sessions were arranged, three involving magistrates, two with justices' clerks and three with social workers, ranging in size from four to six people. The sessions lasted approximately one and a half hours.

Three main areas of discussion were identified for the groups:

1 Were there different views among magistrates and social workers about the punishment and care of young people in general?
2 What perceptions did magistrates, court clerks and social workers have of each other?
3 What were the views of magistrates, court clerks and social workers in relation to certain current local and national issues, such as the closure of a remand centre, the introduction of remands with foster parents, locking up young people, the introduction of a Secure Training Order, and the problems posed by certain types of young offender, especially the young persistent offender?

Participants were given a sheet of questions covering the following issues:

- any particular types of crime that caused them concern;
- particular groups of offenders that caused them concern (e.g. certain age groups), and what they thought could be done about them;
- their views about what the main causes of youth crime might be;
- what they thought the main objectives of the magistrates' court and of Family and Community Services were in relation to youth crime;
- their views regarding such matters as cautioning, remand arrangements for young people, and the sentencing of young offenders.

It was stressed that participants were also free to introduce other matters related to youth crime which they felt were relevant. There were always two researchers present at each group, which was tape recorded, and researchers' notes were compared and written up soon after the session.

The study showed that magistrates, clerks and social workers shared some concerns about persistent offenders, drug use and offending while on bail. However, it also showed how magistrates, clerks and social workers differed in their perceptions of what led young people to get involved in offending and what should be done about it. Those from the court emphasized their role in trying to protect the public, whereas the social workers, while concerned to protect the public, also wanted to protect the young people from themselves and others. The research laid the basis for subsequent discussions between the court and Family and Community Services about how to improve their working relationship and build on what they had in common (Crow 1996).

A third example of the use of focus groups in criminology is a study of women's fear of crime by Esther Madriz (1997a, 1997b). The aim of her research was to explore the attitudes of women towards crime, with a view to untangling the apparent paradox that women have higher levels of fear of crime, even though their levels of victimization are lower than men. She developed a theory that women's fears are exacerbated by stereotypical images of criminals and victims and set out to examine how popular images of criminals and victims were interpreted by a group of women of different ages and backgrounds.

In her research, she used a combination of 18 focus groups and 30 in-depth interviews with women living in the New York area. This is a good example of a research study in which focus groups are combined (or triangulated) with other methods in order to build a more detailed and valid picture of the phenomenon being studied. Another interesting aspect of this study is the approach taken to the sampling. The researcher made a deliberate decision to include more women of colour and teenagers in the sample than were represented in the actual population. This was for two reasons: first, because these groups had not been studied in detail in the existing research on fear of crime; second, because the researcher hypothesized that racial diversity, socio-economic status and age may be important aspects of the images of criminals and victims. The participants were recruited using a snowballing technique (see the section on sampling in Chapter 3). The researcher contacted community organizations and began the process of collecting participants through 'word of mouth'. This meant that the final sample consisted of a range of different women from different socio-economic backgrounds and from different ethnic groups but could not be said to be representative or free from potential bias. However, this was recognized by the researcher and justified as an approach which fitted the aims of the study.

There were 18 focus group sessions with a total of 140 participants (thus approximately seven participants in each group) and each session lasted between one and two hours. The researcher describes how she used a 'discussion guide' which was structured enough to keep some level of consistency between groups, but also flexible to allow for the discussion to flow. The result was that several themes emerged from the discussions. Regardless of the race and socio-economic background of the women, the images of criminals tended to be strongly racialized with Black and Latino men being the most feared. Immigrants were also perceived to be threatening and criminals were often described as being savages or monsters. The women also had a common image of victims. However, although the stereotypical victim was commonly perceived as a white middle-class female, there were differences between some individuals' ideas of the race, socio-economic background, size and appearance of victims. Interestingly, most discussions contained images of women as victims of sexual assault and murder rather than of other, more common types of crime. The researcher concluded that female fear is exacerbated by images of crime contained in the prevailing ideology of crime. Although the images are not consistent, some common themes emerged from the participants' discussions. It is clear from reading about the research that some very interesting themes emerged from the focus group discussions, themes which may have been missed if the researcher had relied upon interviews with individuals. The focus group format allowed the women to share their ideas and experiences and express themselves more fully.

Questionnaires

When are questionnaires appropriate?

When people think of social research, a questionnaire is often the first thing that comes to mind. However, this is only one way of asking questions and gathering information, and it may not be the best one. Questionnaires are usually highly structured, with limited options for responses and involves ticking boxes and scales, which will be coded and analysed numerically. It is important that every respondent is asked the same question, in the same way, and presented with the same response choices. They involve quite a lot of preparation if the options for administration, response and analysis are to produce worthwhile results, and they have significant limitations. Therefore it is important to think about what you hope to get out of a questionnaire, and whether some other form of data collection might be more appropriate before preparing one. Another common belief is that questionnaires are just a matter of common sense, which anyone can undertake regardless of whether or not they have prior experience or training. Both of us can attest to having been asked to rescue someone who thought that doing a questionnaire was easy, who ends up with a large pile of material that is of little real value!

Strengths and weaknesses of questionnaires

First, they make it possible to collect information about a large number of people, or whatever you are studying, relatively easily and quickly.[2] It is possible to collect hundreds of completed questionnaires in a relatively short time by getting people to fill them in at meetings or conferences, in schools or universities, or in some other setting where people are assembled. The same can happen over a matter of days by sending questionnaires to people. Consequently, you can have a large amount of information at your fingertips in a short space of time. This apparent simplicity can, however, be deceptive since your chosen means of administration is not guaranteed to produce reliable results, or a high response rate.

Second, once you have got your completed questionnaires, producing at least some of the results can be relatively quick and easy. As we explain in Chapter 8, numerical analysis can be performed using a software package. If the data is to be entered by hand, this can take time, but these days it is relatively easy to enter data directly into a computer, or set up a pre-coded questionnaire so that the responses can be scanned in to the computer. Again, a note of caution, since problems can be encountered with errors in the data, and more complex and worthwhile results often require data manipulation and an advanced knowledge of statistics.

Third, as long as the sample is a well-founded probability sample (see Chapter 3) and there is a respectable response rate (see below), generalizations can be made to a wider population, and this is one of the great strengths of the survey compared with other means of inquiry.

For these reasons questionnaires have become a popular and extensively used means of inquiry. But they also have their drawbacks. One is that precisely because they have become so widely used they can engender 'questionnaire fatigue' and consequently a reluctance to complete them.

Furthermore, they are a very stilted form of inquiry. The very qualities that make them relatively easy to complete also mean that they tend to simplify things. While they may be a convenient way of collecting factual data, gathering information into categories and producing rankings and scales, a questionnaire is less useful for looking at shades of meaning, and complex processes. There is also a problem of validity: it is difficult to be sure that all the respondents understand a question in the same way.

So questionnaires are probably best used when you have a good idea what it is you want to know, possibly from previous fieldwork, and you want to be able to generalize the results to a much wider population. Because of their limitations questionnaires are best produced only after a reasonable amount of preliminary work and preparation has gone into them, and it is best not to try to use them to achieve something that they cannot do. Examples of when a questionnaire might be appropriate in criminology are:

- crime surveys, where a study is being undertaken of people's experiences of, or views about, crime-related matters;

- questionnaires for criminal justice personnel about some aspect of their work.

If a questionnaire is appropriate, before developing one it is important to check that this really is the only way of getting the information needed. Is the information already available elsewhere, in earlier surveys, official sources or agency records? For example, when doing a study of debt among a sample of fine defaulters, quite a lot of information is likely to be already recorded. Therefore (observing proper ethical practices for obtaining access to these records), it is possible to avoid asking people in the sample questions about information that is already available elsewhere, which could be obtained by means of an abstraction pro forma.

Collecting the data

The term questionnaire actually covers a variety of information collection techniques. These vary depending on the method of collection, and who provides the information (Table 7.1). When people think of a questionnaire survey the image that comes most readily to mind is that of a researcher with a clipboard interviewing a respondent from a sample *face-to-face*. Although quite a common method of administration, it is by no means the only one. It is one of the best because there is both verbal and visual interaction in which the persons concerned can express themselves most clearly.

A common alternative is the *telephone interview*, which is relatively cheap and quick. One of the drawbacks of telephone interviewing used to be that not everyone had access to a telephone, leading to a biased sample. The spread of land-line telephones reduced this problem, but in recent years the spread of mobile telephones has complicated matters, since many people are more likely to rely on their mobile telephone which is harder for a researcher to contact. Since telephone surveys tend to rely on land-lines, they are likely to exclude certain groups who don't have access to a personal land-line, such as those who are not living in

Table 7.1 Data collection

Methods of collection	*Who produces the information*
Face-to-face	Researcher
Telephone	Researcher's assistants
Internet	Agency staff
Postal	Respondent

their own accommodation, in a hostel, or without a home at all. Furthermore, telephone interviewing is less personal than face-to-face interviewing and has become devalued as a result of its use as a marketing tool. But it could still be useful for interviewing people as representatives of businesses or organizations.

The *internet* has also been used as a way of getting people to complete questionnaires online, and has the advantage of providing anonymity. It is likely to be particularly useful for an organization that wants to get information from its staff, students, clients, and so forth – in other words, where the enquirer has access to a database or sampling frame. It is, however, of limited use for surveys of the general population, since a viable sampling frame is more problematic. Furthermore, research in 2003 found that internet polls do not necessarily produce results that are representative of the population as a whole, 'even after very considerable weighting of the results has been undertaken or care exercised to ensure that those who are asked to complete an internet poll are demographically and politically representative of the whole population' (Baker et al. 2003: 27). This could, however, change as technology develops.

Postal questionnaires are a relatively cheap and convenient way of covering a large number of people or organizations. But response rates can be low, especially if the recipient gets the questionnaire 'out of the blue'. The researcher also has very little control over the circumstances in which the questionnaire is filled in, and there is no opportunity to explain any questions that might be interpreted ambiguously by the respondent.

Who produces the information?

Another important consideration is who is involved in the collection process. *Self-completion* means respondents provide the data directly, but care has to be taken to ensure that they understand what is required of them; very precise instructions are needed, and you have less control over the interpretation of questions. If the collection is by *interview*, then by whom? If assistants are being used, then they need to be trained to ensure consistency of collection. Sometimes information can be collected or provided by the *workers in an agency* dealing with the people who are the focus of inquiry. For example, if you are undertaking a study of a victim–offender mediation service, the mediators are likely to be interviewing referrals anyway and can explain that they want to ask questions that will also be used for research purposes. Similarly, in a study of offenders on employment and training programmes, much of the data may be supplied by the project staff completing forms when people start and leave the scheme. However, in such situations it is necessary to consider that the relationship between the worker and client is not the same as that between researcher and respondent, and people may be reluctant to tell project workers certain things. It also has to be borne in mind that while such workers may be practised at what they do, they are not necessarily trained researchers, sensitive to the requirements of research.

A similar principle applies to another form of data collection, where information is *abstracted* from agency records. Information collected for court or hospital files is collected to meet the requirements of the agency concerned, not those of researchers (see Garfinkel 1967, Chapter 6, 'Good organizational reasons for "bad" clinic records', for a good illustration of this). Much sifting of material may need to be done and certain key items of information may not be available, or may not be in a form that is most convenient for researchers. For example, in a study of sentencing in magistrates courts one vital piece of information may be the previous convictions of offenders. However, it is quite possible that this information will not be in court files, having been retained by the police or Crown Prosecution Service after the case was dealt with. Hence these agencies may also need to be approached.

In addition to the foregoing, it is also worth considering the circumstances in which data is collected. Will it be in the street, on the doorstep, in offices? Who will be interviewed if, for example, a family or an agency or a business is involved? The mode of collection has implications for the reliability and validity of the data, and for the likely level of response. Respondents need to be assured of privacy and confidentiality or the information is unlikely to be valid. If questions are asked in different ways by different people, then the information is unlikely to be reliable.

Response rates are important because those who do not respond to a questionnaire may well be different in some way from those who do, and this therefore biases the results. A low response rate reduces your ability to generalize from the sample you have selected to the population from which it is drawn. One example of this is responses to surveys of voting intentions. If those likely to vote for one particular party also don't like being asked how they will vote, then this means that any extrapolation from the survey to likely election results may be wrong – which is what happened during the 1991 General Election. Inevitably those who have committed offences are reluctant to disclose this to a stranger, which makes it difficult (but not impossible) to do accurate surveys of offending rates based on self-report. Postal questionnaires are particularly prone to low response rates if people are not prepared for them. Efforts to overcome the response rate problem have included offering to pay respondents or to offer vouchers or prizes to those who participate. This lends itself to accusations that those who take up such offers will produce unreliable responses because they are doing it for the 'wrong' reason, or may give answers that they think will please the piper who is calling their tune.

The inevitable question that follows is, 'What constitutes an acceptable response rate?', and the inevitable reply is that there is no definitive answer. There is a tradition in social research that in a survey of the general population, using personal contact based on a sound sampling frame, somewhere around 60 per cent would be the minimum that would be regarded as acceptable (Marshall 1994: 358), but this means that four out of ten people in the sample are ignored, and this is a substantial amount of uncertainty. In criminology, the conditions for obtaining a good response are sometimes not ideal because you may be dealing with populations with whom it is difficult to establish contact. However, the answer to this is not to accept a poor response rate but to take steps when designing the research to minimize the likelihood of non-response. This may mean contacting people through an intermediary, such as an agency that they are in contact with. For example if you wanted to contact known offenders, this can be done through the probation or prison services. Alternatively agencies who work with victims or offenders may be a point by which access can be obtained.

Drafting the questionnaire

Content

As we have emphasized in earlier chapters, in any empirical investigation, what goes into a questionnaire is determined by the theoretical basis of the inquiry, and the hypotheses that are being explored or tested. So you start by asking what information is needed to test or develop hypotheses. Ideally each question constitutes a variable,[3] some of which will be dependent variables, some independent variables, and some intervening variables (see Chapter 3). Some variables will be demographic or classificatory data, such as age, sex, ethnic group, marital status, and so on. These are likely to form the independent variables against which dependent variables are compared. Other questions will cover the things that you are most interested in exploring, and these are likely to constitute the dependent variables. So, for example, a very simple survey might be interested in people's views about various aspects of crime and related issues. This might lead to hypotheses such as:

- whether younger people are more in favour of legalizing cannabis than older people;
- whether people from higher income groups are more liberal towards convicted offenders than those from lower income groups;

- whether men have more confidence in the police than women.

In each of these examples the characteristics of the respondent (age, income, gender) form the independent variables, and their views about various topics the dependent variables. There may also be some intervening variables that might be taken into account. For example, in comparing people's views about whether cannabis should be legalized, it might be important to consider whether or not respondents have themselves used cannabis, and look at the effect this has alongside variations in age – a three-way analysis. It is also worth noting that an item might be an independent variable in the context of one hypothesis, but a dependent or intervening variable in relation to another hypothesis. For example, in the second hypothesis above about income and views about offenders, income is the independent variable. But if our hypothesis were that in general men earn more than women, gender is the independent variable, and income is the *dependent* variable.

In constructing a questionnaire, consider why each question is there. Whatever the subject matter, it is always a sound principle to go through the final draft and ask yourself why you are asking each and every question, how you are going to use it in the analysis, and what you are going to do with the results. This is partly a theoretical matter (every question should have a theoretical justification somewhere along the line), partly a pragmatic matter (there is little point in having an unnecessarily long questionnaire where much of the material is wasted), and it also has an ethical component (why are you asking somebody something unless it is really necessary?).

Sequence

When drafting a questionnaire, it is quite important to think about the order in which questions will be asked. There are a variety of reasons for this:

1 One of them is quite simply to think about the *order* that will run most naturally and be most comfortable for respondents. One of the problems here is that ideally you don't want to start by asking people to whom you are likely to be a stranger a lot of personal questions. On the other hand, it may be important to enquire about people's age and background in order to ascertain whether they fall into certain categories that are important for what follows. Furthermore, it's not a bad idea to get some key details recorded in case the questionnaire is not completed for some reason.
2 Another reason for giving careful thought to the sequence of questions is what is referred to as *routeing*. Some questions may be not applicable to all respondents and they need to be directed to the next question that is appropriate for them, for example:

Have you been burgled within the last six months?

If yes, go to Question X; **If no**, go to Question Y.

These are *filter questions* which involve loops. It may be useful to draw up a flow chart to check that respondents will be taken through the questionnaire in the right sequence and not find themselves with nowhere to go.

3 The *timing* of events. If, as an example, you are interviewing someone about their history of employment and offending, it may be necessary to have a question sequence that takes them through a sequence of time, such as since they left school, or over the past three years. This could be done diagrammatically by showing them a dated timeline. Remember that you also need to think about how it is going to be analysed subsequently.
4 *Multiple events*. Some people may have experienced something several times. For example, if you are inquiring into people's experiences of being victimized or a series of fines that led up to them becoming defaulters, some people may have had several such incidents. If several experiences are to be recorded, you may need to take someone through the same sequence of questions several times, once for each occasion. It may be worth considering whether details are needed about all the incidents, or perhaps those within a given period of time (such as within the past year), or the last three such incidents, or just the most recent one. If you have a good, sizeable probability sample, then although you may miss important experiences for particular individuals, the picture will be representative of the sample as a whole. Again, thought needs to be given to how a series of incidents will be analysed.
5 Finally, there is the fact that the order in which questions are asked might affect the way people respond to them. For example, if you were to ask people about the effects that burglaries have on their victims and then ask them about what sentences they think burglars should be given, you may well get different responses if you had first asked people what sentences burglars should get and *then* asked them about how they think burglary affects victims (see Schuman and Presser 1996, for more on such matters).

Question construction

There are a number of important rules about question composition:

1 *Avoid leading or biased questions*. Seldom, if ever, is a research inquiry 'objective' in the pure sense, since the very fact that some questions are asked rather than others means that you are approaching a topic from a particular perspective. However, every

attempt should be made to make questions themselves as neutral as possible. Thus, 'Are you for or against hanging?' is to be preferable to 'Are you in favour of hanging?'.

2 *One idea per question*. A common fault when trying to keep questionnaires as compact as possible is trying to get too much out of each question. The result can be an overly complex question. For example, don't ask, 'How do you usually get to and from work?' People may have different ways of getting back from work than when going to work. Two questions are needed rather than one here.
3 *Use simple sentence construction*, clearly defined terms, and avoid jargon. The more complex a question is, the more chance of a misunderstanding occurring.
4 Beware of *'social desirability' effects*. For example, 'Are you in favour of recycling?' is unlikely to elicit a negative response, but may not reflect people's true views or behaviour. One study has found that children develop the ability to control their responses so as not to express their ethnic prejudices publicly (Rutland 2005; Rutland et al. 2005). Similarly, avoid questions with 'obvious' answers, such as 'Are you afraid of crime?' or 'Are you against cruelty to children?' A better way to approach such matters is to be more specific, or ask hypothetical questions, or you could put such topics in a list of things that might concern people and ask them to say which they regards as most significant.

It is a good idea to put yourself in the position of the respondent and think about how you might answer a question.

Response options

As mentioned earlier, one of the main advantages of questionnaires is that they are a way of getting a lot of information as efficiently as possible. The most common way of obtaining responses to questionnaires is to ask people to tick boxes or circle options which have been pre-determined and pre-coded. But there are in fact a variety of ways in which responses can be recorded, see Box 7.1.

Each of these response types has its advantages and disadvantages. One thing that is important for all of them is to make sure you tell respondents what you want them to do: 'tick one only', 'tick any that apply', 'rank in order'. Where you want people to tick only one option (as in number 2) ensure that the categories are indeed mutually exclusive. When given the option of ticking multiple responses (number 3) note that each option becomes a variable, which will be coded as ticked or not ticked (usually coded 1 or 0). The ranking option (number 4) can produce some confused responses and be more difficult to analyse. For example, how are you

Box 7.1 Response options

1. Quantity or Factual Information

How many years (to the nearest year) have you been a police officer? _____

2. Categories

Have you ever been, or are you now, involved almost full-time in domestic work (e.g. as a carer or houseperson)? Tick one only

Yes, currently ☐ Yes, in the past ☐ Never ☐

3. Multiple Choice

Do you regard your work as a magistrate as any of the following? (Tick any that apply)

a service to the community ☐
an opportunity to help offenders ☐
ensuring offenders get their just deserts ☐
representing the interests of victims ☐
an opportunity for me to learn more ☐
a way of meeting people from diverse backgrounds ☐
None of these ☐
Other ☐
(Please give brief details)

4. Ranking

What do you see as the main benefits of probation work for you personally? Please rank all that are relevant in order, from 1 being the highest:

personal development ☐ career advancement ☐
interesting work ☐ helping others ☐
fulfilling ambition ☐ serving justice ☐
Other ☐
(give brief details)

5. Scale

How would you describe your attitude towards the police?
Please tick **one** of the options below:

very positive	positive	mixed / neutral	negative	very negative	not sure
☐	☐	☐	☐	☐	☐

6. Grid

How beneficial or otherwise do you think Neighbourhood Watch is for each of the following. Please put one tick in each row.

For:	very positive	positive	neutral	negative	very negative	not sure
you	____	____	____	____	____	____
your family	____	____	____	____	____	____
businesses	____	____	____	____	____	____
the country	____	____	____	____	____	____
your community	____	____	____	____	____	____
your friends	____	____	____	____	____	____

7. Open-ended

Do you have any further comments on how you see speed cameras?

going to compare someone who has ranked three of the options to someone who has ranked all six (and perhaps added the 'Other')? The scale or grid (numbers 5 and 6) are generally a much better way of gauging the strength of feeling because you then have an ordinal scale which enables you to compare scores quite easily. These are usually used for exploring attitudes, which often form the dependent variables in a survey. A grid is a way of integrating several scales, and more will be said about attitude measurement shortly.

Response order effects

Just as the order in which questions are asked can affect the kind of responses you might get, so the order in which response options are presented can have a similar effect. Some research suggests that response options that come towards the start of a list tend to get favoured more, a primacy effect, whereas other research suggests a recency effect, where options that are given towards the end of a list are more likely to get chosen (Schuman and Presser 1996). The latter effect is more likely to happen where there are just two options.

Open-ended questions

Questionnaires are usually quite highly structured instruments. But there is often a wish to include open-ended questions, where the respondent can say what they like. It is perfectly reasonable to include such questions, as long as you think about why they are there. They give respondents a feeling that they have been able to get across what they want to say in their own words rather than just being treated like a ticking machine, and they may give the researcher the reassurance that they have not overlooked some important view or experience. However, they need to be used with care. If you feel the need to put a lot of them in a questionnaire, then you should be asking whether a structured questionnaire is the right tool to be using at all; perhaps a less structured interview is more appropriate.

It is also important to be clear about what you are going to do with the answers to open-ended questions. Are you just going to sift through to check for responses that haven't been included under any of your pre-coded categories? Are you going to go through and post-code responses into categories? Are you going to transcribe and qualitatively analyse the information, or perhaps use some of the responses as quotations to illustrate points that will be made in the report? All too often what actually happens is that open-ended responses are simply never analysed and end up getting left on one side until the questionnaires are shredded. Similar considerations apply to the 'Other' option used with more structured responses: what are you going to do with what you get?

An illustration of the kind of effect that the form of the question can have on responses is given in a report of an experiment conducted in America in 1974 (Schuman and Presser 1996), (see Table 7.2). The columns on the left show the percentage of responses received to options that respondents were presented with by the researcher. The columns on the right show the percentages for various responses when participants were asked an open question.

Thus, when presented with prepared options, crime and violence were regarded as the biggest problem by far, but when respondents were allowed to choose their own responses, unemployment was the problem that most concerned people, and there was a more even spread of opinion.

Apart from the response types described above, there are a number of other things to think about when constructing a

Table 7.2 Question form

Closed Form "*Which of these is the* ***most*** *important problem facing this country at present?*"	(%)	(%)	*Open Form* "*What do you think is the* ***most*** *important problem facing this country at present?*"
Food and energy shortages	6.0	1.7	Food, energy, resources
Crime and violence	34.9	15.7	Crime, public order
Inflation	12.6	13.3	Inflation, high prices
Unemployment	19.7	19.1	Unemployment, no jobs
Less trust in government	9.9	3.0	Less trust in government
Bussing	1.1	1.1	Bussing
Breakdown in morals	9.2	5.7	Breakdown in morals
Racial problems	1.6	2.4	Racial, minority problems
		7.0	Quality of leaders, officials
		4.6	People's general faults
		3.0	Defects in social structure
		1.5	Lack of care for the poor
		.9	Too much care for poor
		.4	National defence
		.9	Foreign affairs
		4.6	Next presidential election
		.7	Communism
		3.7	The economy
		5.4	*More than one problem*
Other	*1.8*	*3.0*	*Other*
Don't know	*.2*	*1.1*	*Don't know*
Not available	*3.0*	*1.3*	*Not available*
TOTAL = 436	100	100	TOTAL = 460

questionnaire. This includes situations where a particular question is not answered for some reason, or where the answer is ambiguous:

- *Not Applicable*. There are various reasons why you may need to include this in your response options. The most common is when you have used a preceding filter question. 'Have you been burgled in the last year? If no, go to Question X.' All the questions between this one and Question X need to have a Not Applicable option for those who have not been burgled. Fairly obvious, but it can be overlooked.
- *Don't Knows*. Not surprisingly some people can't make up their mind, can't remember, or just don't know the answer. It is important not to ignore them because sometimes the 'Don't Knows' can tell you a lot. For example, if you are comparing people's attitudes towards sentencing with their knowledge of the criminal justice system, and you ask questions such as, 'How likely do you think it is that a burglar will be sent to prison?', then the proportion of people who don't know can be quite telling. People's knowledge about criminal justice (or the lack of it) may be related to their attitudes. Apart from examples like this, if you get a lot of 'Don't Knows', then it is probably a weak question and you really need to reconsider it. This is one reason why it is a good idea to do a pilot study with a group of people who are similar to those who will take part in the main study, with enough cases to do a pilot analysis (referred to again later). If you don't offer a 'Don't Know' category in an attempt to force people to make up their minds you might get a lot of cases where people don't answer at all.
- *No Answer*. What do you do if someone simply does not give an answer? This is more likely to happen with self-completion questionnaires, but even if you or others are administering the questionnaire you need to know if someone chooses not to answer a question. In order to decide what to do, you have to be able to interpret what the lack of an answer means. It could be another way of saying 'Don't Know', or that it is 'Not Applicable', or that they simply couldn't be bothered to answer the question.

With all these kinds of responses you have to be careful how you code them. If you leave them blank, data analysis packages such as SPSS will treat it as missing data, and sometimes it may not be. If you code zero, then make sure this does not conflict with a genuine zero value, e.g. how many times did you go to the cinema last year – zero or blank could be not at all or don't know. In the case of missing data or 'Don't Knows' you may want to exclude them from the analysis for that question. But bear in mind that if you do so it will have an effect on the remaining data. Thus, if 10 per cent of the cases have said 'Don't Know' and they are excluded from analysis, the percentages for other categories will go up correspondingly, and the analysis of the relationship between the remaining answers and other variables is more likely to be strong and statistically significant.

The middle position

Questions that ask respondents to rank something, or scales which range from 'Strongly Agree' to 'Strongly Disagree', often have a middle position. But this middle position can be problematic. First, as with 'Don't Knows', having a middle position at all can affect how people respond to the question. Not having a middle position means that people will be forced into making a choice or not answering at all. If there is a middle position then it can mean:

- a lack of opinion: a middle position can be a form of 'Don't know';
- a positive wish to adopt a position of neutrality;
- a conservative opinion indicating 'No Change', 'About Right' or 'Stay As It Is'.

So it may be quite important how you label the middle position. It could say 'Neither Agree nor Disagree', and one could have a neutral position *and* an additional box at the end labelled 'Don't Know'.

Researching attitudes

> An attitude is a state of readiness, a tendency to act or react in a certain manner when confronted with certain stimuli. (Oppenheim 2000)
>
> An orientation towards a person, situation, institution or social process, that is held to be indicative of an underlying value or belief. (*Concise Oxford Dictionary of Sociology*, definition of 'attitude' 1994)

Like several of the topics dealt with in this book, attitudes and the study of attitudes deserve much more space than we can give them. They are an important branch of social psychology, and we can only give the kind of brief introduction that deals with the ways that they can be used in researching criminology. Attitudes have several components:

- beliefs – a cognitive (thought) component;
- feelings – an 'affective' (emotional) component;
- behavioural – a potential for acting in a certain way.

They can also range from being very ephemeral to longer-lasting and more deep-seated. Thus, there can be said to be **spectra of attitude**, from

- specific to general
- changeable to stable
- superficial to profound
- opinions to ideology.

When undertaking criminological research, we often want to know about what people think about such things as crime in general, criminal justice policy, and specific aspects of criminal justice. This can be done in a qualitative manner by open-ended, semi-structured, and group interviews. However, one of the most economical ways of enquiring about people's attitudes is to use some kind of a scale, which can form part of a questionnaire. This is what we focus on here.

Types of attitude scale

Inferences about peoples' attitudes are most usually made on the basis of measuring responses to questions or statements that require respondents to indicate whether they have positive or negative feelings about the attitude object: do they favour or oppose, prefer or not prefer, agree or disagree? A scale is usually a list of such statements, or adjectives, which people respond to. Only a brief consideration of some of the best known attitudes scales is given here:

- Bogardus social distance scales
- Osgood semantic differential scales
- Guttman scales
- Thurstone scales
- Likert scales.

Bogardus social distance scales

These involve statements about how close respondents feel to certain people, objects or ideas, for example:

1 I wouldn't be seen dead in a Skoda.
2 I might be prepared to be given a lift in a Skoda in an emergency.
3 I'd be happy to be a passenger in a Skoda.
4 I'd be prepared to drive a Skoda.
5 I would be happy to own a Skoda.

If asked to tick one of these, the higher the number you tick, the lower the distance between you and a Skoda.

Osgood semantic differential scales

These consist of bipolar adjectives such as good–bad, hot–cold, dark–light, fast–slow, with a range of points between the two extremes. They give a profile of your orientation towards someone or something. For example, do you see the leader of a particular political party as warm or cold, generous or mean, active or passive, etc?

Guttman scales

Also known as scalogram analysis, these are scales indicating an increasingly positive attitude towards the object under investigation. Items on a Guttman scale contain statements which show an increasingly positive attitude towards the object under investigation. Their distinguishing characteristic is that an endorsement of any statement implies the endorsement of every less positive statement. The items on a Guttman scale have the properties of being ordinal and cumulative.

Respondents indicate whether they agree or disagree (endorse, do not endorse) a series of both positive and negative statements. The score is the number of statements endorsed. For example, in arithmetic, addition, subtraction, multiplication and the extraction of square roots are increasingly more difficult things to master. It is highly likely that anyone who can multiply can also add, and anyone who can extract square roots can both multiply and add. If we think of a number of items ranked in order of difficulty, then many respondents will endorse the early ones, for example, indicating that they know how to add, subtract, multiply, etc. However, sooner or later they will 'cross over' and fail to endorse the remaining items, for example, solving differential equations or carrying out integrations. This cross-over point is their individual score.

The advantage of a Guttman scale is that the score provides detailed information on the total pattern of results. Because of this it is possible to measure any change in attitude over time, because change becomes an additive score. A higher number than before is more positive, a lower number less positive.

The main disadvantage of a Guttman scale is the large amount of quite difficult work involved in producing it. Items are measured on the basis of a 'coefficient of reproducibility' and a 'coefficient of scalability'. A large pilot test must be carried out to gather enough information to compute the two coefficients. Without going into the statistics involved, one coefficient checks that the items can be graded into an increasingly positive manner, so that everyone who responds positively to the 3rd item also responded favourably to the 1st and 2nd items. The other coefficient measures the possible error for reproducing the result.

Thurstone scales

Thurstone scales cover all the points along a continuum from strongly positive to strongly negative, with equal intervals between the points on the scale. Thurstone's preoccupation was with the problem of equal, or rather equal-appearing, intervals. To develop a proper Thurstone attitude scale requires a lot of development work and statistical knowledge. This involves getting a panel of people to compare attitude statements two at a time and deciding which of the pair is more positive or negative.

Thurstone equal interval scales are formed by the following process:

1 Having a panel of judges who sort several hundred statements about a topic into eleven piles ranging from the most positive to the most negative.
2 Identifying a smaller number of statements (usually between 10 and 20) that are characterized by a high level of agreement among the judges and are spread evenly across the 11 piles.
3 The respondents are instructed to check the two or three statements that are closest to their own positions.

In this way, the respondents are ordered according to the average value of the items they have endorsed. This method of scale construction is relatively laborious and is not widely used by social researchers.

Likert scales

Likert scales are probably the most common type of attitude measure. However, many scales today are only loosely based on the ideas of the Likert scale. Like Thurstone scales, they cover all the points along a continuum from strongly positive to strongly negative. But Likert's primary concern was with uni-dimensionality – making sure that all the items would measure the same thing.

Items are prepared which can be responded to as either favourable or unfavourable towards the object or idea concerned. Usually a five-point response pattern is used: strongly agree, agree, not sure, disagree, strongly disagree. A numerical value is assigned to each response, such as –2 for strongly agree and +2 for strongly disagree, with the mid-point being scored zero.

An 8-step procedure is used for constructing a full Likert scale:

1 Items favourable and unfavourable to the issue are written.
2 Independent judges examine each item to classify whether items are negative, positive, or neutral.
3 Statements unclassifiable or neutral are excluded.
4 Remaining items are placed in random order on paper.

5 Items are piloted tested with a sample group representative of the population under investigation.
6 Statistical correlations are made between the scores of each item and the total summated score.
7 For an item to remain in the scale, the correlation between it and the total scale score must be statistically significant. All other items are dropped.
8 The final form of the scale is prepared with the remaining items.

A common modification that has evolved over the years is to use attitude statements in a questionnaire, but often these statements are unrelated to each other and one statement is given the job of doing all the assessing of an attitude. No matter how well written or well presented, one statement is rarely going to encompass all the twists and turns of people's attitudes, so Likert-style attitude statements are not the same as using a properly formed Likert scale.

Likert scales, or Likert-type scales, are popular because they are fairly easy to construct and easy to complete. The main difficulty is that because it is a summated score you can get the same total score with several different response patterns. In that sense Likert scales provide a good measure of consistent attitudes but are not capable of measuring attitude change to the same extent that Guttman and Thurstone scales do. In practice, Likert scales tend to perform well when it comes to a rough, but reliable ordering of people with regard to a particular attitude. These scales provide more precise information about a respondent's degree of agreement and disagreement. Also it becomes possible to include items that are not obviously related to the attitude in question, enabling subtler and deeper ramifications of an attitude to be explored.

As a guide to a shortened form of developing a Likert-type scale, first produce preliminary hypotheses. Next, explore the topic area by studying the literature, and undertaking some in-depth interviews to get the actual words that people use. It is also worth using items that have already been used by other researchers: (1) to reduce the amount of work that you have to do to create a valid scale; and (2) to enable comparisons. Next, compose an item pool. These are questions or statements derived from exploratory work that appear to measure a particular theoretical construct. Finally, items are selected for inclusion on the basis of how strongly they contribute to a common underlying factor. Box 7.2 shows how a simple Likert-type scale might look in a questionnaire.

In the questionnaire all the statements would be in the same typescript. However, three of them have been written here in italic. You don't have to think about it too long to realize that the statements in italic are about what could be done to reduce burglary, while the statements in ordinary script concern what might be done

Box 7.2 Example of Likert-type scale

Please tick one of the options alongside each statement:

	Strongly Agree	Agree	Disagree	Strongly Disagree	Neither/ Don't Know
Prison should be used more for burglars	_____	_____	_____	_____	_____
The police should do more to catch burglars	_____	_____	_____	_____	_____
We should give burglars the chance to reform	_____	_____	_____	_____	_____
We need more police to deal with burglary	_____	_____	_____	_____	_____
More Neighbourhood Watch schemes would prevent burglary	_____	_____	_____	_____	_____
Burglars should compensate victims	_____	_____	_____	_____	_____

with burglars. We have shown it this way in order to demonstrate a common feature of such scales, which enables them to be used to explore different attitude 'dimensions'. In analysis it might be interesting to explore the hypothesis that one dimension is related to the other.

Presentation and administration of questionnaires

The most important aspects of a questionnaire are its theoretical basis, the hypotheses it will test and where it sits in the research design as a whole. Nonetheless, there are some minor issues that can have a big effect on how it is answered, *whether* it is answered, and what kind of results you get.

Length

A questionnaire needs to be long enough to do its job, and on the whole, having agreed to answer a questionnaire, most people will go through with it. But it is also the case that most people have a limited amount of time, and a limited attention span. So always keep questionnaires as short as possible. There is no hard and fast rule about how long a questionnaire should be. A survey where people are stopped in the street needs to be no more than a few minutes, whereas a pre-arranged questionnaire interview with some who works in a criminal justice agency could be up to an hour. An illustration of what can happen if a questionnaire is too long is given by a survey of schools done for a community safety programme known to us. The pupils were asked to complete the questionnaire in class, so apart from those absent that day the response rates were very good, in the region of 85–90 per cent – for questions at the start of the questionnaire, that is! Unfortunately the questionnaire was so long and complicated, with lots of questions asking much the same kind of thing, that by the time pupils got to the end of the schedule, up to 15 per cent of them were no longer responding to the questions towards the end.

Layout

Use a clear layout and consistent format. Allow plenty of space so that people don't miss a question and have room to write in their replies. Give clear instructions about what they need to do.

Explanation

Introduce the questionnaire properly. A written covering document should be given to every participant, in advance if possible. Its purpose should be as follows:

This should tell people what the research is about.

- It should explain that you need their consent to do the questionnaire. Whenever possible, there should be a consent form which they sign. At the very least the document should tell them that if they do agree to complete the questionnaire, then this will be taken as having given consent to participate in this part of the research.
- They should be told that the information is confidential, that they will not be identified, that the information will be kept securely, and will be destroyed after analysis.
- They should be given details of who you are and, if a face-to-face interview, your identification should be available.
- They should be told who to contact if they have any queries or concerns, and how.
- It may be advisable to tell respondents that the project has been approved by an ethics committee (and give details of the committee).
- If identifying details (such as name, date of birth, address) are obtained (e.g. to enable a follow-up survey later), participants should be told that they will be kept separately from the questionnaire itself, using a cross-reference for the two.
- They should be told how the results will be used, and wherever possible participants should be given feedback on the results, or told where they can find them.

Finally, remember that you are dealing with people, not data. Be respectful. If possible, give respondents an opportunity to ask any questions they may have, and thank them.

Piloting and analysis

We have mentioned several times that when questions are being drafted you need to think about how they are going to be analysed. Although we consider analysis further in Chapter 8, it is worth emphasizing that this is something that needs to be considered at the start of an inquiry, not left until there is a pile of material to be dealt with, only to find it would have been better to have asked the questions a different way. The data needs to be collected in a form that is suitable for whatever analysis is to be carried out. In the case of quantitative data, this means thinking about the appropriate coding categories *before* the data is collected.

The matter of analysis, along with a number of the other issues considered here, often comes most sharply into focus once the actual process of inquiry proper has started. However, by then it may be too late to alter something. You only get one go at data collection – nobody wants you coming back again because you got it wrong the first time. For this reason one of the most important parts of any inquiry is *piloting*. Ideally a pilot study is a full 'dry run' in which all the measures to be used are tested. It should involve people or areas similar to those which will constitute the main study, and the results should be analysed to make sure that the various codings and statistical procedures produce the desired outcomes. If for some reason this is impossible, then at the very least questionnaires and interview schedules *must* be tried out. There is no such thing as a perfect questionnaire, but some errors can be avoided by piloting.

Further reading

Several of the general social research methods books have chapters on questionnaires including Bryman (2004), Burton (2000), Gilbert (1993), and Kane (1985). However, the classic text on questionnaire design and attitude measurement is that by Bram Oppenheim (2000). Although the first edition was published in 1966, a more recent version is available (1996) and is also very readable. Schumann and Presser's book on attitude surveys is very helpful on the best wording for questions. Pat Mayhew's chapter on 'Researching the State of Crime' in King and Wincup, *Doing Research on Crime and Justice* (2000), is a good introduction to the use of crime surveys as she brings her own extensive personal experience to bear on this topic.

Regarding focus groups, Alan Bryman (2004) has a chapter, and David Morgan's work is also worth referring to, a 1996 article in the *Annual Review of Sociology* being most useful. It is also well worth reading the (2005) article by Överlien et al. in the *International Journal of Social Research Methodology*, both for seeing how it was used in relation to a group of young female delinquents, and for their description of the specific techniques used.

8 Analysing criminological research

About analysis

The analysis of material collected in the course of a study can take various forms, and involves a certain amount of detailed knowledge of how to carry out particular kinds of analysis. For example, statistical analysis requires not only a knowledge of the principles and procedures required to undertake statistical tests, but a knowledge of how to operate whatever software package is to be used. Computer packages have also become increasingly employed in the analysis of qualitative information. To master these techniques involves becoming acquainted with statistics and with the procedures needed to analyse non-numerical material. In this book we do not, and cannot, offer a complete guide to statistics, to the use of SPSS (one of the main means of analysing numerical information), or software such as NUD*IST and Atlas (packages for analysing non-numerical material acquired from documents or interviews). This would require additional volumes.

In order to give readers an understanding of what is involved, and how to go about data analysis, we will consider the general principles and procedures of data analysis, and provide some illustrative examples. There are other texts which deal with statistics and qualitative analysis in more detail (see Further Reading). Our aim is to provide a grounding which will enable readers to progress towards the more detailed study required to become familiar with specific techniques.

One of the points we have made throughout this book is the importance of thinking about the analysis of material at an early stage in the research, and making appropriate provision for it. A distinction is commonly made between analysing numerical information (quantitative) and information in the form of words (usually referred to as qualitative). However, we would like to start by cautioning against making too clear-cut a division. Numbers often hide a rich diversity of meaning, as, for example, when examining people's attitudes. What does it mean to say that a certain percentage of a sample of the public favour being 'tough' on crime? Conversely, documentary or interview information can also involve counting things, such as the number of times the word 'tough' is used. Words and numbers often complement each other in criminological research, and the competent criminologist will be adept at analysing both.

One distinction that is worth making is that between descriptive and inferential analysis. Whether words or numbers are being used, there is a certain aspect of any study that involves describing what happened, what was said, or how many times something occurred. This is a necessary and valuable part of any inquiry. Beyond that, however, there is the interpretation of information, and this is where inferential analysis comes in. Inferential analysis involves using the data collected to consider its wider implications. Usually these will be related to hypotheses that are the subject of inquiry. Where quantitative data are involved, then statistics are used to make inferences about a population based on a sample drawn from that population. For example, a descriptive statistic might tell us that the mean number of previous convictions of a *sample* of offenders convicted at a particular court is five. As long as the sample was randomly drawn, it can be inferred that the mean number of previous convictions of *all* those appearing at the court is also going to be about five, give or take a bit. It is unlikely to be exactly five because any statistical inference is an estimate based on a probability that allows for a certain margin of error. This is known as the confidence limit. Making inferences is about making generalizations. Any criminological study hopes to be able to add to the pool of knowledge about a topic. It therefore has to have regard to where the information came from and the extent to which any generalizations are valid, and this will usually depend on what kind of sample it is based. The extent of inference can be estimated numerically where quantitative data are concerned, but this is not possible where non-quantitative material is involved, nonetheless the same principles apply.

Analysis can take the form of either primary or secondary analysis. Analysis is frequently thought of in terms of analysing data collected by the researcher(s) themselves. This will often involve the analysis of interviews, questionnaires or observations. However, as we mentioned in Chapter 5, valuable research can be done using existing data and sources. It might involve using official sources of data, such as the criminal statistics and subjecting them to further analysis than that which has been done already. It can also involve drawing on records and archives, such as court records and historical archives. Secondary analysis may also involve taking information collected by other researchers and analysing it in a different way. Of course, a study can do both, analysing some material already available, and also adding to it by collecting further primary data. Secondary analysis might involve using the ESRC's Economic and Social Data Service, based at the Universities of Essex and Manchester[1] (also referred to in Chapter 5). This is an archive of social science studies which the original researchers have deposited with the ESDS, and requests can be made to re-analyse particular datasets. The archive includes both quantitative and qualitative material. The decennial census is another large source of information which can be used by bona-fide researchers. For criminologists a considerable amount of information is collected by the British Crime Survey (BCS). The Home Office publishes and commissions reports using this information, but cannot examine every facet of the material collected. Chapter 12 describes a study that involved using the BCS. Before assuming that new data needs to be collected, it is well worth any criminologist's while to consider what material might already be extant that could be analysed to cast light on their own research question.

We would also like to take the opportunity to nail what is probably the most commonly used aphorism about statistics, that there are 'lies, damn lies and statistics'[2]. Statistics don't lie; it is the people who use them who either knowingly misuse them, or don't know how to use them. Wrongly applied statistics can be used to support whatever argument you want. Properly applied, data can help to evaluate competing claims. The criminologist needs to acquire good statistical practice, and to recognize when bad practice occurs in the work of others. This does not mean getting to know lots and lots of different statistical procedures, but does involve understanding the principles of good statistical analysis.

Analysing quantitative material: An introduction

The word statistics makes some people nervous, perhaps summoning up memories of struggles experienced in school maths lessons. However, statistics are an important part of criminology, and need not be daunting. Those researching criminology do not necessarily need to be experienced statisticians, but some appreciation of how numerical data is analysed is important in order to understand the possibilities and limitations of quantitative material – both your own and that of others. We have already said something about official statistics in Chapter 5. Here we look mainly at the primary analysis of your own data. In doing this it is necessary to say something about probability and statistical inference, because they are at the heart of analysing quantitative material. However we will come to this shortly. In a Glossary of key terms at the end of this book we have included short descriptions of some of the main concepts applied in doing quantitative analysis.

The Statistics Package for the Social Sciences (SPSS)

Although it is possible to do some analysis using just a calculator, most numerical analysis is done on a computer using a statistics package, such as SPSS, which is the one we will refer to. As we have already said, we aim only to give an introduction to data analysis and therefore do not set out to produce an SPSS user's manual. There are several texts available (see Further Reading at the end of this chapter) which explain procedures in detail.

Like many computer programs, SPSS has menus and buttons at the top of the screen which enable the user to perform various operations, and when first started it shows a grid of rows and columns. The rows contain individual cases, and the columns contain variables. Let's suppose we have been to the local court and extracted from the files some information about 56 cases dealt with in the last month, consisting of information about age, gender, ethnicity, the offence, number of previous convictions and the sentence. This information is shown in full in the appendix on p. 220. The variables have been simplified so that there are just three broadly defined ethnic groups (1 = White, 2 = Black, 3 = Asian), three offence categories (1 = theft, 2 = criminal damage, 3 = violence), and three sentences (1 = a fine, 2 = community sentence, 3 = custody). For convenience the first six cases are shown in Table 8.1.

Thus, the first case is a 21-year-old male, white, who committed an offence of theft, had one previous conviction ('precons' is the number of previous convictions), and was given a fine. The last

Table 8.1 Court abstract data (first six cases)

case	*age*	*gender*	*ethnic*	*offence*	*precons*	*sentence*	*sscore*
1	21	1	1	1	1	1	60
2	17	1	2	1	1	2	80
3	24	2	1	1	4	1	70
4	30	1	1	3	5	3	120
5	19	1	3	1	0	1	50
6	25	1	1	1	3	2	100

variable, 'sscore', is a calculation based on previous variables which reflects the seriousness of the case. We will refer to this data again in due course.

Clicking on a tab at the bottom of the SPSS screen brings up the Variable View, which enables you to insert and look at details of the individual variables. When an operation has been performed a new screen will appear, the Output View, which gives the results of the analysis. This output can be confusing at times because it often contains a lot of information, and although it is all relevant as far as the practised statistician is concerned, it can sometimes be difficult for the novice to know which bits are the important ones to use in a given situation. A good textbook will help to decipher this output (see Further Reading at the end of this chapter).

We will give an overview of three main kinds of numerical analysis. These are:

- univariate analysis – looking at a single variable;
- bivariate analysis – looking at two variables;
- multivariate analysis – more than two variables.

Analysing a single variable

Analysing a set of data often starts by looking at individual variables such as what the mean (average) age of the sample is, what percentage are female and male, how many come from different ethnic groups, and so on. However, there are important differences between the types of variable involved, and this depends on the kind of measurement involved. There are four types of measurement: nominal, ordinal, interval and ratio.

Nominal variables are mutually exclusive categories such as gender (male, female). In the court abstraction data referred to above, four of the variables are of this type (gender, ethnicity, offence, sentence). When analysing variables of this type it is usual to look at the number of cases in each category (the *frequency*) and the *percentage* of cases in each category. For example in the first six cases in the court abstraction table there were five males and one female, which means the percentage of females was $1 \div 6 \times 100 = 16.7$ per cent. The sentencing for the first six cases can be described as shown in Table 8.2.

Ordinal variables are ranked in order. For example: Unsatisfactory, Satisfactory, Good, Excellent. In the example above, the three sentences fine, community sentence, custody could be seen as an ordinal scale of severity. These are often referred to as scales or scores and assigned numerical values ranging from 1 for the 'weakest' to 2, 3, 4, 5, etc. for 'stronger' items. It is quite common for responses to attitude questions to take the form of an ordinal scale:

Table 8.2 Frequencies and percentages

Sentence	*Frequency*	*%*
fine	3	50.0
community	2	33.3
custody	1	16.7
Total	6	100.0

Q: Are you worried about going out alone at night?
A: Not at all – A little – A lot – Very

However, it is important to note that ordinal scales are very imprecise measures, and the intervals between different points on the scale are not necessarily the same; they are not equal intervals. Thus, there may not be much difference between 'A lot' and 'Very' in the example above, but there might be a much bigger distance in people's minds between being a little worried and a lot worried. Similarly many might regard the difference between getting a fine and a community sentence as being not as great as that between getting a community sentence and a custodial sentence.

Interval variables, on the other hand do have equal intervals between each point on the scale (e.g. temperature, time), and *ratio variables* have equal intervals, with a zero point. Examples here are money, age, height, weight, and so on. The fact that there are equal intervals means that more precise interpretations can be made: £20 is twice as much as £10; being sent to prison for 12 months is twice as long as a prison sentence of 6 months. In the court abstraction table shown earlier, there are two interval level variables, age and number of previous convictions. When doing descriptive analysis of these variables you can look at two main attributes:

- where the central point is: a measure of centrality;
- how the cases are spread out between the lowest point and the highest point: their distribution.

Both are important in describing the characteristics of interval and ratio level variables.

Measures of centrality

There are three main ways of describing where the centre of a distribution is. The *mean* is the average of all values. It is the sum of the values for all the cases divided by the number of cases. It is usually shown in calculations as an X with a bar above it: $\overline{X}$. Thus, if we look at the average age of the first six cases given in the court abstraction table we get:

$$\overline{X} = \frac{\text{total of all values}}{\text{no. in sample}} = \frac{21+17+24+30+19+25}{6} = \frac{136}{6} = 22.67$$

The mean is the most commonly used measure, but it has the drawback that a few cases with extreme values will have a big effect. For example, the fines imposed by magistrates courts are generally in the region of £100 to £150, with a mean of £125. However, every so often courts will feel that, while a fine is the right disposal, there is something about a particular case that warrants a heavier fine to mark the gravity of the offence. So they may well impose a fine of £500 or more. This will considerably increase the mean, even though the great majority of offenders are still within the £100 to £150 range.

The *median* avoids this because it is the value above which half the cases lie, and below which the other half of the cases lie (if there is an uneven number of cases it will therefore be the one in the middle). This can be illustrated by taking another example. When awarding a degree classification, an examinations board looks at the mean marks achieved by a student in their second and third years. In borderline cases a wise exam board will also look at the median mark, because one poor result could have an adverse effect on a student's overall pattern of performance, as shown in Table 8.3.

Six subjects are taken in each year. Marks for Year 3 are double weighted to take account of improvement. Had the classification been based solely on the mean, the student would have received a lower second degree because of the mark of 30 in Year 3, but in fact received an upper second when the median was taken into consideration.

The *mode* is simply the most frequently occurring value. Although it may not tell us much on its own, it does give an indication of where most of the cases congregate.

Measures of dispersion

Another way of describing variables with equal intervals is how the number of cases is distributed. *Kurtosis* is a measure of how closely cases cluster around a mean. If there are a lot of cases close to the mean then the distribution will be tall and thin and is called *leptokurtic*. If the cases are widely spread, the distribution will look much flatter and is called *platykurtic* (see Figure 8.1).

Skewness describes the extent to which a distribution is asymmetrical. If most of the cases are to the left of the mean, then the distribution is said to be *positively skewed*. This would be the case if,

Table 8.3 Comparing mean and medium

	Year 2 Marks	*Year 3 Marks*	*Overall*
	55	62	
	48	65	
	48	30	
	65	65	
	55	62	
	62	62	
Total	333	346	
Weighted yr3		692	
mean	55.5	57.7	
Weighted overall mean			56.9
median			62.0
Classification based on mean			2.2
Classification based on median (awarded)			2.1

for example, one was examining the age distribution of a sample of offenders and there were a lot of young people in the sample. If more of the cases are to the right of the mean, then the distribution is said to be *negatively skewed* (see Figure 8.2).

If a distribution is very evenly spread, then it is said to be normally distributed (see Figure 8.3).

In real life, it is rare to find a distribution for a variable that is like this. The normal distribution is an ideal distribution, which has a symmetrical, bell-shaped, curve. It is important in statistics, however, because it has certain properties. The attributes of areas under the curve are known, and can therefore be used as a basis for making comparisons.[3]

Two commonly used measures of spread are the *variance* and the *standard deviation*. If you subtract the value of every case from the mean for the distribution, square this value, add them all up, and divide by the number of cases minus one, then you get the variance for the distribution. If you take the square root of this value, you get the standard deviation. These measures are often used in performing various statistical tests, and SPSS will do the necessary calculations. An example is given in Appendix 2 on p. 222, and more details can be found in one of the books on using SPSS mentioned in the Further Reading at the end of this chapter.

In the curve in Figure 8.3, the solid central line represents the mean. The pair of dashed lines either side of this represent one *standard deviation* either side of the mean. The outer pair of dotted lines beyond the first pair represent two standard deviations either side of the mean. In a normal distribution approximately two-thirds of cases (68.26) lie between the mean and one *standard deviation* either side of the mean. Approximately 95 per cent of cases (95.44) are between plus and minus two standard deviations of the mean. This provides a common standard with which to compare scores taken from different distributions.

Although this is taking us into some detail, these distributions and measures are very important in understanding how statistics can be used in criminology and other areas of social policy; they are the building blocks of subsequent quantitative analysis.

It is also important to appreciate the significance of these different types of variable, because they affect what you can do with the information they represent. In essence, it is possible to do more with equal interval variables like age, and money and time. There are more different ways of examining them, and they meet the requirements for more complex analyses. There may be times when it is necessary to ask respondents for their age group (20–29, 30–39, etc.) or income group (less than £10,000 per annum, £10–14,999 p.a., etc.) for reasons of sensitivity or convenience, but it is generally better to get actual ages, times, and money whenever possible. The actual values can always be grouped later. Ordinal variables, in particular, need to be treated with care because they look as though they can be used like interval level variables, for example using the mean of a scale, when in fact this is not a 'real' mean.[4]

Inferences from single variables

Referring to the distinction we made earlier between descriptive and inferential analysis, the examination of single variables may be purely descriptive. However, when you then seek to apply what has been found to a wider population on which the data is based, this involves inferences from a sample to a **population**. Sometimes such descriptive material can be important and revealing in its own right. For example, from time to time there have been surveys of the prison population (Walmsley et al. 1992; Niven and Olagundaye 2002). These tell us such things as the proportion of people in prison who have been brought up in local authority care, those who are likely to have accommodation problems on release, those who

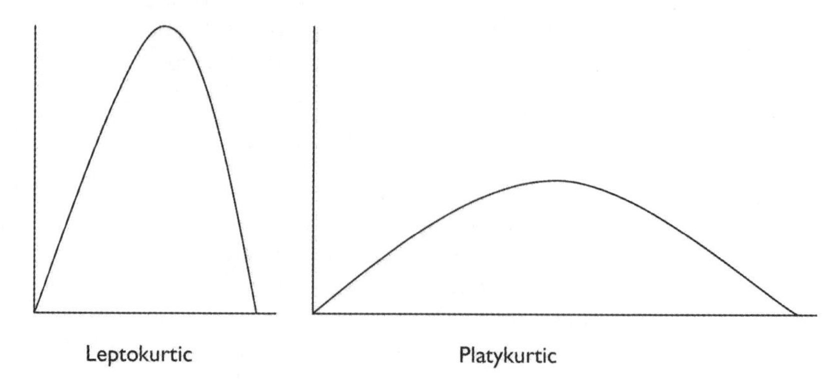

Figure 8.1 Kurtosis

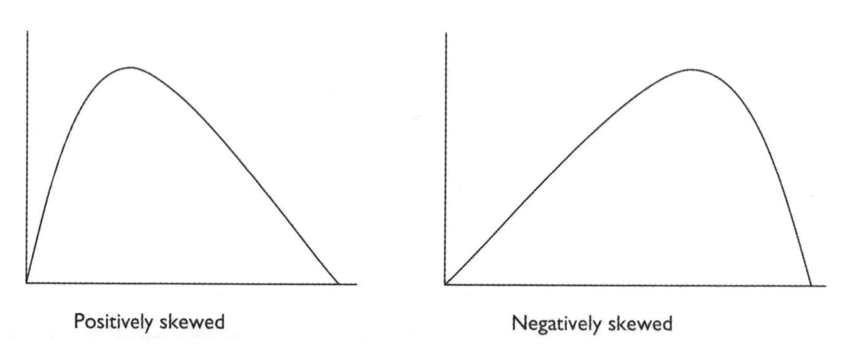

Figure 8.2 Skewness

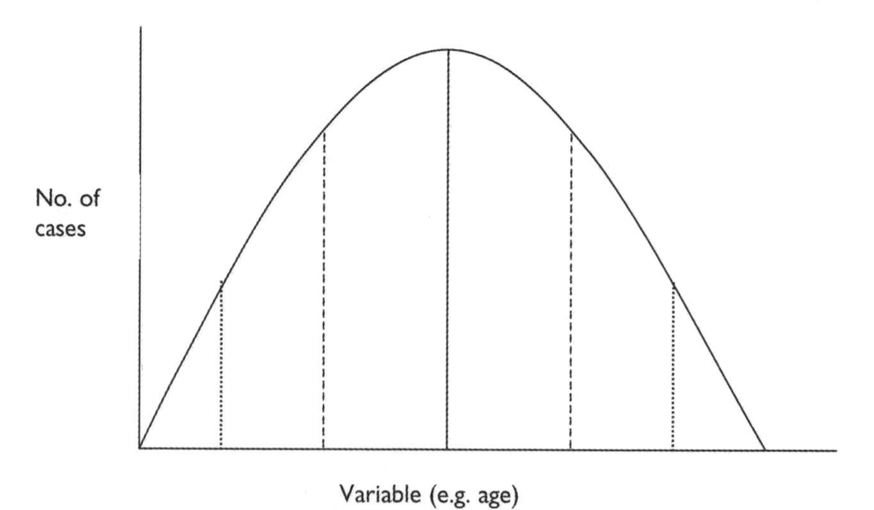

Figure 8.3 Normal distribution

have reading and writing difficulties, and so on. Such information has important policy implications.

Making inferences about a population based on a sample drawn from the population involves an element of uncertainty. If you were to draw several samples from the same population, they wouldn't all have the same characteristics, even if they have all been drawn at random. This is partly a matter of chance (probability) and also because there is always the possibility of errors creeping in one way or another. So any extrapolation from a sample has a margin of error. This is allowed for in any numerical analysis and the margin of error can be estimated from a random sample. It is referred to as the *standard error*. This is something that is used in quite a few statistical calculations.

Let's suppose that we go for a walk one day. When we get back, we are asked how far we walked, and we say 'six miles, give or take a mile'. This 'guesstimate' means that we are saying that we may have walked as little as five miles or as much as seven miles. This means that we have what is referred to in statistics as a *confidence interval* of plus or minus one mile. When doing proper quantitative analysis we can be more precise. The confidence interval is plus or minus two standard errors either side of the mean. The example given in Appendix 2 on p. 222 shows how this would be calculated using the example of the number of previous convictions of a sample of offenders. In the example, the mean number of previous convictions of a sample of 294 offenders was 1.2. By calculating the standard error of this mean, we can be 95 per cent certain that the true mean of the population from which this sample was drawn lies somewhere between 1.06 and 1.34 previous convictions.

Statistical inference can also be used to estimate whether a sample is representative of the population from which it is drawn. Let us say that it is known that for the prison population nationally the mean number of previous convictions is 4.8. If we take a random sample of cases from a local prison, we would not necessarily expect that the mean number of previous convictions for those in that sample would be exactly 4.8. It might be a bit more, or it might be a bit less. But exactly how much is a 'bit'? Let's say that the mean number of previous convictions for our sample is 6.3. Is our sample mean such that it is not significantly different to prisoners generally, or is our sample significantly different, for whatever reason (e.g. perhaps it is a prison that has a particularly hardened bunch of criminals in it)? By calculating the standard error for the mean number of previous convictions of our sample, and the confidence interval for this mean, we can determine whether the national figure lies outside these limits, and therefore whether our sample is significantly different. If it is, we might then be interested in doing further investigations to find out why this might be.

Analysing two variables

So far we have been looking at the analysis of one variable at a time: univariate analysis. However, much of the most interesting research comes from looking at the relationships between two or more variables. In this section we will briefly consider two variable analysis. This mainly involves two kinds of question. Is there a difference between one thing and another, and is there a relationship between one thing and another?

Nominal variables

Here again the distinction between different types of variable is important. The analysis of variables that have categories (nominal variables) is different from those that have equal intervals. Ordinal variables also need to be treated differently. Let's look first at categories, and ask the question, do some groups of people get sentenced differently from other groups of people? Do women get sentenced differently from men? Do people from different ethnic groups get different sentences? Do those who have jobs get different sentences to those who are unemployed (something discussed in more detail in Chapter 9). Sentence, gender, race, and employment status are all categorical variables. Using the court abstraction data referred to earlier, let's look at race and sentencing for the 56 cases.

Table 8.4, produced by SPSS, is a simple descriptive cross-tabulation of the two variables. It tells us, among other things, that six of the 28 White people in the sample got a custodial sentence, ten of the Black people, and none of the Asian people.

Table 8.4 Sentence by race cross-tabulation

Sentence	*Race*			*Total*
	White	*Black*	*Asian*	
fine	11	3	5	19
probation	11	7	3	21
custody	6	10	0	16
Total	28	20	8	56

Table 8.5 Sentence by race, with percentage

Sentence		*Race*			*Total*
		White	*Black*	*Asian*	
fine	Count	11	3	5	19
	% within race	39.3	15.0	62.5	33.9
probation	Count	11	7	3	21
	% within race	39.3	35.0	37.5	37.5
custody	Count	6	10	0	16
	% within race	21.4	50.0	.0	28.6
Total	Count	28	20	8	56
	% within race	100.0	100.0	100.0	100.0

It becomes somewhat more informative if we add in the percentages (see Table 8.5). We can now see more clearly that less than a quarter (21.4 per cent) of the White offenders got custody, compared to exactly half of the Black offenders. However, what we now need to know is whether this is a difference that could have occurred by chance, or is the difference such that it needs to be explained in some other way, because it is not a statistical artefact.

To explain this a bit more, we might be surprised if exactly the same percentage of people always got a custodial sentence, regardless of what group they were in, or whatever the sample that was drawn randomly. Tossing a dice 36 times, we would not necessarily expect to get exactly six 6s, six 5s, six 4s, and so on. There is an element of chance. We might get four 6s or seven 6s. But if we got 12 or more 6s we might think, 'Hang on a minute, someone's been fiddling with this dice!' Similarly if we found that 47 per cent of White offenders got a custodial sentence compared with 53 per cent of Black offenders, we might be unsure whether this is something that could occur by chance, or that we ought to be considering alternative explanations. Statistics enables us to do this by using a test for comparing the proportions within different categories. This is called the *chi-square* test (written algebraically as χ^2). What it does is to compare the observed values for each cell of the cross-tabulation with what the expected values would be if there were no differences between the categories. This gives us a chi-square value that can then be looked up in a table of probabilities to see whether it could have occurred by chance. In practice, SPSS will perform this test for us and tell us the results. We are not going to explain the chi-square test in detail, and recommend referring to one of the statistics texts given in the suggested reading at the end of this chapter. Apart from knowing how a test is done, it is just as important to know when to use it and how to interpret the results.

In the example given, an SPSS analysis tells us that for the cross-tabulation above, chi-square equals 10.33, and that the likelihood of getting a value that large will only occur three times out of every hundred times these groups are studied. This is very unlikely, and we can therefore conclude that such a difference between the sentences the different groups received did not occur by chance. Five times out of every 100 (or 5 per cent, or a probability of .05) is traditionally regarded as the point at which we reject the hypothesis that there is no difference between the groups. This is referred to as the significance level. If we have a probability *lower* than .05, then we can say that the difference is statistically significant. In everyday language the term 'significant' is used loosely to suggest that something is meaningful. However, in statistics referring to a significant difference means something more precise. It means that a certain level of statistical probability has been reached. The 1 per cent level, or probability of .01, is an even more stringent test of significance, and means the likelihood of a difference occurring by chance is one time in a hundred.

It is important to note that what we have done so far is to conduct the test for the whole table, comparing three different sentences for three ethnic groups. While the chi-square test tells us that the differences in sentencing between the three groups is a real one and not just a matter of chance, we still have to consider the differences further. For example, the large chi-square value could reflect not just the fact that a higher proportion of Black offenders get custody than the other two groups, but that the Asian offenders seem to be more likely to get a fine than either of the other two groups. If we specifically want to know whether Black offenders are more likely to get sent to prison than offenders from the other two groups, then we need to do a more specific analysis, comparing Black with other ethnic groups in terms of the likelihood of a custodial rather than a non-custodial sentence. We can do this by means of a bit of simple recoding, which produces the following result, shown in Table 8.6.

Table 8.6 tells us that the proportion of Black offenders getting a custodial sentence is much greater than any other group, and that this is statistically highly significant. The material in the note is statistical shorthand for saying that the value of chi-square is 7.0, and that the probability of this occurring by chance is less than eight times out of every thousand that these particular groups are

Table 8.6 Custody by race

Sentence		*Race*		*Total*
		Not Black	*Black*	
Not Custody	Count	30	10	40
	% within black	83.3	50.0	71.4
Custody	Count	6	10	16
	% within black	16.7	50.0	28.6
Total	Count	36	20	56
	% within black	100.0	100.0	100.0

Note: $X^2 = 7.0$, $p < .008$

examined. We can therefore say that there is a real difference: 16.7 per cent compared with 50.0 per cent may seem to be such a big discrepancy as to convince us that this cannot be explained by chance, but even so we need to check.

Having done this, it is important not to jump to conclusions about *why* this may be the case. Theoretically, various explanations are possible. The Black offenders in the sample might have committed more serious offences than the other two groups, or been more likely to have already received non-custodial sentences, or the sentencers might be racially prejudiced. Each of these possibilities has to be examined to see whether it can be eliminated as an explanation. This brings other variables into play in addition to race and sentence. We will say more about this shortly, but before we do we want to say a bit more about bivariate analysis.

Interval variables

In looking at race and sentencing we have been looking at two nominal variables, where the data is in categories. But suppose we are looking at continuous variables, where the data are in equal intervals, or a mixture of nominal and interval variables, what then? Let's say we want to look at an interval variable, such as age, and a nominal variable, such as gender. Are the women in a sample significantly older or younger than the men in the sample? Taking our data from the court abstraction files we find that the mean age of the men is 21.3 and the mean age of the women is 21.8. To find out whether this is a chance difference or a significant difference we would do a *Students t* test. Using SPSS to do the work for us, we find that $t = -.376$, and that the probability of this occurring by chance is .709 (or 71 times out of a hundred) which is much bigger than 5 per cent, so we can conclude that there is *no* significant difference between the mean ages of the men and the women in the sample.

As a further illustration, let's go back to race and sentencing, where we found that Black offenders were more likely to get a custodial sentence than either of the other two groups. Could this be because the Black offenders in our (fictitious) sample have more previous convictions? A *t* test here tells us that the White offenders have 2.32 previous convictions on average, whereas the Black offenders have 1.8 previous convictions on average. This alone tells us that the greater likelihood of a custodial sentence for Black offenders cannot be explained by their having more of a history of offending, but the *t* test result that $t = 1.0$ and $p = .322$ (again much bigger than .05) also tells us that there is no significant difference between the number of previous convictions of Black and White offenders. For the sake of completeness we should also compare the mean number of previous convictions for Black and Asian offenders, and perhaps for White and Asian Offenders. This could be done by doing two more *t* tests. This is because a *t* test can only compare two groups. If we want to compare the means of more than two groups at once, then we use something called an *analysis of variance.*

As you can see, the number of different statistical tests that a criminologist needs to know about is growing. But this need not be a worry. It takes time to get to know about each, and what it does mean is that we have a range of options to meet different situations. Another statistical procedure, which many people have heard of at some time or other, is *correlation*. The test used for interval level variables is a Pearson's correlation coefficient, and designated by the letter *r*. Here we are again looking at two variables, this time, two interval level variables. However, with correlation we are not looking at differences, but at whether there is an association between two variables. The value of the correlation coefficient can vary from +1 to −1. Plus 1 is a perfect positive correlation and means that for every unit *increase* in one variable there is a corresponding unit *increase* in the other variable. Conversely, −1 means that for every unit increase in one variable there is a corresponding unit *decrease* in the other variable: as one goes up, the other goes down. A correlation coefficient of zero means that there is no relationship at all. Looking at our artificial court abstraction dataset, and using SPSS to perform the calculations for us, we find that there is a correlation between the age of the offenders in our sample and the number of previous convictions they have of $r = 0.269$. This is not a terrifically close relationship, but SPSS also obligingly tells us that for this particular sample it is statistically significant at the

5 per cent level, so not surprisingly we can conclude that in general as people get older, they also have more convictions.

Using SPSS we can also look at the correlation between several variables at once, producing a *correlation matrix*. For example, let's suppose that we are doing a study of crime in 20 local areas, and collect information on conviction rates (per 1000 population), unemployment rate, and household occupancy levels (often regarded as an indicator of socio-economic well-being).[5] We could do three separate correlations and find that:

- r for conviction rate/household occupancy was .656, p = .002;
- r for conviction rate/unemployment was .612, p = .004;
- r for occupancy/unemployment was .163, p = .493, n.s.

However, we can put all three variables into the analysis at the same time and get the following correlation matrix, shown in Table 8.7.

Notice that what you get is a mirror image, with each of the three correlations appearing twice, either side of the cells that form the diagonal. The diagonal cells consist of 1s because obviously there is a perfect correlation between conviction rate and conviction rate. The double asterisks show that for the two significant correlations the results could only have occurred by chance less than one time in a hundred (p < .01). In fact, in one instance the probability is two in a thousand and in the other four in a thousand. One thing to notice is that although correlation matrices include three or more variables, we are still essentially doing bivariate analysis, because we are only comparing one variable at a time with one other variable.

Table 8.7 Correlation matrix of convictions by occupancy by unemployment

		Convictions in ward	*Average occupancy*	*Unemployment rate*
Convictions in ward	Pearson correlation	1	.656(**)	.612(**)
	Sig. (2-tailed)		.002	.004
	N	20	20	20
Average occupancy	Pearson correlation	.656(**)	1	.163
	Sig. (2-tailed)	.002		.493
	N	20	20	20
Unemployment rate	Pearson correlation	.612(**)	.163	1
	Sig. (2-tailed)	.004	.493	
	N	20	20	20

Note: ** Correlation is significant at the 0.01 level (2-tailed).

What matters is whether you are looking at the *relationship* between the variables. We will come onto genuinely multi-variable analysis shortly.

One of the features of correlation is that it is a symmetrical relationship. Variable X is correlated with Y and vice versa; we are not taking any view about which is the dependent variable and which the independent variable. However, in another form of bivariate analysis, we use one variable to predict another variable. This is *linear regression*, where the fact that there is a correlation between two variables is used as a basis for estimating the value of one (usually designated as the Y variable) from the other (usually designated as the X variable):

Dependent variable (Y) ← Independent variable (X)
(e.g. conviction rate) (e.g. occupancy rate)

In the example used here, where we know that unemployment is related to conviction rates, if we know that the unemployment rate in an area is 1.5, a regression analysis enables us to calculate that the likely level of convictions will be 27 per 1000 in the population. This kind of information can be used, for example, to target resources in certain areas – although whether to put more police into an area or to do more to tackle unemployment is a political decision.

Ordinal variables

We've now considered the analysis of two variables where one or both are nominal or interval level variables. What about ordinal variables? Take a series of questions to secondary school children such as the following, where pupils are asked to tick one of the boxes (see Box 8.1).

Box 8.1 Ordinal variables

How wrong do you think it is for someone your age to ...	Very Wrong	Wrong	A bit Wrong	Not Wrong at all
play truant without your parents knowing?	☐	☐	☐	☐
take a weapon to school?	☐	☐	☐	☐
steal something?	☐	☐	☐	☐
attack and hurt someone?	☐	☐	☐	☐

The likelihood is that when coding the responses to each statement, we will give each box a score such as 3 = Very wrong to 0 = Not wrong at all. Suppose we want to see whether there is a relationship between thinking that it is all right to play truant, and all right to steal. Or suppose we want to see whether the attitudes of girls towards these statements are different from those of boys. We can't do the same kind of correlation as for age, or number of previous convictions. We can't use a *t* test to compare means because these are not equal intervals. We could treat each of the boxes as categories and analyse them as though they were nominal variables, comparing the percentage of girls ticking each box with the percentage of boys. There are also certain kinds of statistical test that can be used with such variables. They are called non-parametric statistics, and make fewer assumptions about the type of data for which they can be used. So instead of using a Pearson's *r* correlation coefficient we can use a *Spearman's rho* correlation coefficient, and instead of using a *t* test we can use a *Mann-Witney U* test.

When analysing two variables it is often important to think about which is the dependent variable and which is the independent variable (something that was explained in Chapter 3). In the example above, if we were interested in comparing the attitudes of boys and girls then gender would be the independent variable and the scores for the statements would be the dependent variables – the results that we are interested in. In the example used earlier regarding race and sentencing, ethnic group is the independent variable and sentence is the dependent variable. When analysing research results, it is often the case that the characteristics of the sample, such as gender, ethnic group, occupation, age, etc. will be the independent variables, and things like what happened to them, their responses to attitude statements, and so on will be the dependent variables. This is not always so because there may be times when we want to know, for example, whether the men in a sample are older or younger on average than the women in the sample. The identification of variables as dependent, independent, or intervening variables becomes more important when we embark on multi-variable analysis.

Analysing three or more variables

Multi-variate analysis involves three or more variables, and can take different forms. We've already had a taste of it earlier when looking at the relationship between race and sentencing. Having found that Black offenders were statistically more likely to receive a custodial sentence than the other two groups, we then looked at previous convictions with reference to race to see whether this might explain why this happened – it didn't. In this situation we were using the causal model referred to previously in Chapter 3. Here race was the independent variable, sentence the dependent variable, and previous convictions the potential intervening variable (Figure 8.4).

In this situation we are taking account of, or controlling for, a third variable. In the race/sentencing/previous convictions example, we did it by looking at the relationships two variables at a time. However, there are techniques that enable us to look at three or more variables at the same time. One of these is an extension of correlation called *partial correlation*. This requires three variables, all of which, as in the case of ordinary correlation, are interval level variables.

When we looked at correlation we used the example of conviction rates, occupancy rates and unemployment rates, correlating each variable with each of the other two. But we can also find out to what extent the relationship between two of the variables is affected by the third. Suppose we are doing a study of a particular town and we are interested in the relationship between the households and the conviction levels in the town. We now know that there is a significant relationship because the correlation between conviction rate and occupancy rate was .656, significant at a probability level of .002. But we also know that unemployment is related to conviction rates. What happens to the relationship between occupancy and conviction rates if we control for the effects of unemployment ('partial it out' in statistical language)? If we get SPSS to do a partial correlation for us, it gives us the following output as shown in Table 8.8.

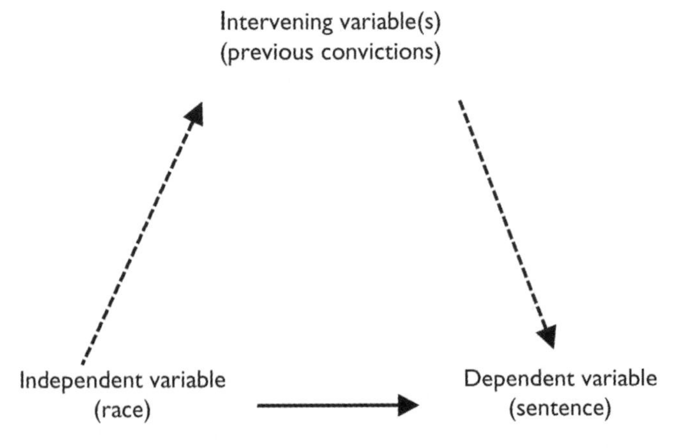

Figure 8.4 Three variable relationships

Table 8.8 Partial correlation

Control variables			*Convictions in ward*	*Average occupancy*
Unemployment rate	Convictions in ward	Correlation	1.000	.713
		Significance (2-tailed)	.	.001
	Average occupancy	Correlation	.713	1.000
		Significance (2-tailed)	.001	.

Table 8.8 shows us that in taking account of the effects of unemployment on the relationship between convictions and occupancy rates, the correlation between convictions and occupancy has now increased to 0.713, and is significant at a probability of 0.001 (i.e. it could only occur by chance one time in a thousand, compared with two times in a thousand previously).

Regression can also be extended to take account of three, and indeed more than three, variables. Using simple regression, we could examine the ability of one independent variable (e.g. occupancy rate) to predict a dependent variable (e.g. conviction rate). By using multiple regression we can achieve a stronger prediction by incorporating several independent variables which contribute towards explaining the dependent variable:

Dependent variable ←independent variable 1 + independent variable 2

(e.g. conviction rate) (e.g. occupancy rate) (e.g. unemployment rate)

Logistic regression can be used where the dependent variable is a dichotomous nominal variable (i.e. it is Yes or No, Black or White, Male or Female).

Where all the variables are nominal, we can do cross-tabulations that show three variables at once (e.g. gender by ethnic group by sentence), but tables with more than three nominal variables will get very confusing to read and, unless there is a very large sample, the numbers in each cell quickly become so small as to be not much use. The statistical procedure for examining several nominal variables is *log linear analysis*.

Summary

In this section we have attempted to give an introduction to some of the possibilities for analysing numerical criminological information. In doing so, we have:

- referred to the different types of numerical variable (nominal, ordinal, interval, ratio);
- introduced the notion of statistical probability;
- considered the analysis of single variables, two variables in relation to each other, and situations which take account of three variables;
- illustrated the distinction between dependent, independent and intervening variables.

We have not, however, attempted to explain in detail how all these procedures work, nor how to use a computer to carry them out. This would take many chapters and it is far better to read texts that are dedicated to doing this. In doing so it will be found that a lot of qualifications need to be added to when and how to use various tests. In order to use multiple regression, for example, a number of assumptions about the nature of the data have to be met. Furthermore, it is one thing to learn how to do a chi-square test, a *t* test, or a correlation, but it is quite another to have a set of data from a questionnaire or abstraction schedule in front of you and know what to do with it, and when to use a particular test. There are a large number of statistical tests, which meet a wide variety of situations, and knowledge of what they are and when to use them will only be acquired over a period of time. We hope that this section gives readers an overview of numerical analysis which will enable you to explore statistical procedures with an understanding of where they fit in to the process of analysis overall.

It may help to summarize the material above, setting out what we have covered by showing the procedures appropriate for nominal and interval level variables depending on whether univariate, bivariate, or multivariate analysis is to be used (see Table 8.9).

Finally, it is important to say something about how quantitative analysis is used. It is easy to become immersed in the minutiae of statistics, or be fascinated by some of the patterns and relationships that emerge. But it is important to use statistics in the context of a theoretical background, the research question being addressed, and the hypotheses being investigated. For example, earlier on we explained how it was possible to produce a correlation matrix in which a series of interval level variables could be correlated with each other. Because this can be done at the press of a button, it is tempting to throw every variable in at once and see what comes out. While we would not say that this should never be done (it may

Table 8.9 Examples of analysis by type of variable and number of variables

Type/Number of variables	Nominal (e.g. red, black, blue)	Interval (e.g. age, height)
univariate	frequencies, percentages	measures of centrality and spread (e.g. mean, variance)
bivariate	two variable tables (e.g. race by sentence) chi-square test	correlation simple regression
multivariate	three-way tables or more (e.g. race by sentence by gender)	multiple regression

throw up some interesting questions worth pursuing), this is something of a 'shotgun' approach to analysis. In general, it is much better to be clear about what one is looking for and why. So, for example, if you are looking at the relationship between unemployment and crime rates, there is a clear rationale for the analysis we did earlier, and for then going on to consider what other factors (such as occupancy) might be involved. Similarly, when using the court abstraction data, the question that needs to be asked is why this data was collected. We have created the dataset to illustrate certain ways of analysing data, but if it were a real dataset, then the likelihood is that these particular pieces of information would have been abstracted from court records in order to investigate what factors influence sentencing. Specific hypotheses would then be developed such as 'Some ethnic groups are sentenced differently to others'. In doing this, dependent and independent variables would be identified. Essentially, therefore, the kind of analysis one does needs to be anticipated when planning criminological research, and the results of analysis need to relate to, and inform the research process outlined in Chapter 1.

Analysing qualitative material: An introduction

We move on now to consider how we analyse qualitative data. We have seen in earlier chapters (especially Chapters 5, 6 and 7) that qualitative data can be collected in a range of different ways.

Interviews, observations, documentary analysis and even surveys (where open-ended questions are used) can all produce qualitative data. Whenever you include these methods in a research study, you soon find yourself in possession of a large, unwieldy database of transcripts, fieldnotes and/or documents and the aim of this discussion is to explain how these data can be managed and analysed. However, unlike quantitative data, there are no clear-cut and widely accepted 'rules' or procedures for qualitative analysis. There are some broad guidelines and we will explain these in this part of the chapter.

Although there is a range of computer packages available for qualitative analysis, we do not refer to them specifically in this discussion. The problem is that there are too many different packages, each capable of different functions, and we cannot refer to each in the same way that we could earlier to SPSS. An excellent overview of the packages that are available (including CISAID, SIMSTAT, NUD*IST and ATLAS) is provided by Lewins (2001) and we refer you there for more detail. You will find that the purpose of these packages is primarily to facilitate the very processes we describe in this chapter.

The skills of qualitative analysis are notoriously hard to master and it is unlikely that a simple reading of this chapter will equip you adequately to conduct analysis of your own. Robson (2002) makes an important observation when he says that traditionally these skills have been taught using an 'apprentice model' with new researchers being guided by more experienced supervisors. We aim simply to provide a detailed introduction to the key processes in qualitative analysis and to explain some of the most commonly used qualitative approaches in criminology. We make some recommendations for further reading at the end of this chapter.

The process of qualitative analysis

We have already seen that quantitative analysis takes place after all the data has been collected and is carried out according to pre-determined principles and statistical procedures. In contrast, qualitative analysis begins soon after the data collection starts and continues throughout the period of study and, as we mentioned in the Introduction, the procedures are far more flexible and adaptable. That is not to say, however, that qualitative analysis does not need careful planning and organizing. In this section, we will explain the basic principles of qualitative analysis and then will go on to describe how these principles have been developed for use with the most common qualitative methodologies in criminology (grounded theory, ethnography, case studies, content analysis and conversation and discourse analysis).

Qualitative analysis always involves two key tasks: coding and fragmenting the data. The task of coding starts almost as soon as the first batch of data has been collected. The first stage is often referred to as 'Basic Coding', and because little analysis takes place, it is simply a labelling process. You begin by reading the transcripts or fieldnotes and reflecting on them. It is a good idea to resist the temptation to write notes on the first reading because it allows you to concentrate on understanding the data as a whole before embarking on the process of splitting it up. On the second reading, you can work through the text and start making a list of the concepts which emerge (the coding process should now be easier because you have a good idea of what is contained in the whole document and this will facilitate the creation of a comprehensive index of concepts). Interestingly, there is no clear definition of what a 'concept' is in this context and often students and new researchers find this frustrating. Bryman (2004) suggests that a good way to start is to list questions such as: What is this about? Who is involved? What question does it raise? What is happening? What are people doing? What do people say they are doing? In the early stages of analysis, the concepts will tend to be descriptive and poorly developed and it should not be a concern if your index becomes rather large and unwieldy. The best approach is to pursue all the different lines of thought and refine the index at a later stage.

When you have developed a well-formed index of concepts, you can begin fragmenting the data. You need to create a file for each concept and then extract all the sections of text (a quote perhaps or a paragraph or longer) which represent that concept for storing in the file. In the days before computers, this was done quite literally by copying, cutting up and gluing together chunks of documents. Today this is made much easier because computers allow you to copy and paste text without scissors or glue! For this, you can use either a simple word processing package or one of the qualitative analysis packages. It is very important that an unviolated version of the original document is kept safe and that excerpts are clearly identified according to their original source. Indeed, it is important to keep in mind that when the data are broken down into small bits, there is a real danger of losing the context once a certain quote or observation has been extracted. It is important, therefore, not to lose sight of the original context.

The next stage of the coding process, often called 'content coding', requires you to identify themes in the data. In identifying themes, you should be able to create 'categories' out of your concepts. Again, there is no accepted definition of a 'category' and this is less than helpful, but perhaps a good way of getting to grips with the idea (especially if you do not have a supervisor or colleague who can guide you) is to read some published work and see how others have done it. There are worked-through examples in several of the methods texts. Although they are too detailed for reproduction here, we do refer to them in the Further Reading section at the end of the chapter. A useful criminological example is Tomsen's (1997) ethnographic study of violence in drinking establishments. Although Tomsen does not explain how he developed his concepts and categories, it is a useful exercise to attempt to identify them (as we have done in Box 8.2).

Box 8.2 An analysis of Tomsen (1997)

Concept	Labels given to phenomena	Drinking rates, speech, gait, mannerisms, threats, assaults, shouting, arguing, brawls, size of groups, working-class males, type of establishment
Category	A group of concepts	Collective drinking, social power, male identity, carnival, rule breaking
Hypotheses	Possible relationships between concepts	• There is a direct causal link between drinking and violence. • There is a power struggle between bouncers/police and patrons. • Collective drinking is related to individual assertion of social power. • Violence is related to masculinity preserving male honour. • Viewing conflict is enjoyable for onlookers.
Theory	Categories related together	There is no direct and obvious tie between violence and the use of alcohol, but there is a complex but powerful link between many incidents of public violence and the social process of collective drinking. This link is built around cultural understandings of the connections between rowdy and violent group drinking, the construction and projection of an empowered masculine identity, and the symbolic rejection of respectable social values.

There comes a point when it is possible to look for initial connections between the concepts and start to draw up hypotheses for testing. In this way, the themes/categories are related to the broader analytical themes. We noted earlier that the process of analysis usually begins early in the data collection and continually feeds back into the collection process itself and this is done through the method of analytic induction. You develop a hypothetical explanation (a set of hypotheses) for the social situation or phenomenon you are to explore and have a look to see whether the data confirm your hypotheses. If not, you must redefine your hypotheses and start the process again. Once you reach the point where you have confirmed your hypotheses and no deviant cases or examples emerge, the data collection ceases and the final conclusions can be drawn. It is particularly important to ensure that there are no cases which contradict your hypothesis, an approach called negative case analysis. A useful example of this process in action is Cressey's article in which he describes the analysis he conducted on embezzlers (1950). This is a particularly good example because he specifically describes how his hypothesis (originally derived from the literature) was reformulated a number of times throughout the study. He notes how his initial hypothesis was 'abandoned almost immediately' (ibid.: 741) and shows exactly how each subsequent hypothesis had to be revised. He concludes that his eventual successful hypothesis is as sound as it can be, but is open to the idea that it might be disproved in the future. He has also included a range of cases in the existing literature as part of his negative case analysis, which is a common approach.

Cressey's article is useful because he does explain how he has carried out the process of analytic induction to the reader. However, often researchers do not take this approach and the reader is left to guess how the hypotheses have been developed and the final conclusions drawn. In order to demonstrate how this may be done, we refer you again to Box 8.2 in which we have listed the hypotheses and subsequent theory which we think we can see in Tomsen's study. The key point to realize is that we could, of course, be wrong in our analysis and that is why it is so important for qualitative researchers to explain how they reached their conclusions (a point we take up again in the final section).

We have now introduced you to the process of qualitative analysis in simple terms. Remember that these are merely guidelines and that the actual process of qualitative analysis is complex, time-consuming and requires considerable skill. We will move on now to see how these basic principles have been used in different qualitative traditions which use a range of methods. You will notice many common themes and approaches but there are also differences, most of which are shaped by the epistemological basis of the approach and the type of data collected. It is often acceptable to utilize elements of different qualitative approaches, but remember that it is always important to ensure that you are maintaining validity and reliability in your research.

Analysing open questions in surveys

It is common to see a combination of both closed and open questions in questionnaires and interviews. Usually, a positivist approach will have been adopted and it will be desirable to combine the quantitative and qualitative data together for the purposes of hypothesis testing. So, in order to analyse the quantitative and qualitative data together, it is necessary to convert the open responses into numbers. The process for doing so is best illustrated through an example and we shall use this excerpt from an interview with local residents about their local area:[6]

> Q: What do you think are the most serious problems faced by people living in this area at the moment?
>
> A: We are having a lot of trouble with kids. They are always on the corner of Bates Street smoking and drinking at night. They make a lot of noise all night and leave chip-shop wrappers and smashed bottles all over the paths. We also have a problem with traffic. People who work at the hospital park on both sides of our street and as everyone uses it as the short cut through to the supermarket, there's a lot of traffic. It makes it hard for cars to pass and there have been crashes in the past.

The first thing you will need to do is make a long list of all the problems mentioned by all the respondents and give each problem a unique numerical code. So, our list here would look like this:

1 Youths hanging around at night
2 Youths making noise at night
3 Youths leaving litter
4 Parked cars obstructing road
5 Heavy traffic.

The list would grow as more interviews are analysed and additional problems mentioned by respondents. You then need to decide how to apply the codes to each case and record them in the data file. There are three possible ways to do this:

1 Create a single variable (PROBLEM) and record only the *first* problem mentioned by the respondent (so, for our respondent in the example, PROBLEM = 1).

2 Create several variables (PROBLEMA, PROBLEMB, PROBLEMC, etc.) and record the *first three* problems mentioned by the respondent (so, for our respondent in the example, PROBLEMA = 1, PROBLEMB = 2, PROBLEMC = 3).
3 Create a variable for each of the problems on the list (PROBLEM1–PROBLEM5). If a respondent mentions the problem, insert the code '1'. If the respondent does not mention the problem, insert the code '0'. (So, for our respondent in the example, PROBLEM1–PROBLEM5 would each be coded as '1' but PROBLEM6–PROBLEM10 would be coded as '0' because they were not mentioned.

Each of these three approaches is valid but the important thing to realize is that a clear decision needs to be made before the analysis begins. Open questions can be very useful in interviews and questionnaires, but they do need to be handled with care. You need to resist the temptation to insert open questions and just wait to see what happens – the risk here is that you end up with a batch of wasted data. It is important, then, to test out the coding process at the stage of piloting to ensure that the coding strategy is suitable. Fielding (2001) also suggests that a Code Book is kept, in which you record exactly how each of your variables are coded and constructed.

Grounded theory studies

The most widely used framework in qualitative analysis is the grounded theory approach. This is where you enter a research situation or environment with no preconceived ideas about it and no hypotheses to test. Instead, you allow the key features and relationships to emerge from the situation and record them accordingly. Thus, the process of data collection is controlled by the emerging theory.

The grounded theory approach utilizes three types of coding (Strauss and Corbin 1998):

1 *Open coding*. Data are separated, concepts and categories are identified and given labels.
2 *Axial coding*. The concepts and categories are interconnected to make theories.
3 *Selective coding*. One core category is selected for in-depth consideration.

Grounded theory studies have some additional special features and there is an extensive methodological literature which we cannot go into here (although there are recommendations for further reading later). Instead, we will simply highlight three of the most important elements. First, you utilize a process of theoretical sampling in which the whole process of data collection is controlled by the emerging theory (what to look for, who to speak to, etc.). Second, an approach called 'theoretical saturation' is used which requires that coding and analysis continue until no new categories emerge and the data no longer illuminates aspects of the concept under development. Finally, the 'constant comparison method' ensures that the relationship between concepts and categories is continually examined by the researcher. Glaser and Strauss (1967) suggest that the researcher uses a tool called a 'memo' to facilitate the constant comparison approach. This is a kind of journal or diary in which the researcher records the analytic decisions s/he makes and explains how concepts and categories have been developed.

There are, however, a number of criticisms of the grounded theory approach which you need to be aware of before beginning this kind of research. Aside from the fact that it is time-consuming and resource-intensive, perhaps the biggest question is whether it is possible to maintain the absolute level of objectively that the approach requires. Robson (2002) notes that this is a particular problem in reality because in order to make proposals for projects (especially where you are bidding for funding) you need to have a clear research question from the outset and to consider the possible implications and uses of your research. There is also a question as to whether this kind of research can actually make a useful contribution to theory since the focus is on generating concepts rather than seeking explanations.

Analysing case studies

This approach, developed by Miles and Huberman (1994), has a strong realist thread and the aim is to look for the mechanisms and processes which can provide causal explanations for events and situations. It is best understood as a qualitative approach with some in-built positivist elements for the purposes of making the research more 'scientific'. This approach has three stages but all form a continuous iterative process. At the data reduction stage, descriptive data are summarized in notes and memoranda. At the data display stage, matrices, charts and networks are used to create structured analysis. There are different types of tools to use and it is worth noting that some of these tools are useful in non-case study approaches too:

- context charts (showing the relationships between organizations, groups and roles);
- event flow networks (showing incidents and events in time sequence);

- flow charts (showing how decisions are made);
- tree diagrams (showing how phenomena are broken down into categories and concepts);
- cognitive maps (showing a person's belief system or thought process);
- casual networks (showing how different concepts relate to each other).

The final stage is conclusion-drawing and verification. It is important to be looking for reliability and validity throughout the process. There is a range of different approaches available and we discuss these later in the section on interpretation, conclusions and presentation.

Analysis in ethnographies

Ethnographic work, you may recall, usually involves a combination of methods and as a result, different types of analysis may be appropriate. Sometimes, a grounded theory approach is taken and sometimes a case-study approach is more suitable. Either way, it is likely that you will need to tailor the analysis to the individual study and this may involve taking different aspects from different approaches to analysing qualitative data.

Wolcott (1994) suggests that there are three stages of analysis in ethnographic work. The first is the 'thinking stage'. This requires you to get to know your data extremely well and to reflect on it fully. This stage should not be rushed and really does require an unhurried, skilled approach. The second stage is the 'categorizing stage' in which categories are created and typologies developed (this is a common approach in ethnographic work: Hammersley and Atkinson 1995). Categories start off poorly defined and descriptive and take time to be developed fully. The third stage is the 'progressing focusing stage' in which the research question is defined and clarified.

Content analysis

If you recall from our discussions in Chapter 5, the name given to the method of analysing documents is content analysis. Content analysis is often used as a supplementary method in a multi-method strategy. It can involve the collection and analysis of both quantitative data (for example, the number of relevant words or paragraphs) and qualitative data (the nature of language or style of pictures). In the criminological context, most studies using a content analysis approach have focused on printed news media and official policy documents.

Content analysis begins with the identification of a focused research question and, where suitable, developed hypotheses. The next stage is to develop a sampling strategy. The sampling frame will depend entirely on the nature of the research question. For example, if the aim is to test the relationship between crime reporting in the news and perceptions of crime rates, the sampling frame would be constructed of relevant national and local newspapers and/or news programmes on television/radio. The sample can be drawn according to a number of different elements, such as time, publication, author and reference to particular events. Again, this will be determined by the nature of the research question.

Arguably, the most crucial stages in content analysis are the development of categories for analysis and the definition of recording units. These categories are usually defined before the analysis begins when the hypotheses are formed. It is not always easy to identify categories effectively, but Holsti (1969) gives an excellent and in-depth explanation of the processes involved in creating 'category systems'. The categories for analysis may be derived directly from the key concepts which, when put together, build the hypotheses and may be quantitative or qualitative. Moreover, categories can be 'manifest' (physically present) or 'latent' (inferred/interpreted by the analyst) (Robson 2002). As in the other approaches to qualitative analysis, these categories must be exhaustive and mutually exclusive. So, if a study were to focus on the relationship between the presentation of crime events in local newspapers and public perceptions of local crime rates, the categories for analysis might include those laid out in Table 8.10.

Once the categories have been designed, they have to be operationalized in accordance with the selected recording units. The most common recording unit is the number of occurrences of words or phrases in a document, but it is possible to use alternatives such as paragraphs, column inches, number of stories, size of headline, colour of text and position on page. The coding scheme should be tested on samples of text and it is advisable to use more than one person in the process so as to assess inter-observer agreement as a measure of validity/reliability. This is especially important where a category system is heavily based on latent content because these categories are more prone to subjectivity or bias.

Finally, once the categories for analysis and recording units are validated, the analysis can begin. Actually, the method used is not dissimilar to using a structured observation schedule where occurrences of the pre-determined categories are counted and recorded using a schedule. Bryman (2004) gives an excellent working example of a coding schedule (including copies of the newspaper articles used). Importantly, the data drawn from the content analysis can then be related to 'outside variables'. For example, the level of crime

Table 8.10 An example of categories for content analysis

Manifest content	*Latent content*
Type of crime: Personal attack, burglary, vandalism, vehicle theft	*Sympathy towards victim:* Words used to describe victim; Quotes from victim
Nature of harm: Death, physical injury, damage to private property, damage to public property	*Condemnation of offender:* Words used to describe offender; Reference to past offences/anti-social lifestyle
Characteristics of victim: Gender, age, height, weight, socio-economic status	*Positive/critical attitude towards police response:* Quotes from police officers; Quotes from members of the public about general policing problems
Outcome of event: Non-detection by police, successful arrest, imprisonment	*Incitement of moral panic:* Criticisms about currently perceived social problems; Use of crime statistics in report

reporting in a newspaper could be analysed to test a relationship with the readers' perceptions of crime rates which are measured using a survey (for an example, see Williams and Dickenson 1993).

Like all methods of research, content analysis has its strengths and weaknesses. On the plus side, the documents under scrutiny have usually been produced for another purpose (i.e. not for the purpose of the research) and content analysis has a clear strength in being unobtrusive and non-reactive. However, this can also cause problems for the researcher as the document can be structured in an unhelpful way, leaving the researcher the tough task of organizing the material. One of the major challenges is to ensure validity in the research, especially where the analyst must distinguish between 'witting evidence' (information which the author of the document intended to convey) and 'unwitting evidence' (any additional information which the analyst can glean through his/her reading of the document). Finally, content analysis is renowned for being a rather laborious and time-consuming process. It is true that computers have eased the labour to some extent. However, one has to be careful because computers are able to analyse text in a restricted mechanical way. For example, it is easy for a computer program to count frequencies of words but it cannot be relied upon to draw inferences, interpret or allow for errors or contexts. As long as one is realistic about the limitations of the computer, it can be a very useful tool in content analysis.

Analysing language – conversation analysis and discourse analysis

It is important to be able to understand language in criminological research, especially where interviews or observations are being conducted, because people use words in particular ways and we need to understand what they actually meant when they used them. This is particularly important where a special vocabulary or 'argot' is used by members of a group or culture, such as drug users. There are two main types of language analysis – conversation analysis and discourse analysis. They are similar in approach but different in terms of the type of communication they can be applied to. Whereas conversation analysis is used to analyse verbal communications between people, discourse analysis can be used to analyse both verbal and written forms of communication.

The method of conversation analysis emerged out of ethnomethodology, which is concerned with understanding the methods used by people in their everyday lives to interact, function and accomplish social order (Garfinkel 1967). The analyst seeks to understand the structures which underlie interactions between people and which contribute to the attainment of social order. So it is not just about what people say, but about how people talk to each other in natural situations. Unlike other kinds of qualitative analysis, conversation analysis does have a relatively clear set of procedures to follow. Indeed, conservation analysis is an interesting mix of principles usually associated with both quantitative and qualitative analysis.

There are three assumptions made by conversation analysts (Heritage 1987):

1 Talk is structured and there are unwritten rules of conversation which we follow; we take it in turns to speak and use words or prompts to progress the conversation.
2 Talk occurs in a context and in order to understand the conversation we have to analyse it in that context.
3 Conversation has to be understood entirely from the data, not through pre-theorizing and constructing hypotheses.

Put very simply, the process of conversation analysis requires going over the transcript of a conversation with a fine-toothed comb, interpreting what has been said and using special symbols to indicate where a person pauses to reflect, hesitate or emphasizes specific words. There are various well-established tools of conversation which are used to conduct the analysis (Wooffitt 2005):

- *Turn-taking*: The idea here is that conversations depend on people knowing when to talk and when to listen. Signals are used to indicate when one person has finished talking and the next person should respond. These signals include greetings, questions and invitations and we all have an innate understanding of how and when they should be used. The analyst seeks to identify if and when they are used in conversation and to what effect.
- *Adjacency pairs*: The questions, invitations and greetings used in a conversation require appropriate responses. A question, for example, should be met with an answer, an invitation with an acceptance or rejection, a greeting with a greeting. Here the analyst will look for the expected response and analyse the effect it has on the progress and content of the conversation.
- *Preference organization*: People who raise questions, invitations and greetings will have a preferred and non-preferred response in mind. So, for example, if I invite a friend to join me for lunch, my preferred response is likely to be 'yes'. If my friend cannot come for lunch, s/he will have to give me my non-preferred response. The analyst will examine how both parties manage the delivery of the preferred or non-preferred response.
- *Accounts*: Accounts are reasons given for not being about to give the preferred response. So, my friend may look for an appropriate way of turning down my lunch invitation without offending me. The analyst will assess whether the account has be used positively, to enforce the value of the original invitation or question, or not.
- *Repair mechanisms*: Of course, conversations do not always follow a strict turn-taking structure. Sometimes, people interrupt each other or start talking at the same time. In these situations, one person will stop speaking or perhaps it will be necessary for the person to repeat a question or invitation. The analyst will examine how the conversation is repaired.

This short summary should give you a flavour of conversation analysis but it is, of course, much more complex than we suggest here. It is a skilled approach to analysis which would probably require some specialist training but it can be useful, especially in ethnographic work. Where a video camera has been used to record a conversation, it may also be interesting to analyse body language.

Let us move on now to consider discourse analysis. As we said earlier, discourse analysis can be applied to written forms of communication as well as spoken forms. It is used in a wide variety of disciplines and there are different variations of how it should be conducted. The focus is slightly different than that for conversation analysis. Here, the assumption is that when people use discourse, they are usually trying to achieve something. Discourse analysis focuses on understanding the tools used as part of this process.

The aim in discourse analysis is to identify the 'interpretative repertoire' (Wooffitt 2005). This is a concept which characterizes the way in which people engage in discourse, so it might be an attitude or belief system. It is common to find more than one repertoire in a study because people may represent their ideas differently in different contexts and to different audiences. Discourse analysis is also used to look at the ways in which facts are presented by different people. Here, the idea is that by analysing the discourse, we come to understand how the originator has attempted to construct an argument and convey facts. These are referred to as 'rhetoric strategies' and can be identified by looking for variations in expression which can alter the impact a series of statements has, evidence that counter-arguments have been anticipated and accounted for and attempts to present accountable arguments.

Unfortunately, it is not possible to go into further detail about the methods of conversation and discourse analysis. It is clear to see how both approaches might be useful in criminological research but neither method is commonly used. It is worth exploring these approaches, however, because even where a true conversation or discourse analysis approach is not adopted, it can be useful to understand more about how conversations work and how they can reveal a great deal about relationships and group contexts.

Interpreting results, drawing conclusions and presenting findings

Finally, we will briefly consider how qualitative data are interpreted and presented. Remember, as researchers we are seeking to produce research which is both valid and reliable, and therefore need to think carefully about how our data are analysed and interpreted to avoid unjustifiable conclusions. There are some very significant potential pitfalls for the qualitative researcher to fall into, all of which have been discussed throughout the preceding chapters, and it is important to consider using a range of methodological and analytical tools to help build a defensible methodology. We summarize these in Table 8.11.

Students of criminology are often frustrated because it is unusual for researchers to explain the details of the analysis process and the methods of interpretation in articles. How, then, can we be sure that the research can be trusted? It can, indeed, be hard to judge whether data has been interpreted correctly by a researcher and this is a significant problem in qualitative research. We would suggest, therefore, that whenever you conduct qualitative work and publish it, you should keep this in mind. You should explain how the process of analytic induction has been carried out, how concepts and categories have been developed and how conclusions have been

Table 8.11 Pitfalls and solutions

Threat to validity/reliability	*Possible solutions*
Representativeness	Random sampling where possible Triangulation (method, data)
Researcher effects	Auditing of analysis by another person Researcher triangulation Weighting (favouring strong data e.g. first hand observations, interviews with trusted subjects etc.)
Unjustified leaps in conclusions (not adequately testing patterns, relationships and explanations)	Checking outliers (not ignoring them) Pursue and develop surprising patterns Look for negative evidence Test hypotheses using 'if-then' tests Rule out spurious relationships Try to replicate findings Consider alternative explanations Get feedback from subjects

drawn. Quotes are often used to illustrate how the data have been interpreted, but you should always ensure that you use them correctly and in context. Only say they are representative of the kinds of responses you had, if they were (this may seem an obvious thing to say but it is very important). Finally, as is almost always the case with qualitative research, there is a problem with generalizability and it is important for researchers to be able to distinguish between the conditions that were *sufficient* for a phenomenon to occur in this research, but not *necessary* in all situations and to recognize that more factors may be relevant in other contexts.

Further reading

Books on quantitative analysis vary from the more traditional statistics textbooks, to ones that aim to reach out and communicate with those who find numbers off-putting. Among the more friendly books on statistics for the non-statistician are: David Rowntree's *Statistics Without Tears: a primer for non-mathematicians* (1991); Frances Clegg's *Simple Statistics* (1990); and Kranzler and Moursund, *Statistics for the Terrified* (1995).

A fuller knowledge can be gained from: Fielding and Gilbert, *Understanding Social Statistics* (2000); Daniel Wright, *Understanding Statistics: An Introduction for the Social Sciences* (1997); and Fink, *How to Analyse Survey Data* (1995).

David de Vaus's book, *Analysing Social Science Data* (2002), also gives a fuller understanding of data analysis, but instead of just writing about various methods takes the approach of telling you how to do different things.

There are also several books about how to use SPSS, which also tell you about the various statistical techniques as well. SPSS changes fairly regularly and the main thing to watch out for is which version of SPSS a particular book covers.

Julie Pallant's *SPSS Survival Manual* (2001) is one of the most user friendly for beginners, which helps you to not only use SPSS but interpret the sometimes confusing output that it produces. Others include: Foster, *Data Analysis Using SPSS for Windows: A Beginner's Guide* (1998); and Norušis, *SPSS for Windows: Base System User's Guide* (1992), produced by the SPSS Corporation itself.

Probably the best all round guide is Andy Field's *Discovering Statistics Using SPSS* (2004). It covers a wide range of statistical applications, explains how to apply them using SPSS, and is also very accessible and well written.

There is a vast literature on qualitative methods, consisting of contributions by researchers in a range of disciplines (including sociology, psychology, history, information studies and communication science). Most textbooks contain quite detailed overviews of the available methods and our students find the texts by Robson (2002) and Bryman (2004) give useful introductions. Fielding (2001) is a good introduction to coding and provides some very useful examples to illustrate the techniques and Miles and Humberman (1994) present their analytic tools very well. For conversation and discourse analysis, Wooffit (2005) is extremely useful and accessible.

Appendix 1: Court sentencing project

Abstration Pro Forma

		Code
Case Number :		❑❑❑ 1
Defendant's Age :		❑❑ 2
Gender :	male = 1 female = 2	❑ 3

Race :	White = 1 Black = 2 Asian = 3	❑ 4
Offence :	theft = 1 damage = 2 violence = 3	❑ 5
Number of Previous Convictions :		❑ 6
Sentence :	fine = 1 community = 2 custody = 3	❑ 7

This is fictional data abstracted from court records at Escafeld Magistrates Court. The variables are simplified. There are 56 cases and 8 variables. These show a case reference number, age, gender, ethnic group, offence, number of previous convictions, sentence, and a score representing the overall seriousness of the case.

case	age	gender	ethnic	offence	precons	sentence	sscore
1	21	1	1	1	1	1	60
2	17	1	2	1	1	2	80
3	24	2	1	1	4	1	70
4	30	1	1	3	5	3	120
5	19	1	3	1	0	1	50
6	25	1	1	1	3	2	100
7	21	1	2	3	1	3	130
8	34	1	1	3	5	3	140
9	17	2	2	1	0	1	50
10	18	1	2	2	1	2	100
11	25	1	1	1	2	1	60
12	27	2	1	2	3	1	80
13	17	1	1	2	0	1	60
14	23	1	1	3	1	2	110
15	18	2	2	1	1	2	90
16	20	1	1	1	4	2	100
17	16	1	2	2	0	1	60
18	16	1	3	1	0	1	50
19	19	1	1	2	2	1	70
20	21	1	2	1	1	2	90
21	22	2	3	1	0	1	50
22	19	1	1	2	4	2	110
23	19	1	2	2	2	3	120
24	32	2	1	1	5	2	100
25	17	1	2	3	0	3	120
26	28	2	2	3	2	3	130
27	30	1	3	1	0	2	80
28	25	1	1	1	0	1	50
29	17	1	1	2	2	2	100
30	21	2	2	1	5	3	120
31	18	1	2	1	2	2	90
32	16	1	1	1	0	1	50
33	21	2	1	1	6	2	100
34	22	1	1	3	5	3	140
35	16	1	3	2	1	2	100
36	18	1	1	3	0	2	100
37	33	1	1	2	1	1	70
38	16	2	2	1	1	2	90

case	age	gender	ethnic	offence	precons	sentence	sscore
39	17	1	2	2	3	3	130
40	24	2	1	1	1	2	90
41	19	1	1	2	3	3	130
42	26	1	3	1	0	1	50
43	19	2	2	1	2	3	110
44	20	1	1	1	1	1	60
45	21	1	1	3	3	3	140
46	16	1	2	1	1	2	90
47	22	2	2	1	6	3	120
48	17	1	1	2	0	2	90
49	19	2	3	2	0	1	60
50	28	1	2	2	1	1	70
51	30	1	1	1	0	1	50
52	17	1	2	2	4	3	130
53	19	2	3	1	0	2	80
54	23	1	2	3	2	3	130
55	20	2	1	1	3	2	100
56	25	1	1	3	1	3	130

Appendix 2: Calculating measures of a distribution

In this appendix we give an example of how the various features of an interval level variable would be calculated. The variable is the number of previous convictions which a sample of offenders have. In practice these calculations can be done by SPSS, but it is also useful to see how the particular measures are derived.

Suppose that in a sample of 294 offenders drawn from a magistrates' court,

103 had no previous convictions
95 had one previous conviction
50 had two previous convictions
33 had three previous convictions
5 had four previous convictions
8 had five previous convictions

We will calculate:

(a) the mean number of previous convictions
(b) the sum of squared deviations from this mean
(c) the variance
(d) the standard deviation
(e) the standard error of the mean, and
(f) the 95% confidence limits for the true mean.

You need to know that:

X is the value of a particular variable
$\bar{X}$ means the mean of X
f is the frequency with which a value occurs
n is the number of cases
Σ means the sum of all the values.

The procedure

The first thing to note is that although you have a ratio level of measurement, the number of previous convictions, you also have frequencies for each step of that variable. You could write down a long column of numbers starting with 103 zeros, followed by 95 1's, followed by 50 2's, etc. (this is how it would appear for 294 cases on an SPSS data sheet). To calculate the answers by hand, however, it is much simpler just to multiply all the zeros by 103 (answer = 0, of course), the 1's by 95 (= 95) and the 2's by 50 (= 100), etc.

Add all these up to get the total sum (354), and divide by 294 to get the mean (= 1.2). You now have the basis for doing the 'sum of squares' calculation by taking each case from the mean, squaring the result and adding all these up (multiplying $(X - \bar{X})^2$ by the frequency for each step of the variable) to get

$$\sum(X-\bar{X})^2 = 445.76.$$

Laid out as a calculation this looks as follows:

X	f	fX	$(X - \bar{X})$	$(X - \bar{X})^2$	$f(X - \bar{X})^2$
0	103	0	- 1.2	1.44	148.32
1	95	95	- 0.2	0.04	3.80
2	50	100	0.8	0.64	32.00
3	33	99	1.8	3.24	106.92
4	5	20	2.8	7.84	39.20
5	8	40	3.8	14.44	115.52
	n = 294	Σ = 354			445.76

$\bar{X} = 1.2$

The *variance* is the sum of squares divided by the number of cases minus 1, which is as follows:

$$s^2 = \frac{445.76}{293} = 1.52$$

The *standard deviation*, the most commonly used measure of the spread of a variable, is the square root of the variance, thus:

$$s = \sqrt{1.52} = 1.23$$

The *standard error of the mean*, a way of estimating the extent to which the sample mean may vary from the population or true mean is obtained by dividing the standard deviation by the square root of the number of cases, thus:

$$SE\bar{X} = \sqrt{294} = 0.07$$

By multiplying this by two and adding and substracting the result from the sample mean we can be 95% confident that the true mean lies between the resulting two boundaries. These are known as the confidence limits, and the difference between them is the confidence interval. Thus,

$$1.2 + 2 * .07 = 1.34 \quad \text{and} \quad 1.2 - 2 * .07 = 1.06$$

So we can be 95% confident that the true mean of the population lies somewhere between 1.06 and 1.34. (This is because in a normal distribution 95 out of 100 sample means lie within approximately 2 [1.96 to be precise] standard errors of the true population mean.)

Part III

Real-world research

9 Researching offenders and employment

Background to the project

When unemployment rises there is often debate about the relationship between unemployment and various other phenomena such as ill health, and crime. During the 1980s, the United Kingdom experienced the highest levels of unemployment since the Second World War. This led to much writing about the possible impact on offending, drawing both on previous economic and social research (Brenner 1976) and new studies (Gormally et al. 1981) and analyses (Farrington et al. 1986). While the main focus of interest was on the relationship between unemployment and crime (Box 1987), there was less awareness of other possible implications. For example, higher unemployment means that it is more difficult for those with a criminal record to get jobs. Since known offenders are more likely to re-offend if unemployed (see Crow et al. 1989: 79), then this means higher rates of re-offending, and of course this in itself becomes an element in the link between higher unemployment and crime. But another important element is what impact unemployment may have for the way offenders are dealt with. In the 1980s the NACRO Research Unit carried out various studies into the implications of unemployment for offenders. Some of these were concerned with employment and training schemes for young and adult offenders, but the project considered here looked at the relationship between employment status and sentencing.

What the chapter shows is:

- the conceptual basis for the study;
- how this was then turned into a series of testable hypotheses;
- the kind of research design that was employed in order to take account of important variables;
- the use of mixed methods;

- the way the data was analysed;
- the implications of these results for the hypotheses;
- the consequent impact on thinking about unemployment and sentencing;
- the implications for practice and policy that followed.

In other words it very much illustrates the application of the research process outlined in Chapter 1, from theory through hypotheses to operationalization, data collection, analysis and interpretation.[1]

Theoretical context

As we explained in Chapter 1, a criminological inquiry should have some theoretical connections, to enable the results to be interpreted in relation to existing knowledge. This does not necessarily mean that the study is putting some grand criminological theory to the test; it may be several steps removed from theories that have been advanced to explain crime and deviance. Nor need it necessarily have a clear conceptual formulation from the start; this may become clearer as the study progresses. However, to pretend that any enquiry is atheoretical is to delude ourselves. Every question has some underlying basis in theory, and the investigator needs to work at making this explicit and exploring its implications. In the case of the study described here, there were three stages of thinking about the consequences of unemployment for offenders: (1) worklessness and criminal justice; (2) worklessness and the way offenders are dealt with; and (3) worklessness and sentencing.

The context for the first of these was a long-standing association between worklessness and the law, going back to the Statute of Labourers of 1349, and the Vagrancy Acts of 1824–35, which were designed to control surplus labour, with references to 'rogues and vagabonds', 'idle and disorderly persons', and 'not having any visible means of support' (Home Office 1974). Offending has long been linked with a background where work is in short supply, intermittent and poorly paid, and criminological theories have included those which argue that the deprivation brought about by little or no job opportunities is at least a factor in explaining criminality. However, our specific interest was in whether the unemployed were likely to be dealt with differently to those who had jobs, and in what ways. Again, there is much material to suggest that a defendant's employment status plays a role at various stages in the criminal justice process. It may be taken to reflect on a person's character, such that having a job and a steady work record will count in his or her favour. Conversely, the lack of stable employment is regarded as an adverse 'risk factor'. Engels portrayed this graphically in his nineteenth-century survey of the English working class:

> But if a poor devil gets into such a position as involves appearing before the Justice of the Peace ... he is regarded from the beginning as guilty; his defence is set aside with a contemptuous 'Oh! We know the excuse', and a fine imposed which he cannot pay and must work out with several months on the treadmill. And if nothing can be proved against him, he is sent to the treadmill nonetheless, as a 'rogue and a vagabond'. (Engels 1969: 306)

The second stage was to try to be more specific about worklessness and the way offenders are dealt with. Much of what had been written about this concerned the relationship between levels of unemployment and the prison population (Box and Hale 1982). However, the studies documenting this were mainly aggregate studies based on trends in criminal justice and economic data (e.g. Brenner 1976), and there was little understanding of why it should happen. One possible explanation for this is that the prison population rises at times of higher unemployment because there is an increase in crime, which in itself results in more imprisonment. But this depends on a variety of other factors, such as whether enforcement and incarceration practices alter. One possible explanation might be that societies, and their criminal justice systems, become less tolerant and more repressive at times of economic hardship (UNSDRI 1976). Our view was that there was probably more to it than this, and we therefore used decision-making theory as the basis for our inquiry. This posited that unemployment restricts the options both of the unemployed and sentencers to impose financial penalties, and meant that both courts and offenders had fewer possibilities open to them than previously. So we did not just want to establish whether there was an association between employment status and sentencing; we wanted to understand something of the mechanisms that might be operating.

If fluctuating crime rates are taken out of the equation, then there are still various ways in which employment status might affect the likely use of prison. These are threefold:

1 *Remand.* The Bail Act 1976 referred to the relevance of 'community ties', including whether the defendant had a steady job, as a consideration influencing whether to remand a defendant in custody or release him or her on bail.
2 *Sentence.* To what extent does the court take into account an offender's work status and record when deciding an appropriate sentence?

3 *Parole*. Again, a prisoner's 'community ties', including employment prospects, may have been considered in deciding on early release.

It is seldom possible when undertaking a research study to cover all the ground you would wish to. We therefore decided to focus on what might be most likely to affect the way that offenders were dealt with, and this was sentencing. This was reinforced by an article in *Justice of the Peace* (1982: 700) which had stated that, 'A man's (*sic*) employment situation has long been considered to be a relevant factor in sentencing'. It also gave us the opportunity to look not just at the use of imprisonment, but at whether unemployment affected other disposals such as fines, community service, and probation. The research question with which we started therefore became, what impact does rising unemployment have on sentencing, and what are the consequences for the individuals concerned, and for criminal justice generally? We could discuss the topic itself at much greater length, but what we want to highlight here is the way in which a topic of general interest at the time became progressively refined into a manageable, researchable question.

The research

Hypotheses

Having defined our terrain, the next step in the research process was to develop hypotheses which could be put to the test. We developed 21 specific hypotheses, which fell into five main groups. These can be summarized as follows:

1 Employment information is important to courts in making decisions about offenders. E.g. *Hypothesis 1:* 'Employment status and history will generally feature as an item of information presented to the courts at various stages of the process.'
2 Unemployed offenders are more likely than those with jobs to be the subject of pre-sentence reports, and to receive different recommendations. E.g. *Hypothesis 14:* 'Unemployed offenders are more likely to be the subject of an SIR.' At the time of the research, pre-sentence reports were called social inquiry reports (SIRs). Whether they were asked for, and how they were drafted, was more variable then than now.
3 Other things being equal, unemployed offenders are likely to receive different sentences to those who are employed. E.g. *Hypothesis 4:* 'Unemployed offenders are more likely to receive a custodial or potentially custodial disposal (such as suspended sentence or committal for sentence) than employed offenders.'

4 Unemployed offenders are likely to receive different *amounts* of sentences to those who are employed. E.g. *Hypothesis 10:* 'Unemployed offenders given probation orders will be more likely to be given longer probation orders than comparable employed offenders.'
5 Local circumstances and sentencing traditions affect the hypothesized disparities in court decisions between employed and unemployed offenders. E.g. *Hypothesis 18:* 'Employment status will be a more important factor in an area of low unemployment than in an area of high unemployment, and intermediate in a transitional area.' This was included because of previous research (Hood 1972; Tarling and Weatheritt 1979) showing that in magistrates' courts there tended to be a 'bench tradition' of favouring some disposals more than others. It was also necessary to take the local social and economic conditions into account. More will be said about these factors below when describing the research design.

Note the way the hypotheses were expressed. This is in the form of an assertion that such-and-such is the case. The purpose of the empirical inquiry is then to put these assertions to the test; in other words, to see whether the hypotheses can be refuted. If they are, then alternative formulations need to be considered. This principle of refutation is based on the proposition that in the social sciences it is seldom possible to prove something categorically. Because many factors are usually in play, and alternative formulations are generally possible, one's task is to eliminate possibilities.

Research design

The next stages in the research process involve developing a project to test the hypotheses, and this means devising a suitable research design, defining terms, operationalizing variables, and deciding on what methods to employ. (For anyone who is tempted to think that research means going out and interviewing people, or analysing statistics, it is worth noting just how far along in the research process the selection of specific methods occurs.) Of course, the hypotheses are framed in the knowledge that this is what has to happen, so they are always likely to be drafted with these considerations in mind. It is not simply a matter of working your way through the process one stage at a time; each part of the process has to be done with the consequences for other stages in mind.

Back to the research design. If you wish to look at the relationship between unemployment and sentencing, what is the best way to do it? Here again some choices have to be made. It is not possible to study every court in any depth. Even a sizeable sample of courts could only be studied at the most superficial level, since the main task would involve having to go through a significant number of cases in order to establish the employment status of defendants. Although we wanted to determine whether and what kind of relationship there was between employment status and sentence, we also wanted to understand what was happening, and what the nature of any relationship was, and this meant studying courts in some detail. We also had to limit our enquiries to magistrates' courts, because obtaining access to Crown Courts at that time would have been very difficult, if not impossible (Ashworth et al. 1984). In addition, the factors operating at Crown Courts may well have been different to those operating at magistrates courts, and would have required a separate study.

The study was defined in two other ways as well: it would be restricted to adults and to men. This is because very different considerations are likely to apply to young people, and also to the relationship between sentencing and the employment situation of women. The reason for this sequence of limitations was in essence that it was important to control for as many variables as possible. Many factors affect sentencing, and although it would have been highly desirable to cover a full range of situations and all types of defendant, not only would an exhaustive study have demanded massive resources, but even then it would have been difficult to take account of all the variables. In effect, one would have had to mount several different studies, and it is generally better to address one aspect of an issue well than to cover all aspects ineffectually. Of course, defining a study in this way also places limits on how far the results can be applied, but the complete picture regarding a topic will usually depend on a number of researchers undertaking studies on different aspects, and there have been several studies of the impact of unemployment on offending and criminal justice, some of them referred to here. Our study contributed something to what was already known, but also left considerable scope for others to contribute.

We also needed to take account of the fact that although unemployment at the time was high, it did vary from one part of the country to another. As explained above, we needed to take into consideration the sentencing perspectives of different benches, and the possibility that the relationship between employment status and sentencing may be different at courts with a more punitive approach to sentencing than at courts which favoured a less punitive approach. Given the resources likely to be available to us we therefore proposed a study which involved six magistrates courts as shown in Table 9.1.

Two courts were selected in the North-East of England to represent an area with historically high levels of unemployment (H1 and H2), where it might be supposed that the courts were used to

Table 9.1 Research design

TABLES AND FIGURES FOR PART THREE

CHAPTER NINE

Table 9.1 Research Design

	Low unemployment	*High unemployment*	*Low to high unemployment*
Below average use of custody	Court L1	Court H1	Court LH1
Above average use of custody	Court L2	Court H2	Court LH2

dealing with an above average proportion of unemployed offenders. To contrast with these, two courts were selected in the South-East of England where, even at a time of high unemployment nationally, levels of joblessness were lower than elsewhere (L1 and L). London was excluded because of the different nature of London courts, and because there was a wide variation in levels of unemployment within London. Finally, two courts were selected in the West Midlands (LH1 and LH2). This was an area that had undergone a transition from relative affluence and low unemployment, to severe recession and high unemployment during the 1980s, and it was therefore an interesting area to study to see what effect this might have had. The levels of unemployment and sentencing patterns were checked by reference to national statistics held by the Government departments concerned.

The research methods

At each of the six courts three methods of data collection were used, summarized in Table 9.2.

Table 9.2 Research methods used

	At each court	*Number*
Case records	At least 500 men sentenced for property offences	3470
Observations	At least 12 sessions	97
	At least 54 defendants at remand or committal	573
	At least 65 offenders at sentence	410
Interviews	At least 8 key people (Chair, Chief Clerk, Senior Probation Officer, Prosecutors, Defenders)	52

- *Case records*: A form was used to abstract information from the case files of over 500 adult males at each court who had been sentenced for property offences, mostly burglary, theft and criminal damage. Again, the selection of property offences aims to limit the amount of variability likely to occur, since other types of offence might be dealt with differently. The information extracted covered the man's offence and criminal record, employment status, the sentence given, any reports that there were, and any other relevant background information.
- *Observations*: These were carried out in order to get a better understanding of the process leading to court decisions, who said what to whom, and where employment status stood in relation to the decision-making process.
- *Interviews*: Semi-structured interviews were undertaken with key people, not in order to obtain a representative sample, but because they occupied an important role with regard to the court process and were able to offer insights and perspectives on how employment status might affect the way the court made decisions.

The methods constituted a form of triangulation (Denzin 1988). The hypotheses could therefore be examined from three vantage points, and support for any hypothesis would be strongest if provided by consistent evidence from all three methods.

Operationalizing the design and conducting the study

The next stage in the research process involved identifying dependent, independent and intervening variables (see Figure 3.1 on p.41) and deciding how they were to be measured. In one sense this was comparatively easy. The dependent variable was clearly the disposal in terms of the sentencing decision, and the independent variable was employment status. However, it is also clear that the sentence a person receives is determined by considerations other than their employment status, in particular by the seriousness of the offence, and their criminal history. It is important to take these into account (control for them) when examining the extent to which employment status plays a part in sentencing. Although one can never be sure that one has taken every facet of a complex decision into account, earlier research offered an insight into the main factors that influenced sentencing (Thorpe 1978; Phillpotts and Lancucki 1979). We therefore developed a composite scale, the 'Offending Score', to take account of these other factors. This score included the current offence, the number of charges, the value of the property involved, the number of previous convictions the offender had, the interval between convictions, the similarity of previous offences, and previous sentences. It ran from a minimum of three points for a first offender convicted of minor criminal damage, to a maximum of 19 points for a serious and persistent burglar. The sentencing outcome was based on a tariff of disposals running from conditional discharge to immediate custody. Thus, the definition of the variables was as shown in Figure 9.1.

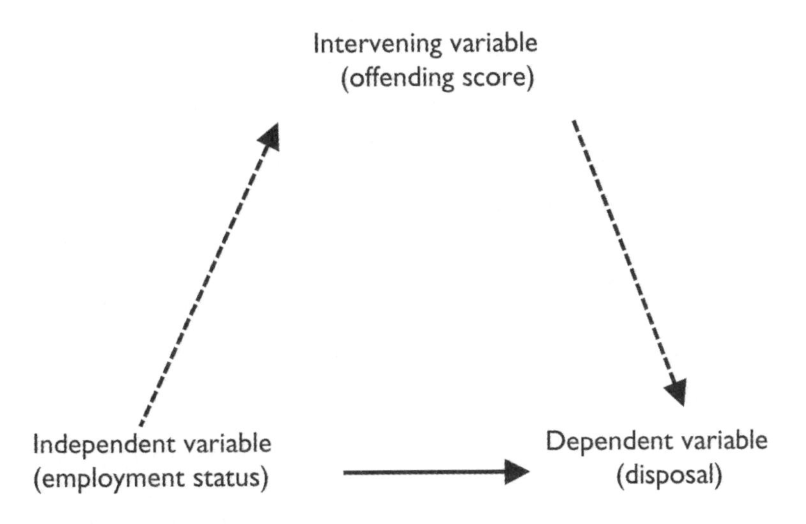

Figure 9.1 Variables used in the study

The fieldwork took place over a period of two years, including a pilot study conducted in a different part of the country from those to be covered by the main study. It involved spending two months at each court. An abstraction form was used for collecting the material from court files. This was not a straightforward process because, while certain information such as the sentence could be easily identified, it often took time reading through the various case files to find other information, such as that relating to employment status. Systematic notes were taken of court observations and interviews, and the interviews were also recorded for subsequent reference.

The analysis of the observations and interviews was largely descriptive, although the hypotheses acted as the main point of reference in recording observations and conducting interviews, and in identifying themes in the interview material. These methods yielded information on attitudes towards the unemployed, and importantly on what information the bench received. The data from the court records was analysed quantitatively, using multiple regression. This attempted to predict, for each type of sentence, the probability of an offender receiving that sentence, as against all others, taking into account, first, the offending score, then employment status, as independent variables. The data did not meet all the statistical assumptions required for multiple linear regression, but further analysis using a multinomial logit model confirmed the general pattern of results.

Results

The main focus of this chapter is on how the research was done, rather than on the substance of the study. However, it might be of some interest to briefly summarize what did come out of the project. One of the first points to emerge, mainly from the observations, was to highlight the important role that information of any kind plays in the court process, which underlines the necessity of getting the best possible information to courts.

More specific conclusions were related to the hypotheses on which the study was based. As outlined earlier, these fell into five main groups, and the findings can therefore be summarized in relation to these:

1 *Employment information is important to courts in making decisions about offenders.* This was supported although, as might be expected, information about employment was subsidiary to details about the offence and offending history of the offender.

2 *Unemployed offenders are more likely than those with jobs to be the subject of pre-sentence reports, and to receive different recommendations.* There was some support for the hypothesis that unemployed offenders were more likely to receive social inquiry reports. Looking at whether courts followed the recommendations of SIRs or not, there was no support for the hypothesis that where courts don't follow recommendations, sentencing was more severe.
3 *Other things being equal, unemployed offenders are likely to receive different sentences to those who are employed.* There was a significant tendency for the unemployed, at the end of the day, to be more likely to go to prison than those in work, but the main impact of unemployment on sentencing lay elsewhere in the range of disposals available to courts at the time. In particular, the unemployed were less likely to be fined and more likely to be given community service orders (CSOs) instead.
4 *Unemployed offenders are likely to receive different amounts of sentences to those who are employed.* This was supported as far as fines were concerned: unemployed offenders were fined less than those who were employed. However, there was no support for this hypothesis in relation to other sentences, such as CSO and imprisonment.
5 *Local circumstances and sentencing traditions affect the hypothesized disparities in court decisions between employed and unemployed offenders.* It was found that what one might call more traditional attitudes towards the unemployed (e.g. that they were shirkers) persisted where unemployment was low and/or custody rates were high. In areas where unemployment was higher, there was some sympathy for the plight of the unemployed, and in fact in one area a number of the magistrates had experienced unemployment.

Although the study was limited in various respects, as outlined above, it was possible to make some extrapolations about the impact that rising unemployment was likely to have on the sentencing of adult male property offenders. The most significant impact was in the use of fines. During the period preceding the study there had been a decline in the use of the fine nationally, and this study helped to explain how that had come about. Unemployment triggered a 'flight from the fine' to other disposals, especially towards the use of community service orders. The research contributed to the debate about the need for fines that were graduated more towards the means of offenders, something which was implemented in the Criminal Justice Act 1991, but subsequently rescinded in the Criminal Justice Act 1993. However, the use of fines and the problem of fine enforcement continues to be an issue to this day. The criminological significance of the study lay in explaining exactly how social and economic changes and criminal justice are interrelated at the level of decision-making rather than just as aggregate phenomena.

Conclusion

So to some final points, to highlight the main features of this study in terms of the practice of criminological research:

- First, the study shows how a broad area of interest becomes progressively defined in order to render it susceptible to empirical investigation.
- Second, it should be noted how the stages which this study went through reflect the research process outlined in Chapter 1. As explained there, this need not always be the way that criminological research proceeds, but elements of that model will be relevant to criminological research at various points in its progress, even if not in that exact order.
- Finally, we would highlight the key role played by the use of hypotheses in linking the parts of the study together. The hypotheses made it possible to turn some general issues into specifically observable events, and then made it possible for the results to be analysed and related to the initial focus of inquiry.

10 Researching the Youth Court

Background to the project

The Youth Court is the successor to the juvenile court, which dealt with children under the age of 16. The Criminal Justice Act 1991, s. 70 replaced the juvenile court with the Youth Court, dealing with a wider age range, from 10 to 17 years old. The study described here was undertaken for the United Kingdom Home Office as part of its plans to change the way that Youth Courts operate in England and Wales. The study shows how a combination of different research methods is used in conjunction with each other. It also illustrates the importance of being able to work with a variety of different people, representing different interests. We will start by describing the background to the project, next explain how the study was carried out, and then discuss the way in which criminal justice research often takes the investigator into engaging with the social and political context in which research operates.

During its first term, from 1997 onwards, the Labour Government was keen to make a number of changes to the administration of justice, especially as regards youth justice. For example, as part of its pledge to speed up the way cases were dealt with, it introduced a system of 'fast-tracking' persistent young offenders, so that they would be dealt with more speedily (Crow and Stubbing 1999). Shortly after coming to power the new Labour Government published a White Paper, *No More Excuses: A New Approach to Tackling Youth Crime in England and Wales* (Home Office 1997). Many of the proposals in this White Paper were implemented in the Crime and Disorder Act 1998. However, the Youth Court Demonstration Project (YCDP) sought to change the culture of the Youth Court without the necessity for legislative change.

The specific impetus for the project was a speech by the former Home Secretary, Jack Straw, that the work of the Youth Court was like a 'secret garden'.[1] This reflected the fact that, while the Youth

Court is in some respects like a junior version of the magistrates' court, many aspects of its work were not open to the public. The court sits in private and there are restrictions on reporting its proceedings, including the identities of those appearing before it. The Youth Court operates with a Panel of magistrates who receive special training. The result is a system that attempts to balance judicial requirements with a regard for the age and limited experience of those who appear in court. But for those not familiar with the Youth Court, there can be a lack of awareness about exactly how it works and what ends it is seeking to achieve.

The aims of the project were twofold. First, it aimed to have an impact on the offending behaviour of those appearing before the court, in the hope of reducing future offending. Second, it sought to increase the confidence of victims and public in the Youth Court. Around the time that the project was taking place, a survey was published showing that the Youth Court was an aspect of the criminal justice system in which the public had little confidence (Mattinson and Mirlees-Black 2000).

The project sought to address these aims through a series of related initiatives. The first was to increase the extent to which magistrates engaged with offenders. Prior to the project it was quite common for young offenders to take little or no part in proceedings. Much of the business was transacted between court officials and lawyers. It was hoped that if magistrates addressed young people directly, they would take more responsibility for their actions.

Second, it was decided to experiment with the layout of the court. Many courtrooms are set out in a very formal fashion in such a way as to 'distance' magistrates and officials from lay persons including defendants, witnesses and the public. In some instances this separation is achieved by the fact that the magistrates are on a platform elevated above others in the courtroom. The extent to which the layout could be changed was limited by the architecture in some of the older courts, but generally attempts were made to make the court less formal, and to bring magistrates and offenders closer together.

A third initiative was to try to open the court up more by encouraging attendance by victims and the press, and to lift reporting restrictions in certain cases. This last practice went under the soubriquet of 'naming and shaming'.

Finally, the project gave feedback to sentencers about sentencing patterns in the courts and other aspects of the court's work. This was intended to enable magistrates to have a better idea of what effects their decisions were having.

Theoretical context

Although much attention has been devoted to youth crime and young offenders by the media, politicians, the public, and criminologists, at the time this study was carried out relatively little research had been done on the Youth Court itself, especially the perceptions of the young offenders appearing there (Allen et al. 2000: 1). However, like many public policy initiatives the YCDP touched on a number of issues, but was not based on a particular, explicit theory. Nonetheless, this does not mean that it was without any theoretical foundations. There were, for example, clearly some implicit notions about the 'responsibilization' (Garland 2001: 124–7) of young offenders. The project also needs to be seen in the context of the historical development of youth justice and the nature of the Youth Court. The juvenile court had a more welfare-oriented approach, but even before it was replaced by the Youth Court in the Criminal Justice Act 1991, cases requiring 'care' had already been removed from its jurisdiction by the Children Act 1989. The decline in rapport and offender involvement reflected the replacement of the juvenile court with a court which mirrored the adult court, and placed more emphasis on just deserts. In the juvenile court there had been more of a sense of 'sitting round a table' to resolve the problems which underlay a young person's offending. The moves to change the layout of the court and to engage with young offenders more could be seen as an acknowledgement of the value of such an approach. However, it did not signal a return to a welfare-based approach to dealing with them; the emphasis was very much on addressing offending behaviour.

The YCDP also had a human rights element, which became more important as the project progressed. There was concern about the rights of young people when they appeared in courts, and this had particular relevance since the Government was at that time committed to introducing a UK Human Rights Act. The project was taking place when the European Court of Human Rights delivered a judgment in the case of two boys convicted of killing the little boy James Bulger in 1993, a case which had attracted considerable publicity and public concern. The judgment stated that the trial of the 10-year-old boys had placed them in a situation in which they were unlikely to understand what was going on. As a result of this, the Lord Chief Justice issued a Practice Direction which, although directed at Crown Courts, related to measures implemented as a result of the YCDP. This meant that in future all courts dealing with young people in the UK would have to have regard to this ruling.

The research

Before introducing any changes on a national basis it was considered advisable to try out some reforms to existing procedure in two areas to evaluate their impact. Consequently, in the summer of 1998 courts around the country were invited to apply to take part in the Demonstration Project. Two areas were selected by the Home Office, and the Project started in October 1998. This means that in effect the research design had already been chosen prior to the research team being involved. One of the areas was a single court located in the centre of a medium-sized town. The other area was a county which had five courts, one of which was in the centre of the main city of the county, and the other four in towns in the county.

The research on the project took place over an 18-month period, and was essentially a process evaluation. This means it was concerned with how changes were implemented and what could be learned from the process of change. Its purpose was to look at how the initiatives were implemented, what problems were encountered and resolved, how the various parties involved responded, and what could be learned prior to the changes being extended to other Youth Courts. In other words, its main aim was to assess the viability of the changes that were made. It was not intended to look at outcomes in terms of any changes in sentencing, or whether the projects affected reconviction rates.

Because of this it was necessary to gather a wide variety of information, both quantitative and qualitative. The main methods employed were observations, semi-structured interviews, questionnaires, and a small number of detailed case studies in each area. These were supplemented by analysis of logbooks in which magistrates and other court users could write comments, feedback on sentencing data supplied by the Home Office, and a telephone survey of ten other courts in the country where similar developments had taken place on the initiative of the individual courts.

Observations

Observations formed the backbone of the study and took two forms. The first was attendance at key meetings, 36 of them in all. These mainly involved meetings related to the project itself, such as Steering Groups and Project Board meetings, and training sessions, but also included 14 of the regular Panel and Court User Group meetings, at which the project was discussed. These meetings enabled the researchers to keep track of the progress of the project and the issues that arose at every stage of its progress.

The other kind of observations were in the courtrooms themselves. The main purpose of these was to examine the interaction between those in the court, in particular, whether the extent and nature of engagement between young offenders and magistrates changed as a result of the Demonstration Project. Altogether 1293 hearings were observed during 110 sessions, but in analysing the data most attention was paid to the 30 per cent of hearings where offenders were sentenced, since this was the occasion when the most important exchanges between magistrates and offenders were likely to occur. When observing interactions such as those taking place in a court, the most important thing is to get as much information down as possible in the limited time available. To do this a one-page pro forma was used to record details of the case and a sociometric diagram was completed to show who spoke to whom, and how often. An illustrative example is shown in Figure 10.1.

This example shows quite a lot of interaction taking place between the magistrates and the defendant and his support (in this case, his mother). The blank boxes could be used if any other people were present, such as a probation officer or social worker. Fuller details can be found in the Appendix to this chapter, which includes the pro forma and shows what kinds of exchanges were recorded.

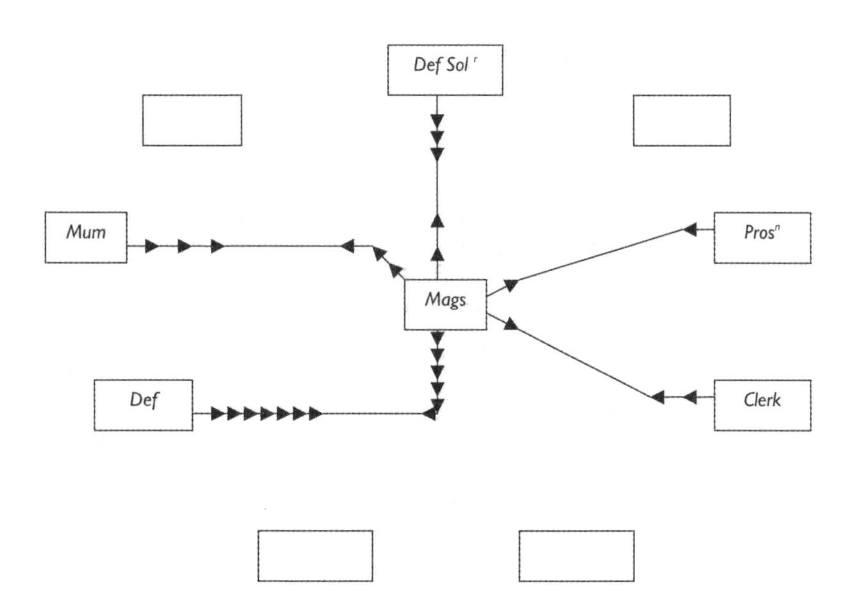

Figure 10.1 Diagram of court interactions

Note: Arrow heads show how many times people speak to each other.

Questionnaires

The other main kind of method used was to ask people questions. Again, this took two forms: questionnaires and interviews. While the main target for the questionnaires was the magistrates, a questionnaire was sent towards the end of the first year of the project to anyone known to be involved with the work of the Youth Courts in both areas, including clerks and other court staff, lawyers, and social workers who attended the court regularly. A follow-up questionnaire was sent to the same groups of people during a follow-up period about six months later.

The questionnaires asked people how much they knew about the YCDP, how they viewed the project, and about the changes that had taken place. The follow-up questionnaire covered similar ground, but also asked whether things had changed in the preceding six months, and explored whether people's attitudes towards the changes had shifted during that time.

An important consideration when using questionnaires is the response rate. One of the main justifications for using questionnaires in this study was that the research was done with the support of the Home Office and Lord Chancellor's Department, and with the willing co-operation of senior magistrates and court staff. A good response rate was therefore expected. However, the response rate to the first questionnaire was 54 per cent and to the follow-up questionnaire 51 per cent. As mentioned in Chapter 6, social researchers generally look for a response rate of around 60 per cent in order to have confidence in their results, and the rate in this study clearly fell short of that target. There were reasons for believing that the responses were not as disappointing as the basic figure suggests. For example, there were a number of magistrates on the register who did not attend court very often, and there were others such as social workers, who only appeared at the Youth Court infrequently. It could also be argued that every effort was made to ensure that those who wished to had the opportunity to make their views known, and that those who did not probably didn't have strong feelings about the demonstration project. Nonetheless this illustrates the difficulty of achieving good response rates for questionnaires, even with considerable support and assistance. Anyone contemplating using a questionnaire needs to think carefully before embarking on something that could involve a lot of time and effort, producing disappointing results. In the case of this project we felt the nature of the enquiry was such as to justify using the results of the questionnaires, but clearly the results need to be qualified.

In addition to the questionnaires, 26 semi-structured interviews were conducted with key personnel such as the Chairs of the Youth Court panels, and the chief clerks, and a selection of magistrates and other court users at three stages of the project: before it started, after it had been in progress for six months, and during the follow-up period. The purpose of these interviews was to gain detailed insights in to how the courts were operating.

Case studies

Twenty cases in each of the two areas were studied in some detail to examine at greater depth how the project affected individual cases. The progress of each case was observed through the court process to sentencing. Afterwards offenders and their support, if in court, were interviewed, as were the magistrates who sat on the case. Defence solicitors were interviewed where possible for an additional perspective. One case study involved an offender who was named in the local newspaper, so there was an additional interest here on the impact of lifting reporting restrictions. Telephone interviews were also carried out with the clerks of ten courts which had introduced some procedures similar to those taking place in the YCDP of their own volition about what had been done and with what results.

Feedback

Although magistrates' courts produce information about their activities, in the past this had tended to focus on administrative and procedural matters such as workload and time intervals in dealing with cases. Before the project started, relatively few details were available about such matters as court sentencing patterns, breaches and reconviction rates. During the course of the project, discussions took place about the type of feedback that magistrates might like to have regarding youth justice matters at their court and, in conjunction with the Home Office Research Development and Statistics Division, newsletters were produced and discussed at subsequent meetings. This development was welcomed by magistrates and other court users, who were particularly interested in receiving information about reconviction rates and the extent to which sentences were breached or completed.

Analysis

The material collected was analysed by a mixture of quantitative and qualitative methods. Written material from interviews, observations, and logbooks was analysed by hand, and ordered in such a way as to reflect the views of various parties towards the different initiatives. It was a source of quotations that could be used to illustrate the various perspectives, such as the comment of a magistrate regarding engagement: 'Defence solicitors speak in well oiled grooves and it is refreshing to hear from defendants; you are hearing something new rather than the standard mitigation.' This was mirrored by the defendant who said, 'At least they know that it's coming from you, and not something that the solicitor's made up.'

Clearly it is important when analysing and using such material not to be selective. It is useful to have a combination of quantitative and qualitative material because they can be used to complement each other. The qualitative material enables one to gain a better understanding of what the figures mean, while the numerical data gives one a broader view of the whole picture than is possible when seeing just a few cases, or talking to just a few people.

The observations yielded both quantitative and qualitative material. Quantitative analysis involved examining the number of times magistrates talked to defendants over a period of months to see whether there was a pattern of increasing engagement, whether they asked more questions, and the number of times that defendants themselves talked. It was also possible to look at whether the level and type of engagement were affected by changes in the layout of the court.

When analysing the questionnaires, distinctions were made between the views of magistrates and those who occupied different positions in the court, such as clerks, solicitors, ushers, guards and police. Differences between the different court locations also had to be considered, and when analysing the follow-up questionnaire comparisons were made with the first questionnaire. Thus, the main independent variables were court occupation, location, and initial versus follow-up questionnaire. The main dependent variables were those which asked people for their views and perceptions, often in the form of Likert-type scales. Usually simple bivariate statistics such as chi-square or *t*-tests were appropriate to establish whether there were statistically significant differences between such things as whether people with different roles in the Youth Court had different views about the changes in the layout of the court.

Policy-makers like the allure of hard 'facts', and there is a danger, where public policy is concerned, that the numbers will dominate the results. It is therefore important to strike the right balance between different methods. One way of achieving this is in the way that the results are presented. For example, the results from this study could have been reported by presenting the results from the questionnaires, followed by the results from the observations, followed by the results of the interviews, and then pulling together the results from the different methods. Not only would this have produced a rather tedious report but it might have given the impression of a 'hierarchy' of results. Instead we opted for a thematic presentation, using material from each method as appropriate. Thus, when reporting the results of attempts to encourage magistrates to engage more with young offenders and their families, material was drawn first from the interviews and questionnaires, then from the case studies, then from the telephone survey of other courts, and then from the court observations, with comments from the logbooks also being used. Further details of how each kind of development was evaluated using each method are given in the Appendix to this chapter.

Results

Although the purpose of this chapter is to focus on the way the research was done, it may be of some interest to note that there was broad agreement with the aims of the project on the part of the majority of those involved. Reservations were expressed by some magistrates and court staff about some aspects of the initiatives, such as court security and whether the changes might reduce the authority of the court. One of the main points noted was the fact that young people change a great deal during the course of the age range covered by the Youth Court; there is a considerable difference between dealing with a 10-year-old first time offender and a 17-year-old for whom a visit to the court has become a familiar experience.

Magistrates engaging with defendants and their families was regarded as one of the most welcome and successful aspects of the Project, but it was noted that training and guidance were needed if this was to be successful. It was also noted that some of the aims conflicted somewhat: a better engagement between magistrates and offenders could be inhibited by the presence of victims and the press, and the prospect of being 'named and shamed'. Although the project was not seen as particularly concerned with changing the way the Youth Court sentenced people, some magistrates said that engaging in discussions with offenders had on occasions caused them to reconsider the sentence they were initially inclined to impose. In one of the areas there was a shift in sentencing patterns, with a significant decrease in the use of fines, supervision orders and being sent to a Young Offender Institution, and an increase in the use of discharges and probation orders.

There were mixed reactions on the part of court personnel and defendants to the changes in layout that were made. Some felt it was possible to get used to the new arrangements and that they facilitated greater engagement. Others felt that space became very restricted, with people sitting uncomfortably close to one another. The indications from a follow-up study were that those involved became more used to the new arrangements with the passage of time, but this aspect of the project was regarded as having had the biggest impact on the culture of the Youth Court.

Attendance by victims was supported in principle, but there were problems in ensuring that it operated satisfactorily. In practice, few victims wished to attend court other than as a witness. What seemed to be most important to victims was knowing about the outcome of a case. Attendance by the press was difficult to ensure in practice and could be counterproductive in unduly increasing concern about youth crime, but the efforts at forging better links with the local press did raise awareness of the need for courts to make more effort to keep in contact with, and have a positive relationship with the press.

Although it was felt that it was useful for magistrates to have the power to lift reporting restrictions on occasions, there was broad agreement that this was a power that would be used only occasionally, in instances where the public needed to know that someone was a serious and persistent menace. It only happened twice during the period of the YCDP itself. There was concern that 'naming' a young offender could be counterproductive and give the young person involved an enhanced and undesirable status among his or her peers.

It is worth noting from both the policy and research point of view that the YCDP also had a general 'galvanizing' effect. It produced more communication, both in the form of such things as newsletters, and in the interactions that took place, not just between magistrates and offenders, but between courts and press, and to some extent between the people involved with the courts. In one area a special meeting was arranged between magistrates and young people to talk about the ways in which each saw the other, and this was an unusual and successful event. This galvanizing quality of research is not unusual. People respond to the fact that what they do is worth studying, but it also means that the researchers do not necessarily get a 'real' (i.e. normal) picture. It also means that whatever happens during a period of research is not necessarily maintained beyond the study period.

Conclusion

If we think of this project in terms of the model of the research process set out in Chapter 1, then at first sight it appears to have only a slight resemblance to the process outlined there. The project did not come about because a criminologist (or group of criminologists) decided that here was an interesting and important research question, derived from theory, with testable hypotheses. It came about because of a Government agenda which required the feasibility of certain developments to be tested before being used more widely. This is a common way for research done by criminologists to occur; remember we did say that the model was an ideal type, and not everything happens exactly that way. But the model is nonetheless relevant. As mentioned earlier, there were implicit theoretical and conceptual issues, and there were implicit hypotheses requiring empirical verification. It's just that these hypotheses related more to the viability of changes, the acceptability of changes to the parties concerned, and what impact the changes had on court functioning. Studies such as the one described here have some, but not all, of the features of what is often referred to as administrative criminology (McLaughlin 2001). This term is sometimes used in a pejorative sense, but such research can play a role in advancing understanding of the criminal justice process, and the way in which changes occur.

The YCDP research can be compared with studies that have taken place in the past, which have evaluated intensive probation. One of the classic studies of intensive probation was the IMPACT study that took place in the early 1970s (Folkard et al. 1976). This focused very much on the outcome of reconviction rates, using a traditional clinical trial research design, with experimental and control groups and random allocation. The largely (but by no means totally) negative results helped to reinforce the perception gaining ground during the 1970s that 'nothing works'. By contrast, a study of another attempt to develop intensive probation some 15 years later took a very different approach (Mair et al. 1994; Mair 1997: 70). The research involved process evaluation, and concentrated more on how the programmes operated. It focused on the viability of such an initiative, whether it reached the target group of high risk offenders, whether it diverted people from custody, and the views and opinions of sentencers and offenders, more than whether it reduced re-offending. It was as much about management as treatment, and reflected a very different theoretical, political and methodological environment to that which had prevailed at the time of the IMPACT experiment. The YCDP research described in this chapter is more like the second intensive probation study than the first. The Government's Crime Reduction Programme, which started in 1998, sought to examine 'what works', and evaluations during the early part of the twenty-first century once again tended to focus on outcomes measured by reconviction data. However, there are advocates of what is referred to as pluralistic evaluation who support a diversity of measures (Smith and Cantley 1984; Gelsthorpe and Sharpe 2006; Israel and Chui 2006). Clear (1997) and Israel and Chui (2006), for example, have suggested that researchers should consider the extent to which initiatives can benefit criminal justice organizations. The study described in this chapter falls into that category.

Another point to note about the YCDP study is the mixture of methods used, and the way in which they interweave with one another. A one-dimensional evaluation concerned purely with reconviction rates may well need to have regard to some process material to determine whether a project was implemented as intended, but is more likely to place statistical material at the centre of analysis to determine the results.

Finally, it is worth noting that the research carried out on the Youth Court Demonstration Project required the researchers to interact with a wide range of people in a variety of settings and contexts. This is a skill that is often overlooked in textbooks on research methods. The criminologist not only needs to know how to design and implement a project, but needs interpersonal skills if the research is to be successful. A 30-page, structured questionnaire has minimal value if one is engaging with homeless, petty persistent offenders who frequently have alcohol and/or other drugs in their bloodstream. Similarly, talking to magistrates and judges requires a certain decorum if one is to gain their confidence in getting them to tell you about their work. The YCDP meant being able to relate to magistrates and young offenders alike. In both cases it involved gaining their trust that what you were told would not only be treated in confidence, but would not disadvantage them. Inevitably when one seeks to change structures, as the YCDP was threatening to do, people feel defensive and guarded. Another party to this research was the Government, or rather officials of the Home Office and then Lord Chancellor's Department who represented the interests of the Government. Organizations at the local level – the Youth Courts in this instance – are often wary of the intentions of central Government, and it can be hard for researchers to tread the line between the two, especially if the central authority is the customer paying for the study. It takes time to overcome people's inhibitions, without at the same time becoming partial to one party or another. It helps to build in occasions when participants will receive feedback on how the research is progressing, as we did in this study.

Appendix: Youth court observation form

Defendant and Hearing	
Name: John Smith	Sex: Male
Date of Birth: 23/10/84 (16)	Ethnicity: White
Court: Ro Court 1	Date of Observation: 8/2/00
Time Started: 2.19	Time Ended: 2.34
List Number: 5	Number of Charges: 1

Type of Charge: Criminal damage – broken window
Number of Previous Hearings: 0
Purpose and Outcome of Hearing: Sentence – 100 compensation order
Date of Next Hearing ? N/a £
Rep. Rest. Application ? No Reason:
Accepted: ? Reason:
Court Layout: traditional ☐ alternative ☐ well of court ☑
Details: Defendant next to Mum
PSR: requested? ☑ used? ☐
Number of retirements: 1

In Court (no. of each)

Magistrates	_3_	Stipendiary	____
Clerk	_1_	Defence solicitor	_1_
Defendant/s	_1_	Prosecution solicitor	_1_
Parents	_1_	Youth Justice	_1_
details:	Mum	Bail support	____
Other family	____	Victim	____
details:		Witnesses	____
Other support	____	Press	____
details:		Probation officer	____
Guards	____	Other Prosecutor	____
Usher	_1_	details:	
Other	____		
details:			
Total No.	_10_		

Note: Rep. Rest Application=Application for reporting restrictions to be lifted

Magistrates' questions

	Def.	Def. Sol.	Parent	Clerk	Social	Pro. Sol.	Other	TOTAL
Present Offence	/	//				/		4
Offence History				/				1
Defendant Details	////		//					6
TOTAL	5	2	2	1		1		11

Use of methods by topic

Topic	*Interviews*	*Questionnaires*	*Case studies*	*Observations*	*Log books*	*Telephone survey*
Engaging with defendants and their support	✓	✓	✓	✓	✓	✓
Court layout	✓	✓	✓	✓	✓	✓
Attendance by victims	✓		✓	✓		
Attendance by press	✓	✓	✓	✓		
Lifting reporting restrictions	✓	✓	✓			
Feedback to sentencers	✓	✓				

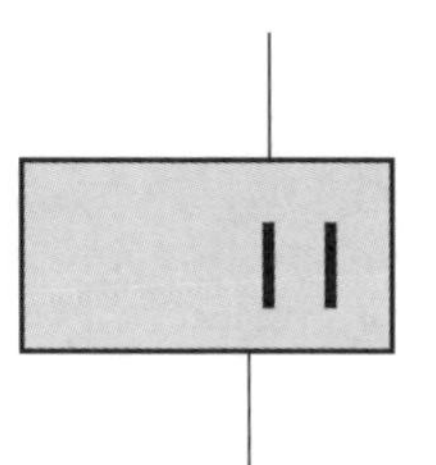

11 Researching a Community Safety Programme

Background to the project

In this chapter we describe an evaluation of a programme, the aim of which was to develop safer neighbourhoods. The specific aim was to reduce the likelihood of certain kinds of problem behaviour developing among young people, and to promote their personal and social development. We have referred elsewhere to the fact that evaluation is one of the most common types of criminological research, but evaluations can take various forms. The one described here is very different to the evaluation of the Youth Court Demonstration Project described in the previous chapter.

We will start by explaining the programme itself. Communities That Care (CTC) involved local people and local agencies working together to apply their knowledge about what factors in a neighbourhood are most likely to put young people at risk of developing social problems such as delinquency, drug misuse, school failure, and school-age pregnancy. The factors can include such things as a disadvantaged neighbourhood, high residential turnover, poorly performing schools, and poor parenting. They try to reduce those 'risk factors', and promote the kind of 'protective factors' that will encourage achievement and social commitment among young people, such as opportunities for pro-social involvement such as availability of youth provision. Even before saying any more you will realize that this is not something that can be achieved overnight, or even over a few months. Determining whether a neighbourhood has been transformed, and whether the children who grow up in this changed environment are indeed different to those who grew up there previously (or have grown up elsewhere), is going to require years. So it is a long-term programme, and this makes it particularly difficult to evaluate.

Communities That Care originated in the United States. In the mid-1990s, the Joseph Rowntree Foundation (JRF) decided to investigate the prospects for introducing a similar scheme into the United Kingdom, and funded a British-based version of the programme, to be run independently by an organization called CTC UK. Three pilot projects were established in the United Kingdom, and in 1998 three of us were commissioned to undertake an independent evaluation. A series of reports and articles have been published reporting the results of this study (France and Crow 2001; Crow et al. 2004; France and Crow 2005; Crow et al. 2006). As is the case with the other examples included in this book, this research involved a team of colleagues, whose work is acknowledged here.

Many initiatives that attempt to reduce crime, or change the behaviour of offenders, have a specific programme or series of activities set out in advance. For example, a programme for the treatment of offenders might be based on cognitive behavioural therapy, or a crime reduction programme might be based on physical changes, such as better street lighting, or better locks and entry systems for blocks of flats. CTC, on the other hand, sets out a process to be followed if the intervention is to be implemented as intended. The first stage involves a central agency (such as CTC UK) assessing and selecting areas that have the kind of conditions that are favourable to receiving a CTC programme (known as 'community readiness'). A community's state of readiness is liable to vary, and affects the chances of success, which means that CTC may not work equally well everywhere. The second stage involves local people and agencies, working through a programme board, in carrying out two audits. One assesses the kind of factors locally that are likely to place young people at risk of growing up to develop problem behaviours, and the other assesses what resources are already in the community that can be used to reduce such risks, and to build protective factors. In the third phase, an action plan is developed. In doing this the local board draws on a guide to programmes that have been shown to be effective in reducing risk, called *Promising Approaches* (Utting 1999) to identify programmes that might tackle risk problems in their area. The fourth stage, implementing the action plan, includes changing working practices and developing new initiatives where the audits suggest they are needed. The final phase should involve a review and re-assessment of risk and protection, so that local communities can evaluate the impact of their work and set new targets.

Theoretical context

CTC does not set out to test a particular theory of juvenile development, but it does have certain conceptual foundations. One of these is the proposition referred to above that certain risk factors within communities are associated with particular types of future problem behaviour. This proposition is supported by empirical evidence which has shown that certain risk factors within communities are associated with particular types of future problem behaviour (Hawkins et al. 1992; Farrington 1996). Risk factors include such things as lack of discipline in families, poor supervision by parents, under-achievement in primary school, lack of neighbourhood attachment, and having friends involved in problem behaviours (Farrington 2000). A risk factor approach to social issues has become widespread in recent years, but when CTC was being developed in the United States, and subsequently in the UK in the 1990s, the risk factor model was still a relatively new development in the social sciences. One of the main proponents of the model was also instrumental in introducing CTC to the UK (Farrington 1996, 2000), so CTC was an early test of the viability of such an approach. A simplified version of the model can be presented as shown in Figure 11.1.

However, it is worth noting that this model is based on correlations, rather than explanations; a theoretical framework is nonetheless required to understand the correlations. It could be argued that in fact CTC involves several theories, for example about the consequences of poor parental supervision and discipline, about disadvantage, about school disorganization, about alienation, and so on. In effect, every risk factor reflects some kind of theoretical position. Consequently, the proposition stated above of a causal relationship between risk factors and causal behaviours begs the question, where does the risk itself come from?

This takes us to the other conceptual basis for CTC, which is the social development model, put forward by Catalano and Hawkins (1996). They argue that child development is influenced by the quality of the interaction between children and adults, and that for children to grow up free from social problems, they need to be given clear standards of behaviour and have positive social bonding with adults. To aid this process, children and young people need to be given opportunities to be valued by, and involved in their families, schools and communities, to gain social and learning skills, and be given recognition and praise, ensuring that their positive behaviour is recognized. The social development model therefore sees the devel-

Figure 11.1 The CTC model

opment of pro-social factors as a means of protecting children from the consequences of risk factors. The CTC approach therefore advocates the reduction of risk factors and the promotion of pro-social factors that will help children to manage their circumstances better (Pollard et al. 1999).

We are including the research on CTC in this book as an example of an evaluation of intervention in a community, as opposed to interventions involving individuals. As such, the CTC evaluation not only constitutes a test of the social development model, but also has international significance because CTC has now been widely adopted in several countries, having expanded from its original base in the USA to countries in Europe, and to Australia. However, the evaluation of CTC has a wider criminological significance because of the role it played in a celebrated dispute concerning the nature of evaluation during the 1990s. It was referred to by those involved as the 'paradigm wars', described in more detail in Chapter 4. The evaluation of CTC featured prominently in that debate, even though it had not yet commenced at the time that several of the articles were written (Pawson and Tilley 1994; Bennett 1996; Pawson and Tilley 1996; Farrington 1997; Pawson and Tilley 1998a; Pawson and Tilley 1998b; Farrington 1998). An exchange of articles in the *British Journal of Criminology*, and the journal *Evaluation* ended with two of the protagonists, Pawson and Tilley, saying 'The UK evaluation of CTC will be under way by the time this exchange is published. Let us see what happens!' (Pawson and Tilley 1998b).

The research

Evaluating a programme such as CTC presents a variety of problems, which we will touch on as we describe what happened. The first thing to do, as described in an earlier chapter, was to define the research question. In the case of CTC there were actually three key questions. First, was CTC implemented successfully? As mentioned above, CTC involves carrying out a series of tasks. Clearly it was important to establish whether the programme had been implemented in the way intended. If it had not, then it would be unreasonable to attribute any failure to achieve the intended outcomes to a failure of the CTC model. The second question was, did any change occur? Since the evaluation only had a three-year life span, this involved establishing to what extent, if any, medium-term measures of risk and protection changed in the three areas (explained further below). The third question was, if there was any change, what might have caused it? To what extent could any changes be attributed to the intervention of CTC rather than to other factors?

Answering these questions involved two kinds of evaluation research: process evaluation and outcome evaluation. It therefore employed the kind of integrated model of evaluation referred to in Chapter 4 (Friendship et al. 2004: 14–15). The process research was important in examining the first of the research questions, and mainly involved qualitative research, including observations and attendance at meetings, analysing documentary sources, and interviews with the key personnel concerned.

The outcome research required to answer the second question was more problematic. The eventual aim of CTC is to reduce four problems among young people: failure at school, school-age pregnancy, drug abuse, and youth crime. Thus, the long-term success of CTC is to be judged by reference to these four measures. However, CTC is a programme which affects children as they grow up, and it may therefore be ten years or more before its full impact can be evaluated. Unfortunately researchers seldom have the opportunity to be around so long. But since the CTC proposition is that these behaviours can be influenced by addressing risk and protective factors, in the medium term it is possible to look at the extent to which there are changes in certain risk and protective factors associated with these longer-term outcomes. The best way of doing this was to see whether the perspectives of young people themselves were changing. In the CTC model a school survey is used as an indicator of community levels of risk and protection. Hence the main tool of analysis was to use surveys of young people going to schools in the areas concerned before the programme was implemented, and again some time later: a before and after research design.

The third research question involved drawing on a combination of both process and outcome research to make inferences about whether any observed changes could be attributed to the intervention, and this is where the research design is crucial. In Chapter 4 we discussed the nature of criminological evaluation and the techniques used. When applied to looking at communities rather than individuals the principles are the same – it is important to compare like with like – but in practical terms this is often more problematic. Although an attempt was made to compare the neighbourhoods where CTC was taking place with similar communities nearby, this did not work out, since the three intended comparison communities turned out to have important differences. Consequently, what we did was to compare young people going to local schools who lived in the areas where the CTC programme was taking place, with young people from the same schools who did not live in those areas. This also had the advantage of controlling for the schools variable – i.e. the possibility that schools might themselves make a difference. We referred to the three areas involved in the pilot study as Northside, Westside and Southside, so our research design took the form as shown in Table 11.1.

We now need to say more about the main method for measuring outcome: the school surveys. In CTC, risk factors are organized under four domains relating to the local community, school, the family, and individuals and their friends. The community risk factors include measures of neighbourhood disadvantage, community neglect, and a lack of neighbourhood attachment. School factors are measured by such things as low school achievement, bullying, truancy, and poor school organization. Family factors include poor parental supervision, family conflict, and parents condoning problem behaviour. Factors related to individual children and their friends are alienation and a lack of social commitment, early involvement in problem behaviour, and having friends who are involved in problem behaviour. The protective factors cover rewards and opportunities for pro-social involvement, such as being valued by parents and teachers and being involved in community activities.

Consequently, the questionnaires included questions about pupils' personal and social circumstances, their families, neighbourhoods, and school experiences, the availability and use of alcohol, tobacco and other drugs, delinquent and anti-social behaviour, and spare time activities. Identical questionnaires were used for both before and after surveys. Altogether, there were 195 separate items of information. Apart from collecting demographic information, much of the questionnaire was devoted to asking about young people's experiences of, and views about these topics. Their views were mostly rated on a four point scale from 'Strongly Agree' to 'Strongly Disagree'. Their responses to the various questions were put together to compose 16 risk factors and seven protective factors. Box 11.1 gives an illustration of five questionnaire items which together constituted a scale showing pupils' overall assessment of a risk factor measuring what kind of neighbourhood they lived in.

Table 11.1 CTC comparative design

	Northside	*Westside*	*Southside*
Pupils living in CTC area	X	X	X
Pupils not living in CTC area	O	O	O

Box 11.1 Risk Factor 2: Community Disorganization and Neglect SCHOOL SURVEY ITEMS	
Q. No.	Question
B2a	There are lots of fights in my neighbourhood
B2c	There is crime and/or drug selling in my neighbourhood
B2e	There are lots of empty or abandoned buildings in my neighbourhood
B2g	There are lots of graffiti in my neighbourhood
B3	How safe do you feel in your neighbourhood after dark

Note: Scored 1–4, Strongly Agree to Strongly Disagree

The questionnaire was administered immediately prior to the implementation of the CTC Action Plans in late 1999 and early 2000, and just over two and a half years later in July 2002. Nearly 11,000 children answered the two school surveys (5516 the first and 5334 the second). The surveys were completed at school, in confidence. Response rates varied somewhat between the areas and from school to school, but in general were very good, and show the advantages of being able to get questionnaires completed in such controlled circumstances. In Northside the response rates were 95 per cent for the first survey and 96 per cent for the second. In Westside they were 82 per cent for the first survey and 84 per cent for the second, and in Southside they were 79 per cent and 68 per cent.

The results were analysed by comparing the proportion of children in each area scoring positive for risk and protective factors between the first and second surveys, as a basis for determining whether any changes had occurred. The more items a child scored for a risk factor, the greater the risk for the child, and similarly for protective factors. It should be noted that this measurement of change was done at an aggregate level. In other words, we were looking at changes within groups of children from CTC and non-CTC areas, rather than looking at the extent to which CTC might have had an impact on individual children.

Results

In the other examples we have used we have reported the results as being incidentally of interest; our main focus has been on the study's methodology. As elsewhere we will report the results briefly, but in the case of this study the results do illustrate some important points about the methodology used.

It will be recalled that the first research question we addressed was whether the intervention (CTC) had been implemented as intended. In fact, only one of the three areas implemented CTC in such a way as to constitute a valid test of the model. In the area we referred to as Northside the project ran into problems about a year after starting, partly as a result of losing the Co-ordinator who was not replaced for some time, which resulted in little activity, and no meaningful interventions. In Westside there was more activity resulting in several initiatives. But these were undertaken alongside other developments taking place in the area, and were not of a kind that were in accordance with the CTC model. This highlights the importance of undertaking a process evaluation in order to see whether an initiative is doing what it set out to do.

Only in Southside was there implementation in accordance with the CTC model. Here 14 out of 21 risk and protective factors examined for this project showed a positive change for children who lived in the CTC area. Only one of these changes was statistically significant, so it is possible that the changes are due to chance, but the overall trend was positive. The analysis of the surveys in all areas showed an overall trend towards increased risk overall, and the indications were that CTC in Southside may have had an inhibiting effect in keeping risk lower than it might otherwise have been. Thus, looking at the picture with regard to medium-term outcomes, the indications were that CTC was of some benefit to Southside, but the results were mixed rather than strikingly advantageous. However, this does not tell the whole story.

It was also relevant to look at the results in relation to the activities taking place in the area. The CTC model requires communities to identify, on the basis of risk and resource audits, the risk factors that it intends to target, and the actions it plans to take. In Southside, most of the interventions implemented were targeted at family factors, and this was where the most encouraging results were found. There was also evidence regarding the reduced availability of drugs that could have been attributed to CTC-initiated activity. On the other hand, intended action relating to school factors was not implemented for various reasons, and the results for the school factors were not encouraging. This holds out the possibility that had more been done in relation to school factors targeted at CTC children, the results for Southside could have been better. In essence, our research showed that, while CTC may indeed be a line of development worth pursuing, it was as yet unproven.

Conclusion

To summarize: a long-term programme, intended to change communities in order to reduce the chances of children who grow up there developing certain social problems was imported from the United States, and tried out in three experimental areas. The initiative was evaluated over a three-year period by studying the process of implementation, and by using a before-and-after survey of children attending secondary schools in the areas concerned to measure the medium term outcome. Their responses were scored according to a series of risk and protective factors which have been found to be related to the probability of children developing social problems, in order to see whether the scores of the children who lived in the CTC areas had improved between the first and second surveys, compared with the children who did not live in those areas. The results showed that the programme was not implemented as intended in two of the areas, and that in the third, while there were promising indications, it was not possible to conclude that the programme had so far demonstrated significant success.

Several issues are raised by this study, some regarding the project itself, others relating to the nature of the research, and inevitably they overlap. To start with, this is a complex programme requiring a number of events to happen over quite a long period. It is more difficult to measure change affecting whole communities over a period of time than it is to evaluate interventions directed at individuals (not that that is easy). Then there is the school survey itself. As we have said, in the medium term, this survey of a large number of schoolchildren is the nearest the developers of CTC have been able to get to measuring what is happening in the neighbourhood that affects them. But like all surveys, we can never be certain that it reflects exactly what is happening. There are, however, various checks within the survey to test for reliability. For example, pupils who claimed to have knowledge of a drug called Derbisol were eliminated from the survey – because it doesn't exist; it was put in to see if children were exaggerating.

It is also important to point out that the evaluation described here occurred during the formative stages of these three projects, and of the use of CTC in the UK generally. There are different views regarding when it is best to evaluate a new initiative. On the one hand, it could be argued that programmes should not be evaluated until they are well established, because only then can there be a valid test of their operation. On the other hand it could also be argued that it is much better to study programmes from the outset because one can observe what is happening and why; if evaluation were delayed much valuable information would be lost. Generally it is the latter view that prevails, but concomitant with this must go the recognition that the results may not truly reflect what a programme is capable of. The fact is that, as noted in an earlier chapter, programmes change throughout their lives, perhaps because people leave and arrive, or circumstances change, so it is probably best to regard any initiative as a dynamic entity, and any evaluation as an analysis at a particular point in time. This is one of the reasons why the evaluation of criminological and other social initiatives is so different to, say, testing a new drug or certain types of medical treatment: the ingredients are more variable.

Alongside this is the importance of recognizing that the very process of being evaluated may have had some effect on the projects concerned, what is referred to as the 'Hawthorne effect' (from an early sociological study of an organization). While the researchers did make it clear that we were independent of the projects and there as observers only, we did give some feedback and produce an interim report (France and Crow 2001), and this was bound to have some effect. In real life, it is difficult to stand back and say nothing whatsoever to people with whom one has close contact over a period of time.

It can also be argued that there were too few instances of the CTC programme in the evaluation for it to have been adequately tested. Two other researchers with experience of community evaluations point out that,

> If the community is the unit of analysis, then the number of communities will be our sample size ... Using a unit of analysis of this size might make it more difficult to reach a sample size adequate for effective statistical inference. (Hollister and Hill 1999: 130)

This raises the question of how many projects are needed to constitute an adequate test of the model, but one of the proponents of CTC has argued that a large number of projects are necessary to evaluate CTC effectively (Farrington 1997). An earlier community safety programme in the UK, Safer Cities, based its analysis on 96 schemes, rather than the three available to us (Ekblom et al. 1996).

It will be recalled that in the model outlined in Chapter 1, the final stage of the research process was defined as interpretation. Regarding the results of this study there are three possible interpretations:

1 *Measurement failure.* This means that the intervention may have been more (or less) successful than described, but that flaws in the research failed to identify this. As we have noted, like any research, this study had its limitations, but we do not think that it was so badly inaccurate that the conclusions are misleading.

2 *Implementation failure.* This is liable to occur in any evaluation study, and clearly did take place as far as two of the projects were concerned.
3 *Theory failure.* This is the key issue. In terms of the model we outlined in Chapter 1, criminological inquiry derives from the examination of some theoretical proposition, and the main purpose of empirical investigation, such as an evaluation study, is to see what conclusions can be drawn about the theory underpinning the inquiry. As we described earlier, CTC does have a particular conceptual basis. However, what we have to infer from the present study is that the results do not allow us to conclude whether the theory underpinning CTC is a failure or not. This happens in research, through no particular fault of the researchers. What it means is that the case is 'not proven'. Lessons can still be learned, both about the interventions and about the way the research was done, but the results of this study showed that more needs to be done before it can be concluded whether CTC, and thus the ideas underlying it, are a success or a failure. Although this particular study has ended, other evaluations of CTC have continued in the UK and elsewhere.

12 Researching the fear of crime

In this chapter, we will describe a research project which focused on one of the most heavily researched topics in criminology – the fear of crime. This project is a particularly good example of how the research process can benefit from a collaboration between researchers who are working for different types of organization. Indeed, it is not uncommon for criminological research to involve a collaboration between an academic researcher or research team and a government department, criminal justice agency or community partnership. Sometimes, agencies will approach academics due to their expertise in a particular field and ask for help with their research; at other times an 'invitation to tender' will be advertised, inviting researchers to bid for the project. Collaboration is an attractive prospect for the academic researcher not only because it can bring funding (often the hardest part of getting a project underway) but also because it may alleviate some significant access problems by giving access to otherwise closed information. This was certainly the case in this project which was facilitated by the development of a relationship between a research team at the Home Office and a university-based researcher. There are, however, potential problems and limitations associated with collaborations like this and we hope that some of these will be illustrated in this chapter.

Background to the project

The research project was carried out during the period 1999–2001 and it is essential to begin by explaining the context in which it took place. In the 1990s, fear of crime had become a primary concern for policy-makers. In his extensive literature review, Hale (1996) had identified more than 200 articles, conference papers, monographs and books on the topic and that number was escalating with great speed. The vast majority of studies of fear of crime used a survey approach and attempted to measure levels of fear by asking people how safe or worried they felt in their everyday lives. This was, more often than not, conducted using structured questionnaires and the main hypotheses tended to focus on establishing who is fearful, what causes fear and how fear manifests itself (all of which are questions which need to be answered if the problem of fear is to be addressed effectively).

There was, however, surprisingly little consensus reached as to what factors influenced and explained fear levels. Gender and age emerged as the most likely explanatory variables, but even these were found to be unreliable predictors in many studies. The reason for this incongruity seemed to stem from inadequacies in the conceptualization and operationalization of fear of crime measures, many of which had existed for many years and had been perpetuated by an almost 'blind' acceptance of them as tried and tested measures by researchers. As a result, the questions which had originally been designed for the US National Crime Victims Survey and the British Crime Survey in the late 1970s/early 1980s were being used as standard, despite a growing body of literature which drew attention to their weaknesses. The study described in this chapter was designed at a time when researchers working in the field of fear of crime had recognized the urgent need to address some of the methodological questions which had emerged during the mid-1990s and sought to make improvements in the conceptualization and measurement of fear of crime.

Theoretical context

The research began with the lengthy process of reviewing the literature on fear of crime. The process of organizing more than 800 items of literature was complex. Once each item had been read, it was photocopied and filed alphabetically in a large cabinet for future reference. Short summaries of each item were written in a word processing package and organized according to topic (for example 'studies about fear and gender' or 'studies about fear and victimization'). Each summary contained details of the topic studies, the methods used and the conclusions drawn, together with a critical statement as to the usefulness or reliability of the work. In addition to the summaries catalogue, a separate chronological catalogue was constructed to try and trace how the concept of fear had been developed over time. This was important because in order to understand the methodological problems that existed, it was necessary to understand how they had evolved.

During this period of reviewing the literature, a whole range of interesting possible research questions emerged and at times the need to restrict my ideas to one broad question was quite overwhelming. There seemed to be so many unanswered questions and possible avenues for making a contribution to the field that it was easy to lose perspective on the research process itself. I was, though, able to eliminate many of the questions through discussions with other researchers and colleagues, many of whom were more experienced than I was. Eventually, one question did emerge which seemed to prompt a curiosity in the reactions of colleagues which was not present in previous discussions. This, for me, was the sign that the question was probably well conceived and worth pursuing! The question was: *how worried are people about financial crimes?*

The question itself had stemmed from my genuine surprise that very few studies on fear of crime had included financial crimes in their conceptual framework. I had read much about the perceived impact of being burgled, mugged or having a car stolen but never about the effect of losing money as a result of fraud. Repeatedly I told myself 'surely someone has researched this' but there was very little evidence that this was the case. The main reason for this *seemed* to be that fraud was not seen as something that had a serious or widespread impact on the lives of individual citizens and thus was not a pressing political concern. In many ways, it was overshadowed by the more 'newsworthy' and immediate crime problems that policy-makers were usually concerned with. This was particularly striking because, at the time, the financial industry had actually been reporting record figures in levels of fraud on credit and debit cards (plastic card fraud). Indeed, media reports were alerting the public to the potential impacts of these crimes, describing how they can affect the credit ratings and financial autonomy of victims. Moreover, concerns were being expressed in the commercial world that 'fear of fraud' was deterring consumers from engaging in e-commerce. However, a lot of this discussion was informed by market research studies and, although useful, they lack the theoretical rigour that criminological research has. It seemed that the time was right to start exploring the possibility of studying the fear and victimization of plastic card fraud more formally, from a well-developed, criminological perspective.

The next stage of the research process, then, was to build a theoretical framework which could be used to identify the key concepts and develop the hypotheses. There were essentially two key areas in need of theoretical development. First, it was necessary to take the broad concept of 'fear of crime' and establish a theoretical framework which utilized 'crime-specific fears'. It was important to know whether people had different levels of fear for different crimes in order to construct some hypotheses as to levels of fear of plastic card fraud. The second area of theoretical development focused on plastic card fraud – how do people use cards? how do they manage their accounts? where and when do they use their cards? and have they any experience of theft or fraud?

Fear of different types of crime

Perhaps the first question to address here was *what is* fear of crime? It was perhaps a little surprising to see that a concrete definition was far from forthcoming in the literature. Indeed, as mentioned at the start of this chapter, it is this weakness in conceptualization which has been cited as the primary cause for contradictory and inconclusive research in the field. The first stage here, then, was to unpack the concept of fear of crime and, through doing so, attempt to re-build a theoretical framework. This involved breaking the concept down into two constituent parts: *fear* and *crime*.

Whilst it is widely acknowledged that *fear* is a term used to describe a whole range of perceptions and emotions from general anxiety through to a state of terror, very little attention has been given to the systematic conceptualization of fear itself. In studies of fear of crime, fear has been loosely conceived in four ways and, although far from comprehensive in conceptual terms, it is helpful to explore the different perspectives that have developed over time. First, as an emotional response to the perceived threat of victimization. This approach might sound as though it has a solid psychological basis but, in reality, researchers have tended to focus only on asking individuals about 'feeling afraid' or, more commonly, 'worrying about crime' in their everyday lives. Only recently has the need to explore the complex psychological and emotional dimensions of fear been recognized. Second, fear is often conceived as a general perception of safety (often referred to as a 'global fear'). Typically, crime surveys include a question asking the respondent how safe s/he feels walking in the local area during the day and at night. However, this kind of measure has been recognized as unreliable because of its over-general nature and the need for respondents to answer hypothetically. The third way of conceiving fear is as a behavioural concept. This approach attempts to measure people's fear by their actions, that is, do they take security precautions or, for example, avoid certain areas at certain times in order to reduce their risk or fear? This is an interesting approach but one which is in its infancy and in need of significant development. Finally, fear may be conceived as a judgement of risk, that is asking people to judge their likelihood of becoming a victim of crime in the future. The now infamous 'fear-risk paradox' (the fact that those least at risk of victimization seem to be the most fearful and vice versa) has been the focus of a considerable amount of research and discussion, often resulting in the conclusion that fear is somehow an irrational response to the reality of crime.

The next stage was to address the *crime* dimension – what is it that people are afraid of? Although fear of crime surveys do tend to include measures of crime specific fears (usually burglary, vehicle crime, mugging, personal attack and rape/sexual attack), it was noted that most articles and research reports conclude with statements summarizing the reactions to crime generally with very few recognizing the implications of crime specific analysis. As Rountree states, '[s]tudies examining the crime-fear linkage tend to estimate the effects of *any* type of victimisation or a total crime rate on fear. Such an approach implies that there are no important differences in the effects of various crime or victimisation types on fear' (1998: 342). The literature review did, however, reveal some studies in which some general distinctions were made between fear of property and personal crimes. It became clear that property crime does evoke reactions different to personal crime (LaGrange and Ferraro 1989) but that the reasons underlying these differences are complex and yet to be explained. At best, we can hypothesize that an individual's attitude towards property crime and personal crime may be influenced by a range of perceptions including the perceived seriousness of the crime, the perceived likelihood of that crime occurring, and the perception of self-vulnerability (Skogan 1987; Rountree 1998). However, this did not bring me particularly close to how fears of financial crimes might manifest.

This process of deconstructing the concept of fear of crime was useful, despite the fact that it raised more questions than answers! It was important to understand that although not all of the conceptual problems could be solved in one study, an awareness of the potential threats to validity and reliability in the research was essential. This part of the theoretical framework had been constructed and the next stage of the theoretical development was to explore the concept of plastic card fraud and make the essential theoretical links between the two frameworks.

Plastic card use and misuse

There are characteristics or behaviours which can increase (or decrease) an individual's risk of becoming a victim of crime and these risk factors have also, to varying degrees, been used to explain different levels of fear of crime. These factors might include age, gender, socio-economic status, health and fitness levels, place of residence and lifestyles (whether an individual socializes, travels, works, etc.). One of the central aims of crime surveys is to measure the effect of these different factors and attempt to identify vulnerable groups in society. It was necessary, then, to find out as much as possible about the factors which can be associated with risk of card fraud victimization and the fear of victimization, to build as complete a picture as possible and inform the process of operationalization.

The starting point was to establish the different ways in which card fraud can be committed in order to build an accurate concept of the crime itself. The information produced by the Association of Payment and Clearing Services (APACS) was helpful at this stage of the research because the rates of card fraud are publicly available and routinely presented according to the source of the fraud. For example, it is possible to compare the rates of fraud on different types of card, the locations of frauds (in the UK or abroad) and the method used by fraudsters. It was this latter category which was of particular interest. Fraudsters use a variety of techniques to commit their crimes and it is important to conceive their 'target' much more broadly than just the plastic card itself. While a considerable proportion of fraud is committed using *physical cards* (either genuine cards which have been lost or stolen or counterfeit cards), fraudsters can also utilise the *card information* (name, number, expiry date, etc.) without being in possession of the card itself. Moreover, a significant proportion of frauds are carried out during the *application process*, so a fraudster may steal an individual's personal details and apply for cards or other forms of credit.

The next stage of building the theoretical framework was to understand how and why cards are used by individuals. This was important because it would provide the context in which the fear and victimization of card fraud manifest. The first thing to become clear was that it is important to distinguish between different types of plastic payment cards. Credit cards, debit cards, store cards and cashpoint cards are the most common card types and all have different uses and features. Credit cards and store cards provide a credit facility, allowing the consumer to borrow money in the short or longer term; in contrast, debit cards and cashpoint cards are used when the consumer wishes the money to be taken straight out of his/her bank account. Because each card type is different in nature, it is important to distinguish between them at a conceptual level. The second point for consideration was where people use their different cards. This allowed me to conclude whether people are most at risk of fraud when they are using cards in shops, restaurants, on the internet, to pay bills, over the telephone or at cashpoints. Similarly, it was important to know how often cards are used to establish whether the risk of victimization increases with card use. All of this was important because it helped to build a picture of the potential impact on a person's life and well-being that fraud victimization might have. So, for example, if a person becomes a victim of credit card fraud, it may be the case that his/her credit rating is affected. Where a debit card is targeted, the victim could lose money direct from the bank account and, perhaps, incur bank charges. In both situations, it is likely to take a lot of time and effort on the part of the victim to sort out the problem.

Another important element of the 'card usage' framework was the fact that individuals seem to manage their finances in different ways. Some people, for example, may simply keep their money in a single account and some have complicated financial interests distributed across many different financial institutions. Where some people have the ability to embark upon complex and profitable accounting enterprises, some people have financial problems which restrict their financial autonomy. Some people have special insurance to protect their financial interests and some protect themselves from fraud with preventative measures such as shredding receipts and only using secure internet sites. The point is that individuals operate within different financial contexts and these contexts may influence the risk of victimization and, indeed, fear. There was very little literature on these aspects, however, and so it was recognized that exploratory work was needed in order to build this part of the theoretical framework.

Theorizing the fear of financial crime

The final step in the theoretical development was to bring the two frameworks (fear of crime and plastic card fraud) together. Due to the limited amount of research carried out from the crime-specific perspective in the field of fear of crime, it was hard to imagine exactly what types of reaction financial crimes do prompt. These could be direct emotional or behavioural responses or they could contribute more indirectly to a general feeling of safety or unease. So, I decided to explore an additional literature base, the literature on white-collar crime, in order to seek guidance on any known reactions and attitudes to financial crimes. A number of useful sources were identified that confirm the serious impact that white-collar crimes can have. Pearce and Tombs (1992) note that when surveys do include questions on white-collar crime, often it has been rated as being more serious than many other types of crime. Ganzini et al. (1990) suggest that the victims of white-collar crime can be compared with victims of violent crime in terms of their responses and reactions to their victimization. Like the victims of violent crime, white-collar victims tend to be older, more affluent and are relatively more likely to be female. In terms of psychiatric outcome, general anxiety disorder and major depressive disorder are the most common psychiatric complications of both types of victimization. Also, for both types of victimization, a previous history of psychiatric illness and the degree of victimization are important variables in predicting the risk of psychiatric problems. Levi and Pithouse concur, arguing that, '[f]or these private victims, the victimisation experience could be likened to a (comparatively mild) sort of rape' (1992: 233).

Although it must be borne in mind that these studies were about white-collar crime generally (thus including crimes like embezzlement, tax evasion, consumer fraud and corruption in their remit), a lot of useful ideas could be drawn from them. There was, in addition, a small amount of literature which focused specifically on the impact of financial frauds and frauds which involved the misuse of personal information (of which credit/debit card details are an important element). First, in a study of pensioners who were victims of the Maxwell affair,[1] Spalek (1995) found that their experiences did indeed have a profound effect on their lives. In particular, their mistrust of financial institutions and advisers left them in serious doubt of their financial stability. Second, Grabosky et al. (2001) argue that to lose control of one's personal information is potentially damaging to quality of life. They allude to a deep psychological harm, 'the loss of one's private life is often accompanied by a decline in spontaneity, creativity, and a diminished sense of self' (ibid.: 176). Both studies were useful in building a picture of the potential impact of plastic card fraud on the victims and, indeed, the impact of the threat of victimization more generally. Finally, the theoretical framework was strong enough to move on to the process of conceptualization and hypotheses building.

The research

So, having explored the topic and identified an interesting gap in the field, the research question was broadly conceived to be 'to what extent are people victims of and fearful of plastic card fraud?'. The theoretical framework had been developed and the next stage was to draw up some hypotheses. However, it was appropriate now to think about the most appropriate research strategy to adopt. There were, actually, several possible research strategies which might have been suited to the aims of the research. As it was a completely new area of research, it might have been appropriate to adopt an interpretivistic approach, using open interviews or focus groups perhaps to properly *explore* the experiences and attitudes of different groups of people. It would, for example, be interesting to explore differences in attitudes between those who had and had not been victimized and this kind of data would be particularly useful both conceptually and theoretically. However, a positivistic approach was another possibility, allowing for the testing of some simple hypotheses using a survey approach. While there would be a reduced scope for theoretical development using this approach, its value lay in the ability to draw data from a larger sample and to make comparisons with data about fear and victimization of other crimes and other studies.

While either approach would have had been useful, there was one factor which ultimately had to be taken into consideration. Because this research was being carried out as part of a PhD thesis, there was no funding available for the empirical work and the scope of the study was limited to that which one person, in a short period of time could achieve. Fortuitously, at this early stage in the project, a rare opportunity arose to form a working relationship with the British Crime Survey team and to contribute some new questions to the British Crime Survey 2000. This was a significant and exciting development because it allowed for new questions to be developed and tested on a well-established, national survey. However, choosing this approach would mean that that there would inevitably be some restrictions placed on the operationalization process and that the analysis process would bring the many challenges associated with analysing somebody else's data (see Chapter 8). These issues will be discussed in some detail, following a brief description of the research itself.

Aims

One of the first things which needed to be established was the set of aims and objectives which would serve the interests of both parties to the research. This was achieved through a series of informal meetings in which possible areas of research were discussed and explored. It was important that everyone involved in these meetings was honest about their own interests and motives and that the boundaries of the research were clearly defined. It was also necessary to negotiate the legal and ethical issues at this stage. So, for example, it was agreed that the data would be anonymized before being handed over for analysis. Also, I agreed to give the Home Office team access to any work before being published. We also had the opportunity to discuss the potential difficulties I might encounter when trying to get to grips with the complex dataset and we were able to arrange training sessions to help alleviate any problems.

Since this was the first time that plastic card fraud would be included in a crime survey, we finally reached agreement that the aim of the research should be to *test the feasibility* of introducing plastic card fraud questions to the BCS. It was, after all, a distinct possibility that this relatively 'new' and potentially rare crime was not suited to the survey approach. This meant that a lot of the more complex theoretical and conceptual questions raised earlier in the research process would remain unanswered by the research but ultimately this was a sensible and more realistic decision. The objectives of the research were, then, as follows:

1 To design and operationalize questions about plastic card fraud.
2 To compare plastic card fraud with the other BCS crimes (in terms of fear and victimization levels).

It was hoped that by gathering this information about plastic card fraud it would be possible to draw some useful conclusions about the potential contribution which could be made to, (1) our understanding of fear of crime through the introduction of a financial crime to the concept; and/or (2) our understanding of plastic card fraud by attempting to assess the extent of victimization and levels of fear that exist.

Identifying key concepts and building hypotheses

Having developed the two theoretical frameworks, the process of conceptualization and hypotheses building could begin. However, at this point a significant design decision was taken by the British Crime Survey team that restricted the scope of the research. It was decided that due to space restrictions on the questionnaire, it was necessary to confine the plastic card fraud section to two questions only. The challenge, then, was to construct some effective hypotheses which could be tested through two questions on the survey (plus, of course, the data which would already be drawn from the existing survey questions).

Two concepts were selected as the key concepts; 'plastic card fraud victimization' and 'worry about plastic card fraud'. 'Worry' was adopted as the measure of fear here because it was identified as the most reliable of the existing BCS fear measures (see below). These were the only concepts needed to construct the primary hypotheses which both focused very simply on the success of operationalization:

1 Card fraud victims are identifiable.
2 Worry about card fraud is measurable.

There were, also, some secondary hypotheses which were developed in order to explore the nature of card fraud in some more depth. There were two lines of development here. First, to make comparisons between the fear and victimization of card fraud with other crimes. The focus here was on establishing whether card fraud was similar to property crimes in terms of victimization and fear levels, or whether it was more closely aligned with the personal crimes. For the purposes of this analysis, burglary and vehicle theft were taken to be 'property crimes' and mugging, violent attack and sexual attack were taken to be 'personal crimes'. Second, to test whether there is a clear relationship between the fear and victimization of card fraud. Accordingly, the following hypotheses were developed:

1 The incidence of card fraud is more similar to the incidence of property crimes than to personal crimes.
2 The levels of worry about card fraud are more similar to the levels of worry about property crimes than to levels of worry about personal crimes.

3 Victims of card fraud are more fearful of card fraud than are non-victims.

Methodology

In terms of methodology, there was little room for external input to elements of the design such as sampling and interview style as the BCS operates according to a well-established and rigid research design (this is explained in depth by Kershaw et al. 2000). In a way, this was a relief inasmuch as the burden of making complex methodological decisions was removed. However, it was extremely important that I developed a good understanding of how the data was collected in order to be able to design effective questions and conduct the analysis.

There was a great deal of work to be done in terms of question design and operationalization. The earlier literature review had not revealed any examples of survey questions used previously to measure victimization or fear of plastic card fraud. The International Crime Victim Survey included a question on consumer fraud (*'has someone, when selling something to you or delivering a service cheated you in terms of quantity or quality of the goods/services?'*) but nothing on plastic card fraud specifically. Thus, the key concepts needed to be operationalized from scratch.

The first stage of question design produced the following two questions:

1. People can steal money from other people's debit and credit cards, either by overcharging them or by copying down their card details/PIN and using them to buy things or withdraw cash. In the last year, has someone stolen money from you in any of these ways?
   a) Yes – overcharged
   b) Yes – card details/PIN used
   c) No
   d) Don't use cards
2. How much do you worry about someone overcharging you on your credit/debit card or using your card details/PIN to buy things or withdraw cash?
   a) Very worried
   b) Fairly worried
   c) Not very worried
   d) Not at all worried
   e) Insured against losses

However, after initial pilots (informal pilots using a small random sample of colleagues and students), these questions were rejected for two reasons. First, in an attempt to incorporate as many of the conceptual considerations as possible into two questions, the questions themselves had become too complicated and in danger of being misinterpreted. Second, it was decided that, in order to make the results directly comparable with the other BCS crimes, the wording needed to match (as far as possible) more closely the wording of the existing BCS questions.

Therefore, the following two questions were redesigned as;

1. As far as you know, including anything we have already talked about, since the first of January 1999 has anyone used your credit card or bank card, or your card details, such as your PIN, to buy things or withdraw cash without your permission?
   a) Yes
   b) No

2. How worried are you about someone using your credit card or bank card details, such as your PIN, to buy things or withdraw cash without your permission?
   a) Very worried
   b) Fairly worried
   c) Not very worried
   d) Not at all worried
   e) (N/A – don't use cards)

Both questions were piloted as part of the formal BCS piloting exercise which occurs before the sweep is conducted (Hales et al. 2000). The questions piloted well and no further changes were necessary. The narrow scope of the questions reduced the range of final conclusions which could be drawn but they did allow the hypotheses to be tested. This ultimately reflected the overarching aim which was, if we recall, to test the feasibility of introducing plastic card fraud to the survey.

Results

The dataset was provided in SPSS format and had already been 'cleaned' by the data collection company to remove discrepancies and any information which may have led to the identification of respondents. This was helpful because it meant that the data were ready for immediate analysis. On opening the dataset, the first thing to strike me was the sheer size of the BCS dataset. It was larger than any dataset I had ever encountered, containing data from more than 20,000 respondents. The challenge, then, was to learn how the dataset was constructed and how it should be handled. An essential tool here was the 'Technical Report', a large document which contained all the information about the survey methodology and the questionnaire. Without this, the analysis of the data would have been almost impossible, for the reasons we outlined earlier in the book in Chapter 8 (analysing official data).

The analysis was conducted in a systematic way, focusing on the hypotheses which had been set earlier in the research process. The results will be presented briefly below, dealing first with the primary hypotheses and then the secondary hypotheses. The implications of these results will be discussed in the section that follows.

Primary hypotheses

1 Card fraud victims are identifiable.

Table 12.1 shows that 2 per cent of respondents had been a victim of card fraud in the last year (12 months from 1/1/99), on a par with victimization levels for theft of a vehicle and mugging/robbery for the same period. Victims of card fraud, it seems, *are* aware of their victimization and *do* report the event to the interviewer.

2 Worry about card fraud is measurable.

Here we were concerned with the question of whether card fraud is something people *actually* worry about, or would inclusion in the survey be fruitless? Table 12.2 shows the distribution of respondents across worry levels for card fraud. Just under half of respondents (49 per cent) were worried about card fraud to some extent (very worried or fairly worried). Indeed, it was encouraging, and somewhat unexpected, to find that 'very worried' levels (used by the

Table 12.1 Percentage of victims for each crime

	Victims (%)
Burglary	3
Card fraud	2
Theft of vehicle	2
Theft from vehicle	9
Mugging/robbery	2
Violent attack	4
Sexual attack	0.4

Source: BCS (2000)

Home Office as an indicator of fear, see Kershaw et al. 2000) for card fraud were comparatively high (18 per cent of respondents were very worried about card fraud). However, there were also a lot of people who said that they were not at all worried about card fraud and this was particularly interesting because the same observation can be made for the personal crimes (when compared with the property crimes).

Secondary hypotheses

If we recall, there were some secondary hypotheses that were designed to make comparisons between the fear and victimization of card fraud with other crimes in an attempt to explore the nature of the phenomenon in some more depth. The focus here was on establishing whether card fraud was similar to property crimes in terms of victimization and fear levels, or whether it was more closely aligned with the personal crimes. The secondary hypotheses were:

1 *The incidence of card fraud is more similar to the incidence of property crimes than to personal crimes.*

As we saw earlier in Table 12.1, 2 per cent of respondents had been a victim of card fraud. This figure was on a par with victimization levels for theft of a vehicle and mugging/robbery, but lower than rates for burglary and mugging. The conclusion here was that victimization rates need to be interpreted independently and cannot be contrasted on the grounds that they are 'personal' or 'property' crimes.

Table 12.2 Worry about crime

	% Very worried	*% Fairly worried*	*% Not very worried*	*% Not at all worried*
Theft of vehicle	20	36	33	11
Burglary	19	38	35	8
Rape	19	13	28	41
Card fraud	18	31	31	20
Attack	18	25	39	19
Mugging	17	27	42	15
Theft from vehicle	15	36	36	12

Source: BCS (2000)

2 The levels of worry about card fraud are more similar to the levels of worry about property crimes than to levels of worry about personal crimes.

In order to address this hypothesis, it was necessary to look more closely at the distribution and dispersion of the worry variables for all of the crimes. Beginning with the worry variables, Table 12.3 shows the distribution and dispersion values. It became clear that worry about card fraud does not follow the same distribution patterns as the other property crimes. First, looking at the average values (mean and mode) for worry about card fraud compared with the other crimes, we can see that the averages for card fraud are closer to the personal crime averages, reflecting the lower levels of worry for those crimes. Indeed, the distributions for worry about burglary, theft of vehicle and theft from vehicle are positively skewed but card fraud, like the four personal crimes, is negatively skewed (but the skewness is notably smaller than for the other personal crimes). Furthermore, card fraud has a higher value of variance and thus, in terms of dispersion, is more similar to worry about rape and attack than the other property crimes (which are less dispersed and more clustered around the average).

To summarize, then, at a crime-specific level one can conclude that there are distinct differences in the distribution and dispersion of respondents across crimes. Card fraud has a similarly shaped distribution to its property crime counterparts but the respondents are well dispersed across the four worry categories, a feature more strongly associated with the personal crimes (especially attack and rape). We might interpret this to mean that worry about card fraud is influenced by a range of factors, people may be more or less worried for a range of different reasons. The analysis does not tell us what those factors are, of course, but it does reinforce the need for a complex theoretical framework in understanding fear of card fraud.

3 Victims of card fraud are more fearful of card fraud than are non-victims.

The results showed that, for each crime, victims are significantly more likely to be worried about that crime. So, for example, victims of burglary are more likely to be 'very worried' about burglary than non-victims of burglary. Similarly, non-victims are more likely to be 'not at all worried' about the crime. Table 12.4 shows that the victims of card fraud have similar worry distributions to the victims of the other property crimes – they are more clustered around the top end of the worry scale and more likely to be very worried. Victims of mugging and attack are less worried than victims of property crime, differing little from their non-victim counterparts in

Table 12.3 Distribution and dispersion of worry variables

	Skewness (S.E.)	*Kurtosis (S.E.)*	*Mean*	*Mode*	*Variance*
Burglary	.069 (.018)	-.751 (.035)	2.3	2	.77
Theft of vehicle	.086 (.021)	-.850 (0.41)	2.4	2	.85
Theft from vehicle	.006 (.021)	-.752 (.041)	2.5	2	.80
Card fraud	-.024 (.027)	-1.065 (.054)	2.5	3	1.00
Mugging	-.205 (.018)	-.854 (.035)	2.5	3	.88
Rape	-.597 (.018)	-1.071 (.037)	2.9	4	1.28
Attack	-.212 (.018)	-.960 (.035)	2.6	3	.96
Insult	-.418 (.018)	-.554 (.035)	2.9	3	.80

Source: BCS (2000)

Note: For the purposes of analysis, the levels of worry were coded as follows: very worried = 1, fairly worried = 2, not very worried = 3 and not at all worried = 4. Therefore, a lower mean/mode score indicates a higher level of worry

worry levels and variance across levels. Rape victims, however, are considerably more worried than non-victims but, interestingly, more dispersed across worry levels than the victims of the other crimes. From this we might conclude that the victims of card fraud have a heightened level of fear but we must be careful not to assume that that victimization *causes* the fear. Further research would be needed to establish a causal link.

Conclusion

There were a number of conclusions to be drawn from the analysis of the data. Most importantly, this was the first attempt to introduce plastic card fraud to a national victimization survey and it was reasonable to conclude that it was a successful enterprise. Despite fears to the contrary, the results reveal a significant level of

Table 12.4 Distribution and dispersion of worry for victims and non-victims of each crime

	Victims					*Non-victims*				
	Mode	*Mean*	*Variance*	*Skewness (SE)*	*Kurtosis (SE)*	*Mode*	*Mean*	*Variance*	*Skewness (SE)*	*Kurtosis (SE)*
Burglary	1	1.9	.79	.72 (.11)	-.38 (.22)	2	2.3	.76	.56 (.02)	-.74 (.04)
Theft of vehicle	1	1.7	.72	1.03 (.13)	.29 (.26)	2	2.4	.84	.07 (.02)	-.84 (.04)
Theft from vehicle	2	2.1	.77	.41 (.07)	-.58 (.14)	3	2.5	.78	-.03 (.02)	-.73 (.04)
Card fraud	1	1.9	.80	.73 (.17)	-.41 (.34)	3	2.6	1.00	.04 (.03)	1.06 (.06)
Mugging	3	2.3	.89	.11 (.11)	-.99 (.23)	3	2.6	.88	-.21 (.02)	-.85 (.04)
Attack	3	2.5	.95	-.05 (.09)	-1.01 (.18)	3	2.6	.96	-.22 (.02)	-.96 (.04)
Sexual attack	1	2.2	1.15	.28 (.27)	-1.25 (.54)	4	2.9	1.28	-.60 (.02)	-1.10 (.04)

Source: BCS (2000)

Note: For the purposes of analysis, the levels of worry were coded as follows: very worried = 1, fairly worried = 2, not very worried = 3 and not at all worried = 4. Therefore, a lower mean/mode score indicates a higher level of worry

victimization, together with an emergent 'fear of plastic card fraud' and the main objective of the research had been achieved.

If you recall, it had been hoped that by gathering this information about plastic card fraud it would be possible to draw some useful conclusions about the potential contribution which could be made to (1) our understanding of fear of crime through the introduction of a financial crime to the concept; and/or (2) our understanding of plastic card fraud by attempting to assess the extent of victimization and levels of fear that exist. Although this research only represents the first step in building a more accurate picture of the phenomenon of fear of crime, it was encouraging to gain some insight into the contribution further survey work might make. In addition to establishing that 2 per cent of respondents had been victims of card fraud in the preceding year, it became clear that worry about card fraud appears to be relatively high. This certainly suggests that inclusion in future survey work has the potential to bring a new and significant conceptual perspective to the fear of crime.

The research did raise a number of questions which clearly need further thought. Reflecting on the original theoretical perspectives, the most interesting question which arises is: *why do so many people worry about card fraud?* Actually, individuals rarely suffer financial loss in the event of fraud, it is usually the retailer or the financial institution which bears the risk so there were two possible explanations for this apparent paradox: *either* cardholders are under the misconception that they, as individuals, are liable for the cost of the fraud, *or* they are worried about some other aspect of the crime, something beyond the simple loss of money. Either way, a great deal could be learned by further exploratory research. Whether such research will take place remains to be seen, however. Following its successful inclusion in the BCS 2000 and a subsequent brief appearance in the 'Technology Crime' module in the 2002 sweep of the BCS, plastic card fraud has since been dropped from the survey. Although this is a frustrating conclusion, it needs to be understood in the context of policy-driven research. In this case, the Home Office do have a responsibility to research areas of public concern and it simply is not possible to measure everything. Anyway, future developments may indeed be better suited to quite different methodologies and the very fact that this research establishes a foundation to be built upon should not be under-valued.

Final reflections on the research process itself were positive. Were it not for the opportunity to collaborate with the British Crime Survey team, a project of this scale would simply not have been possible. In practical terms, I did not have to run extensive piloting, train interviewers, organize access or even pay for the research! I was able to avoid a lot of problems of the more complicated decisions relating to sampling and questionnaire design, allowing me to concentrate on the development of my small section of the questionnaire. However, there were also some disadvantages. The most significant disadvantage was the restriction on the number of questions I was permitted to use. This meant that many of the conceptual distinctions I had made earlier in the research process had to be set aside. Ultimately, then, my hypotheses were limited. Also, the fact that I had no control over the methodology could be seen as a disadvantage. When a researcher surrenders control of the research design, s/he loses control over the issues of validity and reliability. This was a particular issue when it came to wording the new survey questions. There was a continual tension between maintaining consistency within the questionnaire itself and allowing for conceptual innovation. Finally, the amount of time it took to learn to navigate the dataset could be seen as a disadvantage. It is difficult at the best of times to use a dataset that someone else has designed, but with a dataset as large as this one it was particularly challenging. That having been said, I was provided with the Technical Report and this was a great help.

We hope that this chapter has helped to illustrate a number of important issues. It is, as we said at the start of the chapter, quite common for criminological research to be conducted through a collaboration of researchers or research teams. Such collaborations can be extremely positive but they do require careful consideration. Compromise and negotiation will be necessary and it is important that you are clear from the outset what it is you wish to achieve out of the collaboration. You have to be very clear of the principles you will prioritize because, at the end of the day, you want to produce research that is valid and useful.

13 Concluding comments: Taking it further

'Research methods' is sometimes thought to be a rather dry subject, something that has to be endured before getting on to the more interesting topics. Research is, in fact, a rewarding journey of discovery. It is where substantive criminology comes from; it is the production of knowledge, and what could be more exciting than that? It also requires creativity and innovation. First, you need to have ideas, and while these can be stimulated by reading and discussion, it is your own experiences, observations and thoughts that will produce the ideas for research. Second, you need to be prepared to adapt and think laterally. Books such as this can give you a basic knowledge, but inevitably the day comes when you have to think it out for yourself. To give an example from one of our own experiences, when you find yourself being asked to do some research on a day centre for homeless alcoholics, you suddenly realize that a 30-page questionnaire has limited value and that you'd better think of something else!

In this book we have sought to explain that criminological research is part of an integrated process of inquiry. We have described some of the methods that are used to further that inquiry, and we have given examples of the ways in which inquiries can be pursued. Inevitably there are many things that we have not done. We could have covered some topics in more detail, and we could have covered many others not touched on. For example, much criminological research now has an international and comparative dimension. This requires the consideration of a whole range of issues that are beyond the scope of this book, although the same kind of principles apply to comparative research as to other forms of inquiry. We hope we have produced an introduction to researching criminology that can be used as the basis for further exploration. We end by briefly indicating how you might extend your understanding of what is involved in researching criminology, and start thinking about conducting your own research.

The first thing to say is that the opportunities for researching criminology are greater than ever before, for both students and practitioners. There are more criminology courses available at universities than previously, and many of those (including our own) will include the opportunity for students to do a research project at first hand. We believe that there should be a strong emphasis on 'learning through research' in criminology, encouraging students to work individually or in groups on research projects under the guidance of an experienced member of staff. What is exciting about this approach is that those studying criminology can make a genuine contribution to the discipline by means of online student journals, student conferences, and sessions dedicated to work by students at major conferences (such as the annual British Criminology Conference and the European Criminology Conference). There are also opportunities to work with academic staff on projects they are engaged in. In all this, of course, it is important to ensure that the safety and well-being of students and participants are protected and therefore student research needs to be carefully organized and supervised.

For those people working outside of academia, there are also many opportunities to contribute to the field of criminology (and often have a more direct impact on crime policy). However, becoming involved with criminological research in the longer term requires developing a new range of skills and information. Perhaps the biggest hurdle is the fact that you need money to conduct research, so it is important that you know how to go about getting it (and how to spend it once you have it!). Sadly crime and criminality are a major cause of concern in society, but this does mean that the need to know more about it produces a range of resources for research. The most common sources of funding include the following:[1]

- Research Councils. The main research council covering the social sciences, including criminology, is the Economic and Social Research Council (ESRC). However, other funding councils may also be relevant, including the Arts and Humanities Research Board (AHRB) if one is interested in, say, historical research on crime, or other forms of inquiry that do not include empirical social science. The Engineering and Physical Sciences Research Council (EPSRC) has funded a programme called 'Think Crime'. It is important to check out the research council's requirements to ensure that you choose the right one.
- Government departments and agencies. A major source of funding for criminological research has been the Home Office, which in May 2007 was reorganized to create a Ministry of Justice. Other government agencies include the Statistics Commission, and the Law Commission, and the Scottish Office funds research north of the border.
- Charitable foundations. A valuable source of funding for criminologists is a wide range of charitable trusts. The larger national ones include the Nuffield Foundation, the Joseph Rowntree Foundation, and the Leverhume Trust. However, there are others

which can be found in the Directory of Grant Making Trusts. If you are considering focusing on a particular geographical area it is also worth seeking out local funding agencies. The Barrow Cadbury Trust, for example, can fund research particularly concerned with the West Midlands area.

- Specialist agencies. There are certain agencies working in criminal justice which from time to time need research into issues that they are addressing, such as Crime and Disorder Partnerships, police forces, Victim Support, NACRO, and community groups. However, they tend not to have research funding as such and it is really a matter of working alongside them to understand what is needed. If they are able to fund any research the amounts are likely to be limited.
- International funders. At the other end of the scale is international funding, such as the European Union (EU), which has run a series of Framework Programmes, usually quite wide-ranging in scope, but often with the possibility of covering topics of interest to criminologists.

In order to obtain funding you will need to produce a research proposal. This is not the place to explain in detail how this is done, but in effect a good research plan covers many of the topics covered in this book. It needs to have clear aims, and a research design and methods that address those aims. It also needs to have a timetable and costing, and specify what the research outputs will be: reports, conference papers, publications. It may also be appropriate to say who will be most interested in the research apart from academics, such as practitioners and policy-makers. Texts which cover the writing of research proposals in more detail include Keith F. Punch's *Developing Effective Research Proposals* (2nd edition), and Nigel Gilbert's *From Postgraduate to Social Scientist* (2006). In all instances it is not a bad idea to contact the potential funding source to discuss your ideas informally before submitting a formal application.

The final point we want to make is the importance of research skills. We have covered a wide range of methods and approaches in this book and have highlighted the wide range of skills which are needed. A good researcher needs strong interpersonal, communication and observation skills but that is not the full story! The drafting and execution of a research project require skills that go beyond knowing about research design, methods and analysis. Research projects require management skills. The successful researcher will need presentational skills, and be good at both time management and the management of resources. By and large these are capabilities that can be acquired. However, he or she will also need good personal skills to manage relationships with staff, agencies and participants, and be capable of taking on board constructive criticism, and be adaptable and imaginative.

If you are the kind of person who relishes such opportunities, then you may wish to think about not only learning how criminological research is done, but how you could become someone who contributes to it. Ultimately, we have sought to give you a good grounding in the research process in this book to enable you to take your interests further. We can only hope that we have managed to convey our own enthusiasm about criminological research and encourage you to make creative and confident decisions in your own research. We finish by quoting one of our own students:

> When you understand how research is carried out, you start to look at criminology in a different way. I think I see the authors of the things I read in a different light now – I understand their motivations and inspirations. I suppose criminology has come alive! I want to be part of it now … I am itching to discover something new for myself. (Student (anonymous), University of Sheffield, 2005–6)

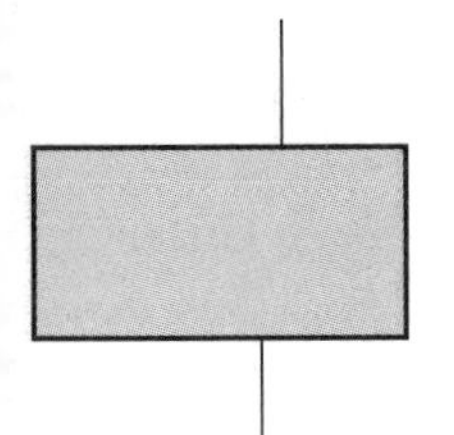

Glossary

Various terms used in social research have specific meanings, especially in relation to numerical analysis. These terms are described in statistical texts, and there are dictionaries that are likely to be particularly useful for the criminological researcher.[1] However, we felt that it would be useful for readers of this book to have a few of the more commonly used terms ready to hand, and therefore offer some brief descriptions, in alphabetical order.

Analysis by type of data and number of variables It is common to make a distinction between variables that are analysed using categories (e.g. sex has the categories 'male' and 'female'), and those that aren't. This roughly corresponds to the distinction between nominal data and interval or ratio level data. Information (usually referred to as data) may be analysed for one variable at a time (univariate analysis), two variables at a time (bivariate analysis), and in situations which involve analysing more than two variables (multi-variate analysis). Table G1 is a kind of 'map' showing which kind of analysis can be done in particular circumstances.

Degrees of freedom Having carried out a statistical test and got a result, you may have to look the result up in statistical tables in order to determine whether the result is significant at a certain level of confidence. In doing this you are quite likely to have to know how many *degrees of freedom* were involved in the calculation. This

Table G1 Types of analysis

Number/type of variables	*Categorical*	*Non-categorical*
univariate	frequencies, percentages, proportions	central: mean, etc. spread: SD, etc.
bivariate	two-way tables, chi-square	correlation
multi-variate	three-way tables or more	multiple regression

refers to the number of cases that are free to vary, and will usually be $n - 1$ or something similar, where n is the number of cases or the number of pairs in your sample.[2]

Just to illustrate the concept, consider the following equation:

$$7 + 3 + ? = 12$$

What is the question mark? It is obviously 2. If the answer is 12, then once the 7 and the 3 have been determined, the remaining term in the equation *must* be 2 – it has no freedom to vary. For example, we could have:

$$6 + 4 + ? = 12$$

The remaining term would still have to be 2. So, given the answer 12 and three terms in the equation, two have the freedom to vary, the third does not. In other words there are two degrees of freedom, or (where n equals the number of terms on the left-hand side of the equation) $n - 1 = 2$.

Usually it will be made clear to you how many degrees of freedom there are for a particular test, so all you have to do is look them up in the appropriate row or column of a statistical table (or better still, SPSS does it for you).

Hypothesis testing The simplest analyses are sometimes called descriptive analyses because by and large all we are doing is saying how many people there are in a particular category, what the mean of a variable is, or how it is dispersed around the mean.

However, the main reason why we use statistics is to ask questions – inferential statistics: if we know the mean age of a sample, can we make any inferences about the mean age of the population from which it is drawn? If we find that more people from one group are sent to prison (or are fined more) than people from another group, is this a real difference, or could it have occurred by chance? If we observe that the children of those who have more money get better exam results, how strong does this relationship have to be before we say that there is a real association? (Note that being able to answer these questions does not necessarily enable us to *explain* these phenomena; for that we have to refer to the theories that caused us to ask such questions in the first place.)

Answering such questions involves testing hypotheses to estimate the probability of a particular event occurring by chance. The examples given above are also examples of the main types of hypothesis testing that are employed by social researchers, i.e.

- whether a sample is representative of the population it is drawn from;
- whether there is a difference between one sample and another;

- whether there is an association between two phenomena.

Hypotheses are derived from the theories held by the researcher. In order to test them statistically, they need to be stated in a particular way.

Measurement 'The assignment of numbers to objects or events according to rules' (S.S. Stevens, 1951, *Handbook of Experimental Psychology*). There is a hierarchy of measurement which consists of four main types of measure:

Nominal – classification by name

Ordinal – ranking items in order

Interval – equal intervals between points on the scale

Ratio – equal interval with zero point

The level of measurement that applies to a variable affects what you can do with it: how it can be analysed and what kinds of statistical test can be used. For example, in a class of students we might be interested in students' ages and which sex they are. We can count how many are 20 years old, how many are 21 years old, etc. We can also count up how many men there are and how many women. These are the *frequencies* of particular ages and genders. However, gender is a nominal variable, whereas age is a ratio variable. For age we can calculate the average (or more properly the mean) age. But we can't have an average gender; all we can do is count the number of people who are in a particular category. Having said that, it is sometimes useful to calculate the *proportion* of people in a particular category – i.e. what proportion in the class are women – and in this way you can apply certain other statistical tests.

Scales are sometimes developed to measure hypothetical constructs such as attitudes. For example, one might ask a sample of solicitors whether they are happy with a particular piece of legislation and score them on a scale:

1 =	2 =	3 =	4 =	5 =
very unhappy	unhappy	neutral	happy	very happy

Scores may also be developed to measure such things as seriousness of offence, or severity of sentence. These may be comprised of several variables. For example, to develop a score of how serious a case is, one might combine scales reflecting the gravity of the offence, the offender's number of previous convictions, how long ago it was since his/her last conviction, and other factors such as the amount of damage caused or the amount stolen.

Null hypothesis The most common form of statistical hypothesis is the null hypothesis: a hypothesis that there is no statistically significant difference between your observations and what would be expected, other things being equal. The null hypothesis is designated as H_0. For example, if you have a set of data concerning the sentencing of black and white offenders, and you are interested in finding out whether they are sentenced differently, your null hypothesis is that there is *no difference* between the two groups. You then carry out a statistical test to test this hypothesis, and you may then *reject* the null hypothesis at a given level of confidence. Note that this does not necessarily tell you that black people are discriminated against in sentencing, because you then need to consider other possible explanations.

One-tailed and two-tailed tests A test may be one-tailed, if you are expecting a difference in a particular direction, or two-tailed if you are simply looking at whether there is a difference, but not in any particular direction. For example, you might be studying whether support and counselling for the victims of crime have any effect on their anxiety levels, and give them a scale to measure anxiety before counselling and again afterwards. If you simply want to see whether there is a difference, you would use a two-tailed test to compare the scores before and after. But if you are expecting that the level of anxiety will have decreased, you can use a one-tailed test. Using the one-tailed test means that statistical significance is more likely to be obtained. (This is because you are only using one end of the distribution of scores, so you don't have to split the probability between both ends of the distribution of scores. This may become clearer as one learns more about distributions and probability levels.)

Populations and samples A population is the universe of cases or units (people, things, events) with which we are concerned, and about which inferences are to be made, e.g. all magistrates courts *or* all the magistrates in a particular court. A sample is part of a population acquired such that it is representative of the population. The characteristics of a population are called parameters, while the characteristics of a sample are statistics. Much depends on how a sample is drawn; whether it is random or non-random.

Probability The concept of probability is central to statistical analysis and *is* important. We can only test hypotheses at a given level of probability. Derived from gambling in the seventeenth century by Pascal and others, probability theory as a subject in its own right stems from the publication of *The Analytic Theory of Probabilities* by Laplace in 1812. Probability is concerned with the analysis of quantities derived from observations of phenomena whose occurrence involves a chance element. It is the basis for hypothesis testing, calculating the chances of an event occurring out of the possibilities available:

$$P = \frac{\text{Number of “successes”}}{\text{Number of possible outcomes}} = \frac{\text{Heads}}{\text{Heads or Tails}} = \frac{1}{2} = .5$$

If a dice is thrown 36 times, you would expect to get 6 sixes. If you get it less or more than this, is it just chance or do we conclude that the dice is loaded, i.e. at what point do we reject the null hypothesis that the dice is not loaded?

Similarly, if we pick *at random* a sample from the general population then in theory half should be female and half should be male. On the other hand perhaps we are studying sentencing at a particular magistrates' courts, and we know from Home Office figures that 17% of those convicted of crime in a given year are female. In our sample 18% are female. Do we conclude that more females are dealt with at our court than nationally or is this attributable to some slight and not significant variation? At what point do we reject the null hypothesis that there is no difference between our sample and what we would expect, other things being equal: at 19%? 20%? 21%? To test such a hypothesis we calculate the probabilities using an appropriate statistical test. (A good explanation of the relevance of probability to statistical analysis can be found in Cramer and Howitt 2004.) Such analyses can only be applied to random samples, but there are *non-parametric* tests, which are not based on random probability.

Significance Test A calculation made to see whether a result that has been obtained varies more than would be expected by chance. On the basis of a significance test one may accept or reject a null hypothesis. Since it is seldom possible to be certain about what the result should be, a significance test is usually expressed in terms of the probability of its being correct, i.e. as a 95% chance that your result is different from what you would expect, alternatively expressed as $p < 0.05$ probability of being wrong. This is the 5% *confidence level*, i.e. we are willing to accept that 5 per cent of the time we are wrong in rejecting the null hypothesis. 5% is the level used most often, but there is nothing 'magic' about it; sometimes we might be more stringent and apply a 1% level of certainty, but it is in the nature of probability that we can never be totally certain.

In some circumstances we use *confidence limits*. If I go for a walk in the countryside and when I get back someone asks me how far have I walked I may say 'about ten miles, give or take a couple of miles'. In other words I estimate with reasonable confidence that I have walked at least eight miles and no more than twelve miles. These are my confidence limits, and two miles is my *confidence interval*, in other words 10 ± 2. In statistics, we are rather more precise and after an appropriate calculation we might say that we are 95% confident that the distance walked lies between eight and ten miles. Similarly, referring to the example used earlier where 17% of those appearing in court nationally are female, we can calculate that if the proportion of females in our sample lies outside the range 14–20% (the confidence interval being calculated as 3% in this case), then we can reject the null hypothesis that there is no difference between our sample and what we would expect, and we might conclude that, for whatever reason, women are more likely or less likely to be convicted at this court than in the country as a whole. (In the example 18% of our sample were female, and since this is within the limits we are prepared to accept our sample as being within the confidence limits, and therefore, on this variable, one on which we can base national generalizations.)

Type I and Type II errors If we only have a certain level of confidence in our results then, as explained above, we have to accept that sometimes the null hypothesis will not be rejected when it should have been, or be rejected when it should not have been. The first is called a Type I error and the second a Type II error (Table G2).

Variables As the name suggests, a variable is a characteristic that varies: age, height, gender, ethnic group, etc. Variables need to be unitary and clearly defined.

Some appear only as categories (gender, race, occupation, etc.). Others are more continuous in nature (time, money, length, etc.).

A variable is usually represented algebraically as x. Where there are several variables, x_1, x_2, x_3 etc. X is one value for a variable. Variables take different forms: dependent, independent and intervening.

Table G2 Type I and Type II errors

	Null Hypothesis Rejected	*Null Hypothesis Not Rejected*
There is a real difference	Correct	Type II
There is no real difference	Type I	Correct

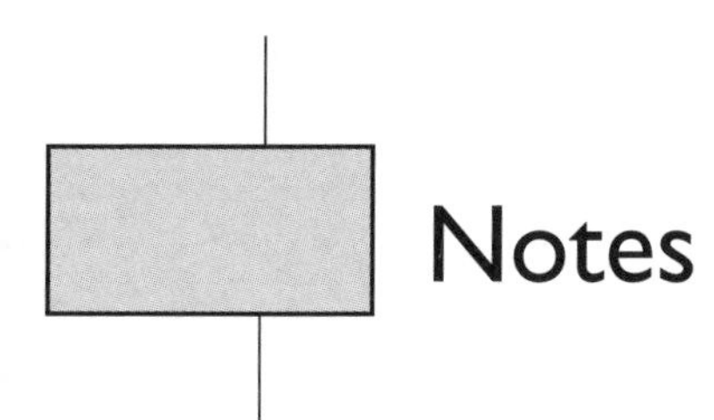

Notes

1 The research process

1. For a good explanation of the different forms of positivism and the distinction between positivism and the scientific method, see the entry on 'Positivism' by Malcolm Williams in the *Sage Dictionary of Social Research Methods* (Jupp 2006).
2. The use of observations and attitude scales are discussed later in the book, in Chapters 6 and 7 respectively.
3. See, for example, the July 2005 issue of the *International Journal of Social Research Methodology*, Vol. 8, No. 3, and Bryman (2006).
4. We lay no claim to this being a particularly original formulation. It can be found in one form or another in various texts. See, for example, Bryman and Cramer (1990: 3).
5. Attempts to do this may involve some supposedly 'objective' measure, such as having a certain socio-economic position, or by means of an attitude scale, whereby respondents are asked to say to what extent they agree that certain statements such as 'I don't feel that I belong to this society' apply to them. More is said about attitude scales in Chapter 7.
6. Observational notes are defined as 'Statements bearing upon events experienced principally through watching and listening', involving as little interpretation as possible. Theoretical notes 'represent self-conscious, controlled attempts to derive meaning from any one or several observational notes', and are reflections on what is observed. Methodological notes are 'A statement that reflects an operational act completed or planned; an instruction to oneself, a reminder, a critique of one's own tactics', and are observational notes on the researcher him or herself.
7. Organizations such as the Home Office, or the Joseph Rowntree Foundation, who fund research will want to produce a 4–6 page summary of findings.

2 The principles of researching criminology

1. The earliest theories about crime emerged from the Classical School in the early part of the nineteenth century. Both Bentham and Beccaria were part of this movement, focusing on the development of theories of crime, criminal justice, penology and explaining crime by human nature. They did not to base their

conclusions on systematic empirical work, drawing instead on 'common-sense observations and armchair reflections' (Bottoms 2000: 26).

2 The Chicago School led the way in these developments. They developed the positivistic approach in their ecological analysis of crime in the urban context. The city was their 'laboratory' and they advocated a scientific approach, but they incorporated anthropological methods of observation which were distinctly non-positivistic.

3 Designing criminological research

1 Defined here as the effect that one variable has on another: X brings about Y.
2 Of course, it is important to define what is meant by 'well off', and arrive at an appropriate measure of well-offness, which could be things like car ownership, council tax bands, proportion of children qualifying for free school meals, and so on.
3 A cross-tabulation is a table with one variable forming the columns and another variable forming the rows.
4 If repeated random samples were drawn from the same population then the mean of all the sample means gives an estimate of the true mean. This is what is known as the Central Limit Theorem. The standard deviation of the sampling distribution of the mean is referred to as the *standard error of the mean.* The standard error of the mean ($S.E.\bar{X}$) is obtained by dividing the standard deviation by the square root of the sample size:

$$S.E.\bar{X} = \frac{s}{\sqrt{n}}$$

The normal distribution has the property that 95 per cent of sample means fall within an area enclosed by 1.96 standard errors either side of the population mean. Thus the true mean will lie somewhere between $\pm$ 1.96 × $S.E.\bar{X}$. Thus, if we take a sample of offenders and find that their mean age is 21 years and calculate that the standard error of that mean is 1.2, then there is a 95 per cent probability that the true age of the population of offenders from which the sample was drawn is somewhere between 18.7 years (21 − 1.96 × 1.2) and 23.3 years (21 + 1.96 × 1.2).
5 Several papers presenting contrasting views were published by the Survey Methods Centre following a seminar on the topic (1994).
6 A brief, but useful discussion of snowballing can be found in the University of Surrey's occasional series on social research techniques (Atkinson and Flint 2001).
7 http://www.britsoccrim.org/ethical.htm.
8 This can be found at: http://www.esrcsocietytoday.ac.uk/ESRCInfoCentre/Images/ESRC_Re_Ethics_Frame_tcm6-11291.pdf
9 The basis for these can be found in Beauchamp, T. L. and Childress, J. F. (2001) *Principles of Biomedical Ethics* (5th edn). Oxford: Oxford University Press.

4 Criminological evaluation

1 It is, of course, possible that the initiators are being entirely cynical and only using evaluation to give some kind of scientific veneer to what was going to be done anyway, but it is to be hoped that this never actually happens.

2 This applies just as much to medical situations. For example, it was reported that a clinical trial of a drug (Tykerb) which might extend the life expectancy of women with breast cancer had been stopped early because of good results. When it became clear that progression of the disease was slowed compared with the standard treatment, the trial was stopped on the basis that it would be unethical to deny treatment to a comparison group that was keeping others alive longer (reported in *The Guardian*, 4.4.2006, and at http://www.gsk.com).
3 Internal validity is defined as a study's ability to determine cause and effect, while external validity is the ability to generalize the findings of the study to analogous situations.
4 A technique for analysing data that are hierarchically structured. For example, we may wish to make comparisons involving regions, towns, districts, wards and streets.

5 Researching by reading

1 http://www.esds.ac.uk/qualidata/about/introduction.asp
2 Hall et al. (1978) famously illustrated that statistics were deliberately used to manufacture moral panics and crime waves through his analysis of the treatment of mugging cases in the 1970s.
3 There has been much criticism of the fact that the Home Office is responsible for the administration of both the British Crime Survey and the Recorded Crime Statistics and it is recommended that control of the BCS should be transferred to the Office of National Statistics (the police statistics should remain with the Home Office as they are an output of Home Office administrative systems).

7 Researching by asking and listening

1 That is, social research relating to the law in general, rather than specifically criminological research. It is also sometimes referred to as law in its social context.
2 Often this will be individual people, but not necessarily. For example, to enquire about what methods different magistrate's courts use to chase up fine defaulters, questionnaires could be sent to the clerks of all or a sample of magistrate's courts.
3 Although just to confuse matters, sometimes the responses to a particular question need to be coded as separate variables. Types of response are mentioned later, and the way such data is analysed is explained in Chapter 8.

8 Analysing criminological research

1 To quote the ESDS's own description, it is 'a national data service providing access and support for an extensive range of key economic and social data, both quantitative and qualitative, spanning many disciplines and themes. ESDS

provides an integrated service offering enhanced support for the secondary use of data across the research, learning and teaching communities.' Access can be obtained at www.esds.ac.uk.

2 Variously attributed to Mark Twain, Benjamin Disraeli, and others.
3 SPSS can be used to display graphs of variables, and there is an option called the Explore command which will show the measure of skewness and kurtosis, along with other attributes of each variable. You need to read one of the books mentioned in Further Reading for a detailed explanation of how to use these facilities.
4 There are special kinds of statistics, called non-parametric statistics, that do not require the same levels of measurement as equal interval variables.
5 Because we are examining areas, not individuals, this is called *ecological correlation*. It is important not to confuse the correlation of one kind of unit (such as areas) with another kind of unit (individuals). The fact that there is a relationship between unemployment rate and conviction rate across areas does NOT mean that there would necessarily be a correlation between unemployment and conviction among individuals.
6 This data comes from an unpublished local study conducted in 1999, looking at fear of crime, using a postal questionnaire.

9 Researching offenders and employment

1 Full details of the study were published in Crow and Simon (1987), and a less detailed account in Crow et al. (1989).

10 Researching the Youth Court

1 Speech to the Labour Party Conference, 2 October, 1997.

12 Researching the fear of crime

1 In the early 1990s, it emerged that the proprietor of the Mirror Newspaper, Robert Maxwell, had used the company pension fund to finance his business interests. After his death in an unexplained accident in 1991, campaigners for the 30,000 Mirror Group pensioners mounted a three-year campaign for compensation. Their funds were largely recovered thanks to a £100m government payout and a £276m out-of-court settlement with City institutions and the remnants of Robert Maxwell's media group.

13 Concluding comments

1 All the sources mentioned have websites which can easily be found using a search engine.

Glossary

1 *The Sage Dictionary of Criminology*, compiled and edited by Eugene McLaughlin and John Muncie (2001), *The Sage Dictionary of Statistics*, compiled by Duncan Cramer and Dennis Howitt (2004), and *The Sage Dictionary of Social Research Methods*, edited and compiled by Victor Jupp (2006).

2 This is because the laws of chance on which probability is based assume that observations are independent and have the freedom to vary. However, when we use deviation scores the sum of deviations is zero, so that one of the scores is determined as soon as all the others are known, so only $n - 1$ of them are free to vary. Therefore a correction has to be made for any loss of independence or the estimate of the population parameter will be biased.

References

Allen, C., Crow, I. and Cavadino, M. (2000) *Evaluation of the Youth Court Demonstration Project*. Home Office Research Study 214. London: Home Office.

Arber, S. (2001) Secondary analysis of survey data. In N. Gilbert, (ed.) *Researching Social Life*. London: Sage Publications.

Ashworth, A., Genders, E., Mansfield, G., Peay, J. and Player, E. (1984) *Sentencing in the Crown Court: Report of an Exploratory Study*. Occasional Paper No. 10. Oxford: University of Oxford, Centre for Criminological Research.

Atkinson, P. (1981) Transition from school to working life. Sociological Research Unit, Cardiff (unpublished memorandum).

Atkinson, R. and Flint, J. (2001) *Accessing Hidden and Hard-to-Reach Populations: Snowball Research Strategies*. University of Surrey, Social Research Update, Issue 33.

Baker, K., Curtice, J. and Sparrow, N. (2003) *Internet Poll Trial: Research Report*. ICM. Available at: http://www.icmresearch.co.uk/reviews/2002/Internet-polling-paper-jan-03.htm

Beauchamp, T. L. and Childress, J. F. (2001) *Principles of Biomedical Ethics, 5th edn*. Oxford: OUP.

Beck, U. (1992) *Risk Society*. London: Sage Publications.

Becker, H. (1958) Problems of inference and proof in participant observation. *American Sociological Review*, 23: 652–60.

Becker, H. (1963) *Outsiders: Studies in the Sociology of Deviance*. New York: Free Press.

Bennett, T. (1991) The effectiveness of a police-initiated fear-reducing strategy. *British Journal of Criminology*, 31: 1–14.

Bennett, T. (1996) What's new in evaluation research? A note on the Pawson and Tilley article. *British Journal of Criminology*, 36(4): 567–73.

Bottoms, A. (2000) The relationship between theory and research in criminology. In R. D. King and E. Wincup, *Doing Research on Crime and Justice*. Oxford: Oxford University Press.

Bowers, K. J., Johnson, S. D. and Hirschfield, A. F. G. (2003) *Pushing Back the Boundaries: New Techniques for Assessing the Impact of Burglary Schemes*. Home Office Online report 24/03. London: Home Office.

Box, S. (1987) *Recession, Crime and Punishment*. Basingstoke: Macmillan.

Box, S. and Hale, C. (1982) Economic crisis and the rising prisoner population in England and Wales. *Crime and Social Justice*, 17: 20–35.

Brenner, M. H. (1976) Time Series Analysis – effects of the economy on criminal behaviour and the administration of criminal justice. In United Nations Social Defence Research Institute, *Economic Crises and Crime*. Rome: UNSDRI.

British Association for the Advancement of Science (1874) *Notes and Queries on Anthropology*. London.

Browne, D., Francis, E. and Crow, I. (1993) Black people, mental health and the criminal justice system. In W. Watson and A. Grounds (eds) *The Mentally Disordered Offender in an Era of Community Care*. Cambridge: Cambridge University Press.

Bryman, A. (2004) *Social Research Methods 2nd edn*. Oxford: Oxford University Press.

Bryman, A. (2006) *Mixed Methods*. London: Sage.

Bryman, A. and Cramer, D. (1990) *Quantitative Data Analysis for Social Scientists*. London: Routledge.

Bulmer, M. (edn.) (1982) *Social Research Ethics*. London: Macmillan.

Burton, D. (ed.) (2000) *Research Training for Social Scientists*. London: Sage.

Catalano, R. and Hawkins, J. D. (1996) The social development model: a theory of antisocial behaviour. In J. D. Hawkins (ed.) *Delinquency and Crime*. Cambridge: Cambridge University Press.

Cavadino, M., Crow, I. and Dignan, J. (2000) *Criminal Justice 2000: Strategies for a New Century*. Winchester: Waterside Press.

Clear, T. (1997) Evaluating intensive probation: the American experience. In G. Mair (ed.) *Evaluating the Effectiveness of Community Penalties*. Aldershot: Avebury.

Clegg, F. (1990) *Simple Statistics*. Cambridge: Cambridge University Press.

Coffey, A., Delamont, S. and Atkinson, P. (2007) *Handbook of Ethnography*. London: Sage.

Cohen, A. (1973) *Folk Devils and Moral Panics: The Creation of the Mods and Rockers*. London: Paladin.

Cook, T. D. and Campbell, D. T. (1979). *Quasi-Experimentation*. Chicago: Rand-McNally.

Cooper, H. M. (1989) *Integrating Research: A Guide for Literature Reviews*. London: Sage.

Cramer, D. and Howitt, D. (2004) *The Sage Dictionary of Criminology*. London: Sage.

Cressey, D. (1950) The criminal violation of financial trust. *American Sociological Review*, 15: 738–43.

Creswell, J. W. (2002) *Research Design: Qualitative, Quantitative and Mixed Methods Approaches*, 2nd edn. London: Sage.

Crow, I. (1996) *Approaches to Youth Crime: A Study of the Views of Magistrates, Justices' Clerks and Social Workers*. Sheffield: University of Sheffield, Centre for Criminological and Legal Research.

Crow, I. (2000) Evaluating initiatives in the community. In V. Jupp, P. Davies and P. Francis (eds) *Doing Criminological Research*. London: Sage.

Crow, I. (2001) *The Treatment and Rehabilitation of Offenders*. London: Sage.

Crow, I., Cavadino, M., Dignan, J., Johnston, V. and Walker, M. (1996) *Changing Criminal Justice: The Impact of the Criminal Justice Act 1991 in Four Areas of the North of England*. Sheffield: University of Sheffield, Centre for Criminological and Legal Research.

Crow, I., France, A., Hacking, S. and Hart, M. (2004) *Does Communities that Care Work? An Evaluation of a Community-based Risk Prevention Programme in Three Neighbourhoods*. York: Joseph Rowntree Foundation.

Crow, I., France, A. and Hacking, S. (2006) The evaluation of three Communities That Care projects in the UK, *Security Journal*, 19(1): 45–57.

Crow, I., Howells, G. and Moroney, M. (1993) Credit and debt: choices for poorer consumers. In G. Howells, I. Crow and M. Moroney (eds) *Aspects of Credit and Debt*. London: Sweet and Maxwell.

Crow, I., Richardson, P., Riddington, C. and Simon, F. (1989) *Unemployment, Crime and Offenders*. London: Routledge.

Crow, I. and Simon, F. (1987) *Unemployment and Magistrates Courts*. London: NACRO.

Crow, I. and Stubbing, T. (1999) Fast tracking persistent young offenders: to what effect? *Liverpool Law Review*, 21(2–3): 169–96.

Dale, A., Arber, S. and Proctor, M. (1988) *Doing Secondary Analysis*. London: Unwin Hyman.

Delanty, G. and Strydom, P. (2003) *Philosophies of Social Science: The Classic and Contemporary Readings*. Milton Keynes: Open University Press.

Denzin, N. K. (1988) *The Research Act: A Theoretical Introduction to Sociological Methods*. Englewood Cliffs, N. J. : Prentice Hall.

De Vaus, D. (2002) *Analysing Social Science Data: 50 Key Problems in Data Analysis*. London: Sage.

Ditchfield, J. and Marshall, P. (1990) A review of recent literature evaluating treatments for sex offenders in prison. *Prison Service Journal*, 81: 24–8.

Ditton, J. (1977) *Part Time Crime: An Ethnography of Fiddling and Pilferage*. London: Macmillan.

Ditton, J. (2000) Crime surveys and the measurement problem: fear of crime. In V. Jupp, P. Davies and P. Francis, *Doing Criminological Research*. London: Sage.

Ekblom, P., Law, H. and Sutton, M. (1996) *Safer Cities and Domestic Burglary*. Home Office Research Study 164. London: Home Office.

Engels, F. (1969) *The Condition of the Working Class in England*. London: Panther.

Falshaw, L., Friendship, C. and Bates, A. (2003) *Sexual Offenders: Measuring Reconviction, Reoffending and Recidivism*. Home Office Research, Development and Statistics Directorate Research Findings No. 183. London: Home Office.

Farrington, D. P., Gallagher, B., Morley, L., St Ledger, R. J. and West, D. J. (1986) Unemployment, school leaving and crime. *British Journal of Criminology*, 23(3): 229–48.

Farrington, D. (1996) *Understanding and Preventing Youth Crime.* York: Joseph Rowntree Foundation.

Farrington, D. P. (1997) Evaluating a community crime prevention program, *Evaluation*, 3(2): 157–73.

Farrington, D. P. (1998) Evaluating 'Communities That Care': realistic scientific considerations. *Evaluation*, 4(2): 204–10.

Farrington, D. (2000) Explaining and preventing crime: the globalisation of knowledge. Key note Address to the American Society for Criminology, 1999. *Criminology*, 38(1): 1–23.

Field, A. (2004) *Discovering Statistics Using SPSS.* London: Sage.

Fielding, J. (2001) Coding and managing data. In N. Gilbert (ed.) *Researching Social Life.* London: Sage Publications.

Fielding, J. and Gilbert, N. (2000) *Understanding Social Statistics.* London: Sage.

Fink, A. (1995) *How to Analyse Survey Data.* London: Sage.

Fischer, F. (1998) Beyond empiricism: policy inquiry in postpositivist perspective. *Policy Studies Journal*, 26(1): 129–46.

Folkard, M. S., Smith, D. E. and Smith, D. D. (1976) *IMPACT Volume II.* Home Office Research Study 36. London: Home Office.

Foster, J. J. (2001) *Data Analysis Using SPSS for Windows.* London: Sage.

France, A. and Crow, I. (2001) *CTC – The Story So Far: An Interim Evaluation of Communities That Care.* York: Joseph Rowntree Foundation.

France, A. and Crow, I. (2005) Using the 'Risk Factor Paradigm' in prevention: lessons from the Evaluation of Communities that Care. *Children and Society*, 19: 172–84.

Friendship, C., Beech, A. R. and Browne, K. D. (2002) Reconviction as an outcome in research: a methodological note. *British Journal of Criminology*, 42: 442–4.

Friendship, C., Street, R., Cann, J. and Harper, G. (2004) Introduction: the policy context and assessing the evidence. In G. Harper and C. Chitty (eds) *The Impact of Corrections on Re-Offending: A Review of 'What Works'.* Home Office Research Study 291. London: Home Office.

Ganzini, L., McFarland, B. and Bloom, J. (1990) Victims of fraud. *Bulletin of the American Academy of Psychiatry and Law*, 18: 55–63.

Garfinkel, H. (1967) *Studies in Ethnomethodology*. Englewood Cliffs, NJ: Prentice-Hall.

Garland, D. (2001) *The Culture of Control: Crime and Social Order in Contemporary Society*. Oxford: Oxford University Press.

Garland, D. (2002) Of crime and criminals: the development of criminology in Britain. In M. Maguire, R. Morgan and R. Reiner (eds) *The Oxford Handbook of Criminology*. Oxford: Oxford University Press.

Gelsthorpe, L. and Sharpe, G. (2006) Criminological research: typologies versus hierarchies. *Criminal Justice Matters*, 62: 8–43.

Gewirth, A. (1996) *The Community of Rights*. Chicago: University of Chicago Press.

Gilbert, N. (ed.) (1993) *Researching Social Life*. London: Sage.

Gilbert, N. (2006) *From Postgraduate to Social Scientist*. London: Sage.

Glaser, B. G. and Strauss, A. L. (1967) *The Discovery of Grounded Theory: Strategies for Qualitative Research*. New York: Aldine Publishing.

Goffman, E. (1961) *Asylums: Essays on the Social Situation of Mental Patients and Other Inmates*. New York: Doubleday.

Gold, R.L. (1958) Roles in sociological fieldwork. *Social Forces*, 36: 217–23.

Gormally, B., Lyner, O., Mulligan, G. and Warden, M. (1981) *Unemployment and Young Offenders in Northern Ireland*. Belfast: NIACRO.

Grabosky, P., Smith, R. G. and Dempsey, G. (2001) *Electronic Theft: Unlawful Acquisition in Cyberspace*. Cambridge: Cambridge University Press.

Green, A. and Preston, J. (2005) Speaking in tongues: diversity in mixed methods research. *International Journal of Social Research Methodology*, 8(3): 167–71.

Hale, C. (1996) Fear of crime: a review of the literature. *International Review of Victimology*, 4: 79–150.

Hales, J., Henderson, L., Collins, D. and Becher, H. (2000) *2000 British Crime Survey Technical Report*. London: National Centre for Social Research.

Hall, S., Critcher, C., Jefferson, T. and Roberts, B. (1978) *Policing the Crisis*. London: Macmillan.

Hammersley, M. (1992) *What's Wrong with Ethnography*? London: Routledge.

Hammersley, M. and Atkinson, P. (1983) *Ethnography: Principles in Practice*. London: Tavistock Publications.

Hammersley, M. and Atkinson, P. (1995) *Ethnography: Principles in Practice*. London: Routledge.

Hargreaves, D. H., Hesterr, S. and Mellor, F. (1975) *Deviance in Classrooms*. London: Routledge and Kegan Paul.

Harper, G. and Chitty, C. (eds) (2004) *The Impact of Corrections on Re-Offending: A review of 'What Works'*. Home Office Research Study 291. London: Home Office.

Hart, C. (1998) *Doing a Literature Review: Releasing the Social Science Research Imagination*. London: Sage.

Hawkins, J. D., Catalano, R. and Miller, J. (1992) Risk and protective factors for alcohol and other drug problems in adolescence and early adulthood: implications for substance abuse prevention. *Psychological Bulletin*, 112(1): 66–105.

Hedderman, C. and Sugg, D. (1996) *Does Treating Sex Offenders Reduce Reoffending?* Research Findings No. 45, Home Office Research and Statistics Directorate. London: Home Office.

Heritage, J. (1987) Ethnomethodology. In A. Giddens and J. Turner (eds) *Social Theory Today*. Cambridge: Polity.

Hobbs, D. (1988) *Doing the Business: Entrepreneurship, the Working Class and Detectives in the East End of London*. Oxford: Oxford University Press.

Holdaway, S. (1983) *Inside the British Police: A Force at Work*. Oxford: Blackwell.

Hollister, R. and Hill, J. (1999) Problems in the evaluation of community-wide initiatives. In J. Connell, A. Kubisch, L. Schorr and C. Weiss (eds) *New Approaches to Evaluating Community Initiatives*. Vol. 1. New Jersey: The Aspen Institute.

Holsti, O. (1969) *Content Analysis for the Social Sciences and Humanities*. Reading, MA: Addison-Wesley.

Home Office (1974) *Working Party on Vagrancy and Street Offences Working Paper*. Appendix A. London: HMSO.

Home Office (1997) *No More Excuses: A New Approach to Tackling Youth Crime in England and Wales*. Cm 3809. London: The Stationery Office.

Home Office (2000) *Review of Crime Statistics: A Discussion Document.* London: Home Office.

Hood, R. (1972) *Sentencing the Motoring Offender.* Cambridge Studies in Criminology. London: Heinemann.

Hope, T. (2004) Pretend it works: evidence and governance in the evaluation of the reducing burglary initiative. *Criminal Justice*, 4(3): 287–308.

Hough, M., Clancy, A., McSweeney, T. and Turnbull, P. J. (2003) *The Impact of Drug Treatment and Testing Orders on Offending: Two-year Reconviction Results.* Home Office Research Findings 184. London: Home Office.

House of Commons Science and Technology Committee (2006) *Scientific Advice, Risk and Evidence Based Policy Making. HC900–1, 7th Report of Session 2005–6 (Vol. 1). London:* The Stationery Office.

Hughes, J. (1990) *The Philosophy of Social Research,* 2nd edn. London: Longman.

Hullin, R. (1985) The Leeds Truancy Project. *Justice of the Peace*, 488–91.

Israel, M. and Chui, W. H. (2006) If 'Something works' is the answer, what is the question? Supporting pluralist evaluation in community corrections in the United Kingdom. *European Journal of Criminology*, 3(2): 181–200.

Johnson, J. (1975) *Doing Field Research.* New York: Free Press.

Jupp, V. (2006) *The Sage Dictionary of Social Research Methods.* London: Sage.

Jupp, V., Davies, P. and Francis, P. (eds) (2000) *Doing Criminological Research.* London: Sage Publications.

Justice of the Peace (1982) A job to go to Monday: notes of the week. *Justice of the Peace.*

Kane, E. (1985) *Doing Your Own Research.* London: Marion Boyars Publishing.

Kant, I. (1871) *Critique of Pure Reason.* Trans. J. M. D. Meiklejohn. New York: Dover Publications Inc.

Kelle, U. (1997) Capabilities for theory building and hypothesis testing in software for computer-aided qualitative data analysis. *The Data Archive Bulletin*, 65, May 1997, 12–14.

Kemp, C., Norris, C. and Fielding, N. (1992) *Negotiating Nothing: Police Decision-Making in Disputes*. Aldershot: Avebury.

Kershaw, C. (1998) Interpreting reconviction Rates. In *The Use and Impact of Community Supervision*, Research Bulletin No. 39, Special Edition, 9–16. Home Office Research and Statistics Directorate. London: Home Office.

Kershaw, C., Budd, T., Kinshott, G., Mattinson, J., Mayhew, P. and Myhill, A. (2000) *The 2000 British Crime Survey*. Home Office Statistical Bulletin 18/00. London: Home Office.

King, R. D. and Wincup, E. (2000) *Doing Research on Crime and Justice*. Oxford: Oxford University Press.

Kranzler, G. and Moursund, J. (1995) *Statistics for the Terrified*. Englewood Cliffs, NJ: Prentice Hall.

Lacey, N. (2007) Legal constructions of crime. In M. Maguire, R. Morgan and R. Reiner (eds) *The Oxford Handbook of Criminology*, 4th edn. Oxford: Oxford University Press.

LaGrange, R. L. and Ferraro, K. F. (1989) Assessing age and gender differences in perceived risk and fear of crime. *Criminology*, 27: 697–719.

Levi, M. and Pithouse, A. (1992) The victims of fraud. In D. Downes (ed.) *Unravelling Criminal Justice*. London: Macmillan Press Ltd, pp. 229–46.

Lewins, A. (2001) Computer assisted qualitative data analysis. In N. Gilbert (ed.) *Researching Social Life*. London: Sage Publications.

Lloyd, C., Mair, G. and Hough, M. (1994) *Explaining Reconviction Rates: A Critical Analysis*. Home Office Research Study 136. London: Home Office.

Loftland, L. H. (1973) A World of Strangers: Order and Action in Urban Public Space. New York: Basic Books.

Madriz, E. (1997a) Images of criminals and victims: a study on women's fear and social control. *Gender and Society*, 11(3): 342–56.

Madriz, E. (1997b) *Nothing Bad Happens to Good Girls: Fear of Crime on Women's Lives*. Berkeley, CA: University of California Press.

Maguire, M. (2002) Crime statistics: the 'data explosion' and its implications. In M. Maguire, R. Morgan and R. Reiner, *The Oxford Handbook of Criminology*. 3rd edn. Oxford: Oxford University Press.

Maguire, M. (2007) Crime data and statistics. In M. Maguire, R. Morgan and R. Reiner, *The Oxford Handbook of Criminology*, 4th edn. Oxford: Oxford University Press.

Mair, G. (ed.) (1997) *Evaluating the Effectiveness of Community Penalties*. Aldershot: Avebury.

Mair, G. (ed.) (2004) *What Matters in Probation*. Cullompton, Devon: Willan Publishing.

Mair, G. et al. (1994) *Intensive Probation in England and Wales: An Evaluation*. Home Office Research Study 133. London: Home Office.

Marshall, G. (ed.) (1994) *The Concise Oxford Dictionary of Sociology*. Oxford: Oxford University Press.

Marshall, P. (1994) Reconviction of imprisoned sexual offenders. *Research Bulletin*, 36. London: Home Office Research and Statistics Department.

Mattinson, J. and Mirlees-Black, C. (2000) *Attitudes to Crime and Criminal Justice: Findings from the 1998 British Crime Survey*. Home Office Research Study No. 200. London: Home Office.

Mayhew, P. (2000) Researching the state of crime: local, national and international victim surveys. In R. King and E. Wincup, *Doing Research on Crime and Justice*. Oxford: Oxford University Press.

McLaughlin, E. (2001) Administrative criminology. In E. McLaughlin and J. Muncie (eds) *The Sage Dictionary of Criminology*. London: Sage.

McLaughlin, E. and Muncie, J. (eds) *The Sage Dictionary of Criminology*. London: Sage.

Merton, R. K. (1967) *On Theoretical Sociology*. New York: Free Press.

Merton, R. K., Fiske, M. and Kendall, P. L. (1956) *The Focused Interview*. New York: Free Press.

Miles, M. B. and Huberman, A. M. (1994) *Qualitative Data Analysis: An Expanded Sourcebook*, 2nd edn. Thousand Oaks, CA: Sage Publications.

Morgan, D. L. (1992) Designing focus group research. In M. Stewart (ed.) *Tools for Primary Care Research*. Thousand Oaks, CA: Sage.

Morgan, D. L. (1996) Focus groups. *Annual Review of Sociology*, 22: 129–52.

Morgan, D. L. (2006) Focus groups. In V. Jupp (ed.) *The Sage Dictionary of Social Research Methods*. London: Sage.

Morgan, D. L. and Krueger, R. A. (1993) When to use focus groups and why. In D. L. Morgan (ed.) *Successful Focus Groups: Advancing the State of the Art*. Newbury Park, CA: Sage.

Moyser, G. and Wagstaffe, M. (1987) *Research Methods for Elite Studies*. London: Allen and Unwin.

Niven, S. and Olagundaye, J. (2002) *Jobs and Homes: A Survey of Prisoners Nearing Release*. Home Office Research Findings 173. London: Home Office.

Norris, C. (1993) Some ethical considerations on field-work with the police. In D. Hobbs and T. May, *Interpreting the Field: Accounts of Ethnography*. Oxford: Clarendon Press.

Norusis, M. J. (1992) *SPSS for Windows: Base System User's Guide*. Chicago: SPSS Inc.

O'Leary, Z. (2004) *The Essential Guide to Doing Research*. London: Sage Publications.

Oppenheim, A. N. (2000) *Questionnaire Design, Interviewing and Attitude Measurement*. London: Continuum.

Överlien, C., Aronsson, K. and Hydén, M. (2005) The focus group interview as an in-depth method? Young women talking about sexuality. *International Journal of Social Research Methodology*, 8(4): 331–44.

Pallant, J. (2001) *SPSS Survival Manual*. Buckingham: Open University Press.

Palmer, C. and Hart, M. (1996) *A PACE in the Right Direction?* Sheffield: University of Sheffield, Institute for the Study of the Legal Profession.

Patterson, A. and Thorpe, K. (2006) Public preparations. In A. Walker, C. Kershaw and S. Nicholas, *Crime in England and Wales 2005/06*. London: Home Office.

Pawson, R. and Tilley, N. (1994) What works in evaluation research? *British Journal of Criminology*, 34(3): 291–306.

Pawson, R. and Tilley, N. (1996) What's crucial in evaluation research: a reply to Bennett. *British Journal of Criminology*, 36(4): 574–8.

Pawson, R. and Tilley, N. (1997) *Realistic Evaluation*. London: Sage Publications.

Pawson, R. and Tilley, N. (1998a) Caring communities, paradigm polemics, design debates. *Evaluation*, 4(1): 73–90.

Pawson, R. and Tilley, N. (1998b) Cook-book methods and disastrous recipes: a rejoinder to Farrington. *Evaluation,* 4(2): 211–13.

Pearce, F. and Tombs, S. (1992) Realism and corporate Crime. In R. Matthews and J. Young (eds) *Issues in Realist Criminology.* London: Sage.

Phillpotts, G. J. O. and Lancucki, L. B. (1979) *Previous Convictions, Sentence and Reconviction.* Home Office Research Study No. 53. London: HMSO.

Pollard, J., Hawkins, J. and Arthur, W. (1999) Risk and protection: are both necessary to understand diverse outcomes in adolescence? *Social Work Research*, 23(3): 145–58.

Popper, K. (1959) *The Logic of Scientific Discovery.* London: Hutchinson.

Punch, M. (1979) *Policing the Inner City: A Study of Amsterdam's Warmoesstraat.* London: Macmillan.

Punch, K. (2006) *Developing Effective Research Proposals*, 2nd edn. London: Sage.

Raynor, P. and Robinson, G. (2005) *Rehabilitation, Crime and Justice.* Basingstoke: Palgrave.

Robinson, W. S. (1950) Ecological correlations and the behaviour of individuals. *American Sociological Review*, 15: 351–7.

Robson, C. (2002) *Real World Research*, 2nd edn. Oxford: Blackwell Publishing.

Rose, G. (1982) *Deciphering Sociological Research.* London: Macmillan.

Rountree, P. W. (1998) A re-examination of the crime-fear linkage. *Journal of Research in Crime and Delinquency*, 35(3): 341–72.

Rowntree, D. (1991) *Statistics Without Tears: A Primer for Non-mathematicians.* London: Penguin.

Rutland, A. (2005) The development and regulation of prejudice in children. ESRC Society Today. available at: http://www.esrcsocietytoday.ac.uk/ESRCInfoCentre/index.aspx

Rutland, A., Cameron, L., Milne, A. and McGeorge (2005) Social norms and self-presentation: children's implicit and explicit intergroup attitudes. *Child Development,* 76: 451–66.

Sampson, R. and Raudenbush, S. (1999) Systematic social observation of public spaces: a new look at disorder in urban neighborhoods. *American Journal of Sociology*, 105(3): 603–51.

Sandel, M. (1982) *Liberalism and the Limits of Justice*. Cambridge: Cambridge University Press.

Schatzman, L. and Strauss, A. L. (1973) *Field Research: Strategies for a Natural Sociology*. Englewood Cliffs, NJ: Prentice Hall.

Schuman, H. and Presser, S. (1996) *Questions and Answers in Attitude Surveys: Experiments on Question Form, Wording, and Context*. London: Sage.

Shapland, J., Wiles, P. and Wilcox, P. (1994) *Targeted Crime Reduction for Local Areas*. London: Home Office, Police Research Group.

Sherman, L. W., Gottfredson, D. C., MacKenzie, D. L., Eck, J., Reuter, P. and Bushway, S. D. (1998) *Preventing Crime: What Works, What Doesn't, and What's Promising*. Washington, DC: U.S. Department of Justice, National Institute of Justice.

Shrum, W. and Kilburn, J. (1996) Ritual disrobement at Mardi Gras. *Social Forces*, 75(2): 423–58.

Skogan, W. G. (1987) The impact of victimisation on fear. *Crime and Delinquency*, 33: 135–54.

Smellie, E. and Crow, I. (1991) *Black Peoples' Experiences of Criminal Justice*. London: NACRO.

Smith, G. and Cantley, C. (1984) Pluralistic evaluation. In J. Lishman (ed.) *Evaluation*, Research Highlights in Social Work 26. London: Jessica Kingsley.

Smith, J. K. (1983) Quantitative versus qualitative research: an attempt to clarify the issue. *Educational Researcher*, 12: 6–13.

Smith, J. K. and Heshusius, L. (1986) Closing down the conversation: the end of the quantitative-qualitative debate among educational enquirers. *Educational Researcher*, 15: 4–12.

Spalek, B. (1995) Trust as an ideology: exploring fear of white collar crime. Paper presented to the British Criminology Conference. Loughborough University, 18–21 July 1995.

Statistics Commission (2006) *Crime Statistics: User Perspectives*, Report No. 30. London: Stationery Office.

Stinchcombe, A. L. (1968) *Constructing Social Theories*. New York: Harcourt, Brace and World.

Strauss, A. and Corbin, J.M. (1998) *Basics of Qualitative Research: Techniques and Procedures for Developing Grounded Theory*. Thousand Oaks, CA: Sage.

Survey Methods Centre (1994) *Quota Versus Probability Sampling, Report of the First Cathie Marsh Memorial Seminar*, Newsletter, 15(1).

Tarling, R. (1982) Unemployment and crime. *Research Bulletin No. 14*. London: Home Office.

Tarling, R. and Weatheritt, M. (1979) *Sentencing Practice in Magistrates' Courts*. Home Office Research Study No. 56. London: HMSO.

Taylor, I., Walton, P. and Young, J. (1973) *The New Criminology*. London: Routledge and Kegan Paul.

Thorpe, J. (1978) *Social Enquiry Reports: A Survey*. Home Office Research Study No. 48. London: HMSO.

Thrasher, F. M. (1947) *The Gang*. Chicago: University of Chicago Press.

Tomsen, S. (1997) A top night: social protest, masculinity and the culture of drinking violence. *British Journal of Criminology*, 37: 90–102.

United Nations Social Defence Research Institute (1976) *Economic Crises and Crime*. Rome: UNSDRI.

Utting, D. (1999) *A Guide to Promising Approaches*. York: Joseph Rowntree Foundation.

Vold, G. B. and Snipes, J. B. (2001) *Theoretical Criminology*. New York: Oxford University Press.

Walmsley, R., Howard, L. and White, S. (1992) *The National Prison Survey 1991: Main Findings*. Home Office Research Study 128. London: HMSO.

Weiss, C. H. (1998) *Evaluation: Methods for Studying Programs and Policies*, 2nd edn. Englewood Cliffs, NJ: Prentice Hall.

Whyte, W. (1981) *Street Corner Society: The Social Structure of an Italian Slum*. Chicago: University of Chicago Press.

Williams, M. (2006) Positivism. In V. Jupp (ed.) *The Sage Dictionary of Social Research Methods*. London: Sage.

Williams, P. and Dickenson, J. (1993) Fear of crime: read all about it? *British Journal of Criminology*, 33: 33–56.

Wolcott, H. F. (1994) *Transforming Qualitative Data: Description, Analysis and Interpretation*. Thousand Oaks, CA: Sage Publications.

Wooffitt, R. (2005) *Conversation Analysis and Discourse Analysis*. London: Sage.

Wright, D. B. (1997) *Understanding Statistics: An Introduction for the Social Sciences*. London: Sage.

Index

Locators shown in *italics* refer to boxes, figures and tables.

access, researcher
  decisions necessary when carrying out observation, 105–7
accidental samples, 49
accuracy, sample, 46
administration, questionnaire, 149–51
aims and objectives, research
  case study involving development of, 244–5
analysis, causal
  as element of evaluation, 58–62, *58, 59, 60, 61*
  characteristics, 35–6, *35*
  see also types eg experimental studies; non-experimental studies; quasi-experimental studies
analysis, data
  characteristics, process and role, 16–17, 85–95, 153–89, *156, 158, 160, 162, 164, 165, 167, 169, 170, 172, 173, 175, 178, 185, 189*
  decisions necessary when carrying out observation, 112–13
  guidelines for research publications analysis, 97–9
  selection of methods of, 31–2
see also analysis types eg content analysis; conversation analysis; discourse analysis; multivariate analysis; univariate analysis
anti-positivism and positivism
  in relation to criminology research, 25–6
anxieties fears and anxieties
  case study of crime fears influence, 240–54, *248, 249, 251, 252*
  definition of concept, 238–40
Arber, S., 87
Association of Payment and Clearing Services (APACS), 240–41
Atkinson, P., 102, 109, 110
attitudes, personal
  research process investigating, 144–9
availability samples, 49
Bail Act (1976), 201
Beauchamp, T., 52
Beck, U., 94
Becker, H., 29
behaviour, problematic
  association between risk and problem behaviour, 226–8, *227,*
Bennett, T., 63–5
Bentham, J., 51
bias, sample, 46
bivariate analysis, 164–71, *164, 165, 166, 167, 169, 170,* 175, *175, 259*
Bogardus social distance scale of personal attitudes, 145
British Cohort Study, The (1970), 88
British Crime Survey, The, 10, 48, 91–3, 155, 237
British Household Panel Survey, 10
British Social Attitudes Survey, 88
Bryman, A., 28–9, 108, 114, 184–5
burglary and burglaries
  Safer City programme statistics, *74*
Cambridge Study of Delinquent Development, 39
cards, financial transaction
  existence as influence on fear of crime, 240–42
case studies
  Communities That Care UK, 226–35, *227, 230–31*
  influence of crime fears, 240–54, *248, 249, 251, 252*
  literature reviewing, 237–8
  offender sentencing project, 190–93, 200–210, *206, 207*
  research aims and objectives, 244–5
  research design selection, 40–43, *41*, 203–5, *205*
  use of focus groups, 127–30

case studies–*contd*
Youth Court Demonstration Project, 213–24, *215*
cataloguing and storage of observation data, 112–13
centrality, measurement of, 158–9, *160*
Chicago School of ethnography, 101–2
Children Act (1989), 213
Childress, J., 52
Chui, W., 221
Clear, T., 221
closed questions
role in questionnaire design, 141–4, *142*
cluster samples, 48
coding
of qualitative data, 177–8, *178*
collection, data
characteristics and role, 16
decisions necessary when carrying out observation, 109–12
selection of methods of, 28–9
see also methods and sources eg information, abstracted; internet; interviews; observation and observers; questionnaires; records, case
communities, safety of
projects enhancing *see* Communities That Care (CTC) UK
Communities That Care (CTC) UK
case study of, 226–35, *227, 230–31*
history and characteristics of project, 225–6
'complete participant' observation role, 107–8
'complete observer' role, 109
conclusions and findings, research
interpretation and presentation, 188–9, *189*
writing up of, 123
see also subject and name of studies of use eg Communities That Care project; criminals and crime; sentencing, offender; Youth Court Demonstration Project
confidentiality
as ethical dilemma within criminological research, 53–4, *54*
consent, informed
as ethical dilemma within criminological research, 53
content analysis
definition and characteristics, 95–6
qualitative analysis of, 183–6, *185*
content and sequence
of questionnaires, 135–7
conversation analysis, 186–7
Corbin, J., 181
correlation
process of, 168–70, *169*, 172–3, *172, 173*
correlation studies, 37–8
covert research
ethical dilemmas within criminological research, 52–3
Cressey, D., 179
Criminal Justice Act (1991), 209, 211, 213
Criminal Justice Act (1993), 209
Criminal Statistics, The, 90
criminals and crime
case study of crime relationship with unemployment, 40–43, *41*
case study of sentencing, 190–93, 200–210, *206, 207*
definition of concept, 238–40
impact and case study of fear of crime, 240–54, *248, 249, 251, 252*
reduction of as intervention outcome, 71–3
see also burglary and burglaries; white collar crime
criminal justice, systems of
case study of offender sentencing, 190–93, 200–210
impact and relationship with concept of unemployment, 200–202
recent policy developments, 211–12
cross-sectional studies
case study of use of, 41–2
characteristics, 39
cross-tabulation, 164–7, *164, 165, 167*
courts, youth
developmental pilot projects *see* Youth Court Demonstration Project
data
analysis *see* analysis, data
collection *see* collection, data
see also types eg qualitative data; quantitative data

deception
  as ethical dilemma within criminological research, 53–4, *54*, 55, *55*
Denzin, N., 11, 117–18, 122, 123
Descartes, R., 24
designs, research
  case study of selection of, 40–43, *41*, 203–5, *205*
  definition and characteristics, 34–6, *35*
  types, 38–40
  see also evaluation, research; operationalization, research
Developing Effective Research Proposals (Punch), 257
Dewey, J., 24
discourse analysis, 187–8
dispersion, measurement of, 159–61, *162*
distribution, measurement of, 193–5
Ditton, J., 108
Drug Treatment and Testing Orders (DTTOs), 72–3
Durkheim, D., 25
Economic and Social Research Council (ESRC), 52–3
Economic and Social Data Service (ESDS), 86, 155
empiricism, 23–4, 26–7
Engels, F., 201
epistemology
  role in research planning, 23–7
errors
  sampling, 45–7
  Type I and Type II, 264, *264*
ESDS (Economic and Social Data Service), 86, 155
ESRC (Economic and Social Research Council), 52–3
ethics and ethicality
  principles in relation to criminology research, 50–55, *54, 55*
ethnography
  historical development and characteristics, 101–103
  qualitative analysis of, 183
  see also elements and decisions eg access, researcher; sampling and samples
evaluation, research
  and criminological theory debates, 62–7, *66*
  case study of use in Youth Court Demonstration Project, 217
evaluation, research–*contd*
  complexity of strategies and processes, 73–5, *74*
  definition and characteristics, 57–8
  identification of aims and purpose, 67–9, *68*
  models of, 58–62, *58, 60, 61*
  of intervention/programme integrity assessment, 69–70
  of outcomes criteria assessment, 70–73
  socio-political context, 75–7
  see also analysis, causal; feedback, research; outcomes; process evaluation
evaluation studies, 39–40
experimental studies, 36–7
Farrington, D., 63–5
fears and anxieties
  case study of crime fears influence, 240–54, *248, 249, 251, 252*
  definition of concept, 238–40
feedback, research
  case study of use in Youth Court Demonstration Project, 219–20
  see also evaluation, research
filming
  as observation method, 112
  of focus groups, 127
findings and conclusions, research
  interpretation and presentation, 188–9, *189*
  writing up of, 123
  see also subject and name of studies of use eg Communities That Care project; criminals and crime; sentencing, offender; Youth Court Demonstration Project
focus groups
  case studies of use of, 127–30
  characteristics, limitations and process, 123–7
fractions, sampling, 44
fragmentation
  of qualitative data, 177–8, *178*
frames, sampling, 44
fraud, financial
  case study of impact on fear of crime, 240–43
'freedom', degrees of, 259–60
Freud, S., 25
Friendship, C., 67, *68*
From Postgraduate to Social Scientist (Gilbert), 257
funding, criminology research, 256–7

Ganzini, L., 242
General Household Survey, 88
Gilbert, N., 257
Glaser, B., 182
Goffman, E., 114
Gold, R., 107–9
Grabosky, P., 243
Green, A., 11
grounded theory
  approach to qualitative analysis, 181–2
  characteristics, 32
groups, focus
  case studies of use of, 127–30
  characteristics, limitations and process, 123–7
Guttman scales of personal attitudes, 146
Hammersley, M., 102, 109, 110
Hargreaves, D., 102
hypotheses
  building of in case study of crime fear, 245–6, 248–51, *248, 249, 251*
  case study of development of concerning offender sentencing, 202–3
  characteristics and role in criminology research, 13–15
  development of as element of research methods, 29
  testing of, 260–61
  see also null-hypothesis
Heritage, J., 186
Hill, J., 234
Holdaway, S., 106, 107–8
Hollister, R., 234
Holsti, O., 184
Hope, T., 94
Huberman, A., 182
induction, analytic
  as applied to qualitative analysis, 179–80
  characteristics, 122–3
inferences
  applicability to samples, 45–7
  characteristics and role, 17, 153–5
  from single quantitative variables, 161, 163
information, abstracted
  as mode for questionnaire data collection, 134, 154–5
inquiry, research
  types, 9–12, *10, 12*
integrity, programme
  assessment of as element within evaluation, 69–70
International Crime Victim Survey, 246
internet
  as mode for questionnaire data collection, 133
interval variables, 158, 167–70, *169,* 193–5
interventions
  as purpose and outcome of criminological evaluation, 67–9, *68*
interviews
  case study of use in offender sentencing research, 205–8, *206, 207*
  characteristics and process, 117–23
  see also focus groups
interviews, telephone
  as mode for questionnaire data collection, 132–3, *132*
Israel, M., 221
judgemental samples, 49
justice, criminal *see* criminal justice, systems of
Kant, I., 24, 51–2
Kelle, U., 14
Kemp, C., 113
Labour Force Survey, 88
language
  qualitative analysis of, 186–8
Levi, M., 242
Lickert scales of personal attitudes, 147–9, *149*
Lindesmith, A., 122–3
Loftland, L., 109
logistic regression, 173
Lombroso, C., 25
longitudinal studies
  case study of use of, 42–3
  characteristics, 39
Madriz, E., 129–30
Maguire, M., 92
Maryland Scale of Scientific Methods, 60–62, *60, 61*
measurement (concept)
  definition, 261
  see also element measured eg centrality; dispersion; distribution
Merton, R., 124

methods, research
definition and characteristics, 34–6, *35*
future development pathway, 255–8
selection and development of, 28–31
see also elements and outcomes eg aims and objectives, research; evaluation, research; strategies, research
see also type eg interviews; observation and observers; questionnaires
Miles, M., 182
Mill, J.S., 51
Millennium Cohort Study, The, 88
'mixed method' research, 11
models
of evaluation, 58–62, *58, 59, 60, 61,* 67–9
of research process, *12*
moderators
role in focus groups, 126
Morgan, D., 126
multistage samples, 48
multivariate analysis, 171–5, *172, 173, 175, 259*
National Child Development Study (NCDS), 39, 87–8
National Crime Victims Survey (USA), 237
neighbourhoods, safety of
projects enhancing *see* Communities That Care (CTC) UK
Newburn, T., 94
New Criminology, The (Taylor), 93
nominal variables, 157, 164–7, *164, 265, 167*
No More Excuses: a new approach to Tackling Youth Crime (1997), 211
non-experimental studies, 37–8
non-probability sampling, 30
non-random samples, 49–50
non-schedule-standardized interviews, 118
non-standardized interviews, 118
null hypothesis, 262
objectives and aims, research
case study involving development of, 244–5
observation and observers
case study of use in offender sentencing research, 205–8, *206, 207*
observation and observers–*contd*
case study of use in Youth Court Demonstration Project research, 214–15, *216*, 222–4
historical development and characteristics, 100–103
role of observer, 107–9
types and models, 110–12
weaknesses of as method, 114–15
see also process elements and decisions eg access, researcher; analysis, data; collection, data; sampling and samples; storage and cataloguing
'observer-as-participant' role, 108–9
offenders and offending *see* criminals and crime
O'Leary, Z., 82, 84
'open' observation, 110–11
open questions
qualitative analysis of, 180–81
role in questionnaire design, 141–4, *142*
operationalization, research
characteristics and role in criminology research, 15–16
experience of use in case study of offender sentencing, 206–8, *207*
involvement in case study of crime fear, 246–7
Oppenheim, A., 144
opportunities, criminology research
future outlook, 255–6
ordinal variables, 157–8 170–71, *170*
Osgood semantic differential scales of personal attitudes, 146[check exact tit]
outcomes
assessment of intervention outcomes as element within evaluation, 70–73
case study of use of outcomes evaluation, 228–31, *230–31*
Överlein, C., 127
OXO model of causality evaluation, 59, 62–3
packages, computer *see name eg* Statistical Package for the Social Sciences
'paradigm wars' concerning evaluation theories, 62–7, *66*
partial correlation, 172–3, 172, 173
'participant-as-observer' role, 108
participants, research
unintended 'manipulation' of researcher by, 116–17

Pawson, R., 62–7
Pearce, F., 242
Peirce, C., 24
pilot studies, questionnaire, 151
Pithouse, P., 242
planning, research
  role of epistemology, 23–7
politics
  relationship with criminological research process, 93–5
populations
  definition of, 262
positivism and anti-positivism
  in relation to criminology research, 25–6
pragmatism, 24–5, 26–7
presentation, questionnaire, 149–51
Preston, J., 11
primary data analysis
  characteristics, 154–5
probability (concept)
  definition, 262–3
  samples and sampling, 30, 47–8
process evaluation
  case study of use of, 228–31, *230–31*
Promising Approaches (Utting), 226
prospective studies, 38–9
publications, research
  guidelines for analysis of, 97–9
Punch, K., 257
qualitative data
  case study of use in Youth Court Demonstration Project research, 217–19
  process of analysis, 175–89, *178, 185, 189*
quantitative data
  case study of use in Youth Court Demonstration Project research, 217–19
process of analysis, 155–75, *156, 158, 160, 162, 164, 165, 167, 169, 170, 172, 173, 175*
quasi-experimental studies, 37–8
questionnaires
  case study of use in Communities That Care project, 230–31, *231*
  case study of use in Youth Court Demonstration Project research, 216–7
  characteristics, limitations and design, 130–51, *132, 139, 140, 142, 149*
questionnaires–*contd*
  modes of data collection, 132–4, *132,* 154–5
questions, research
  characteristics and importance, 20–22
  design for specific case studies, 228–30, 237–43, 246–7
  design of in questionnaire surveys, 137–8
  see also closed questions; open questions
  see also processes and features involving eg hypotheses; operationalization, research; theories
quota samples, 49
random samples, 47–8
rates, response
  in questionnaire surveys, 134–5
rationalism, 24, 26–7
Raudenbush, S., 109
Raynor, P., 94
realism
  in relation to criminology research, 26
Realistic Evaluation (Pawson and Tilley), 65
reasoning
  inductive and deductive, 31
Recorded Crime Statistics, The, 90–91, 93
recording, tape and video
  as observation method, 112
  of focus groups, 127
  see also writing up
records, case
  case study of use in offender sentencing research, 205–8, *206, 207*
regression, 173
reliability
  in qualitative research, *189*
  relevance in research, *20*
representativeness
  of samples, 45–6
  see also validity
research and researchers, criminology
  definition, characteristics and process of, 7–17, *10, 12*
  ethical dilemmas within, 50–55, *54, 55*
  future development pathway, 255–8
  manipulation by participants, 116–17

research and researchers, criminology–*contd*
relationship with political agendas and expediency, 93–5
role of researchers, 30–31
see also methods, research; planning, research; results, research; skills, research
see also approaches to eg positivism and antipositivism; realism
see also elements of process eg analysis, data; collection, data; induction, analytic; operationalization, research; questions, research
respondents
unintended 'manipulation' of researcher by, 116–17
responses
options and order within questionnaire surveys, 138–41, *139, 140*
rates of in questionnaire surveys, 134–5
results, research
interpretation and presentation, 188–9, *189*
writing up of, 123
see also subjects and name of studies eg Communities That Care project; criminals and crime; sentencing, offender; Youth Court Demonstration Project
retrospective studies, 38–9
reviews, literature
case study of use of, 237–8
sources and processes, 82–5
risks
association between risk factors and problem behaviour, 226–8, *227*
case study of, involving Communities That Care, 228–35, *230–31*
Robinson, G., 94
Robson, C., 21, 108, 110–11, 182
Rowntree Foundation, 226
Safer Cities Programme, 73–4
safety, neighbourhood
projects enhancing *see* Communities That Care (CTC) UK
sampling and samples
decisions necessary when embracing observation, 103–4
definition and characteristics, 43–5, *44, 45,* 262
sampling and sample–*contd*
selection of methods of, 30
types, 47–50
see also elements and outcomes eg accuracy, samples; errors, sampling; inferences; representativeness
Sampson, R., 109
scales, personal attitude, 145–9
schedules, interview, 120
schedule-standardized interviews, 118
searches and searching, literature
sources and processes, 82–5
secondary data
case study of use in offender sentencing research, 205–8, *206, 207,* 240–54, *248, 249, 251, 252*
definition, characteristics and process of analysis, 85–95, 154–5
self-completion questionnaires, 133–4
semi-structured interviews, 118–23
sentencing, offender
case study of, 190–93, 200–210, *206, 207*
services, postal
as mode for questionnaire data collection, 133
Shapland, J., 111
Sherman, L., 60
significance tests, 263
simple random samples, 47
skills, research
importance and need for, 257–8
snowball samples, 49
Spalek, B., 243
Statistical Package for the Social Sciences (SPSS), 156–7, *156*
statistics (as data) *see* quantitative data
statistics, official
of social and crime trends, 89–93
Statute of Labourers (1349), 200
storage and cataloguing
of observation data, 112–13
strategies, research
definition and characteristics, 34–6, *35*
selection of, 22–7
see also methods, research
see also aims and objectives, research; outcomes
stratified random samples, 47–8
Strauss, A., 181, 182
Straw, J., 211–12
structured observation, 111–12

studies (research method) *see name eg* experimental studies; longitudinal studies; prospective studies
surveys
crime and social trends, 87–8
questionnaire *see* questionnaires
systems, postal
as mode for questionnaire data collection, 133
tape recording
as observation method, 112
of focus groups, 127
Taylor, I., 93
tests and testing
of significance, 263
theories
characteristics and role in criminology research, 12–13, 22
concerning evaluation-criminology theory debates, 62–7, *66*
Thurstone scales of personal attitudes, 147
Tilley, N., 62–7
time series analysis
case study of use of, 42
Tombs, S., 242
Tomsen, S., 102, 178
tools, research *see* methods, research
trends, crime, 89–93
triangulation, 11, 29
Type I and Type II errors, 264, *264*
UK Data Archive, 85–6
UK Safer Cities Programme, 73–4
unemployment
case study of unemployment relationship with crime, 40–4 *41*
impact and relationship with concept and reality of crimina justice systems, 200–202
univariate analysis, 157–63, 175, *15 160, 162, 175(tab), 259*
unstructured observation, 110–11
Utting, D., 226
Vagrancy Acts (1824–35), 200
validity
in qualitative research, *189*
relevance in research, *20*
see also representativeness
variables
definition and characteristics, 15 164–71, *164, 165 167, 169, 1* 264
inferences from, 161, 163
video recording
as observation method, 112
of focus groups, 127
Weiss, C., 66–7
'What works?' agenda, 74–5
white collar crime
impact on fear of crime, 240–43
Whyte, W., 105
Wolcott, H., 183
worklessness *see* unemployment
writing up
of findings, 123
Youth Court Demonstration Project (YCDP)
case study of, 213–24, *215, 216*
history of, 211–12

POLICY TRANSFER AND CRIMINAL JUSTICE
Exploring US Influence over British Crime Control Policy

Trevor Jones and Tim Newburn

A very interesting book and excellent at setting the context of criminal justice policies in the UK. Thoroughly researched and written in an engaging style."

Tina Eadie, Senior Lecturer, De Montfort University

Since the late 1980s, it seems that policy-makers and politicians in the UK have increasingly looked West across the Atlantic for inspiration in the field of crime control. More broadly, recent years have seen a growing focus upon the extent to which, and ways in which, policy ideas and practices travel within and across national boundaries. Scholars from a number of disciplines have become increasingly interested in the concepts of 'policy transfer' and related ideas.

This book contains the first major empirical study of policy transfer in the field of criminal justice and crime control. It focuses upon policy transfer from the USA to the UK, and undertakes a detailed examination of the processes of policy change in three key areas that have been widely perceived as imports from the USA: the privatization of corrections, 'two' and 'three strikes' sentencing, and 'zero tolerance' policing. Drawing upon a wealth of documentary evidence and interviews with leading politicians, policy makers and other key players in policy developments, the authors explore the complex processes involved in policy transfer and analyse the nature and degree of US influence in these areas.

Contents: *Acknowledgements - Convergence and divergence in crime control - Policy-making and policy transfer - Privatizing punishment - 'Three strikes' and mandatory sentencing - Zero tolerance policing - Policy transfer in crime control - Notes - References - Index.*

2006 208pp
978-0-335-21668-0 (Paperback) 978-0-335-21669-7 (Hardback)

UNDERSTANDING MODERNISATION IN CRIMINAL JUSTICE

Paul Senior, Chris Crowther-Dowey and Matt Long

- How have different criminal justice agencies responded to the modernization process?
- What forms does modernisation take?
- What lessons can be drawn to influence the future shape of criminal justice policy?

Understanding Modernisation in Criminal Justice is the first book to theorize modernisation in the context of criminal justice. It provides a historically informed account tracing the evolving links between new public management and modernisation as well as proposing a conceptual framework for understanding the impact of policies on each criminal justice agency in England and Wales.

A variety of political strategies and tactics are identified, which contribute to the reform process. The extent of vulnerability, capacity for resistance or potential for transformation in each individual key agency is explored, including strategies of censure, compliance and commitment. The authors go on to analyse how these processes have occurred in an international context, in particular, the relationship between drivers of global crime and their impact in the context of England and Wales. This will challenge policy makers in all jurisdictions to consider the potential impact of new public management.

The book concludes with a look ahead, anticipating developments in criminal justice sector after the departure of Tony Blair and potentially post a new Labour administration.

Understanding Modernisation in Criminal Justice is invaluable reading for those concerned with the administration of criminal justice at both a policy and managerial level; from students and academics wishing to understand the way agencies are responding to this agenda through to penal reformers and commentators.

Contents: Series editor's foreword - List of acronyms - Introduction - Part One - Understanding the concept of modernisation - From welfare to new public managerialism: 1945-97 - Understanding the modernisation policy process - Part Two - Modernisation and youth justice - Modernisation and the correctional services - Modernisation and community safety - Modernisation and the court system - Modernisation and the police - Modernisation and the voluntary and community sector - Part Three - Conclusions and way forward - References - Index.

2007 200pp
978-0-335-22065-6 (Paperback) 978-0-335-22066-3 (Hardback)

UNDERSTANDING CRIMINOLOGY 3/e

Current Theoretical Debates

Sandra Walklate

"Provides a very clear, easily readable introduction to the wide range of criminological theories."

Anne Rees, University of Portsmouth, UK

- What does contemporary criminological theory look like?
- What impact, if any, does it have on policy?

The new edition of this bestselling text updates a key title in the Crime and Justice series, whilst maintaining it's trademark theory-intensive approach to Criminology. In this third edition, the author pays particular attention to the development of the policy agenda under New Labour.

The book examines the development of criminological theory over the past twenty five years, with detailed analysis of the relationship between criminological theorizing, criminal justice, social justice, and politics. It also provides:

- A detailed examination of the role of the media in relation to the fear of crime
- Expanded discussion of classical criminology, adding discussion of cultural criminology
- Special reference to young people and victims of crime
- A critical consideration of current policies concerned with rebalancing the criminal justice system
- Increased emphasis on issues related to risk and terrorism
- A comprehensive update of policy and research throughout

Understanding Criminology is key reading for students who are new to the discipline, but also contains the rigourous analysis required by all levels of undergraduate student.

Contents: *Preface and Acknowledgements - Introduction: Understanding some key features of criminology - Perspectives in criminological theory - Understanding 'right realism' - Understanding 'left realism' - Gendering the criminal - Crime, politics and welfare - Criminal victimization, politics and welfare - Conclusions: New directions for criminology - Glossary - References - Index.*

2007 208pp
978-0-335-22123-3 (Paperback)

IMAGINING THE VICTIM OF CRIME

Sandra Walklate

Concern for the victims of crime first emerged with the formation of the Criminal Injuries Compensation Board in 1964 and this has continued with the increase in crime rates since the 1970s and 1980s and in the aftermath of a number of high profile trials.

In this book Sandra Walklate offers an introduction to the key theoretical, methodological and substantive issues in victimology and criminal victimisation. She situates the contemporary preoccupation with criminal victimisation within the broader social and cultural changes of the last twenty-five years.

Written in the context of post-September 11, and alongside the events in Madrid of 2004 and London in July 2005, it questions who can be considered a victim of crime and what the response to such victimisation might look like.

Topics include:

- Theoretical perspectives - positivist, radical and critical victimology
- Victimisation, risk and fear
- The re-politicisation of the crime victim
- The impact of global processes and global change on both the politics and the policy process

The book concludes with an examination of future possibilities for both victimology and victims' policies in the light of contemporary political preoccupations.

Imagining the Victim of Crime is key reading for students of criminal justice and victimology.

Contents: *Are we all victims now? - Ways of thinking about victims and victimology - Exploring victimization and its impact - Victimisation, risk and fear - Responding to victims' needs or harnessing victims' rights? - Crime, victims and justice - Conclusion: Criminal victimization, globalization and cosmopolitanism - References - Index.*

2006 224pp
978-0-335-21727-4 (Paperback) 978-0-335-21728-1 (Hardback)

UNDERSTANDING RACE AND CRIME

Colin Webster

- Why are some ethnic minorities associated with higher levels of offending?
- How can racist violence be explained?
- Are the police and criminal justice system racist?
- Are the reasons for offending and victimization among ethnic minorities different from those among ethnic majorities?

Understanding Race and Crime provides a comprehensive and critical introduction to the debates and controversies about race, crime and criminal justice. While focusing on Britain and America, it also takes a broader international perspective, with case studies including the historical legacy of lynching in the United States and racist state crime in the Nazi and Rwandan genocides.

The book provides a conceptual framework in which racism, race and crime might be better understood. It traces the historical origins of how thinking about crime came to be associated with racism and how fears and anxieties about race and crime become rooted in places destabilized by rapid social change. The book questions whether race and ethnicity alone are significant enough factors to explain differing offending and victimization patterns between ethnic groups.

Issues examined include:

- Contact/conflict with the police
- Public disorder
- Involvement with the criminal justice system

Understanding Race and Crime is essential reading for students from a range of social science disciplines and for a variety of crime-related courses. It is also useful to practitioners in the criminal justice field and those interested in understanding the issues behind debates on 'race' and crime.

Contents: Series editor's foreword - Acknowledgements - Conceptualising 'race' and crime: Racialisation and criminalisation - Origins: Criminology, eugenics and 'the criminal type' - Context: Race, place and fear of crime - Offending and victimisation - Racist violence - Race, policing and disorder - Race, criminal justice and penality - 'Race', class, masculinities and crime: family, schooling and peer groups - The African-American 'underclass' and the American Dream - State crime: The racial state and genocide - Understanding race and crime: Some concluding thoughts - References - Index.

2007 256pp
978-0-335-20477-9 (Paperback) 978-0-335-20478-6 (Hardback)